The Diary
of Samuel Sewall

The Diary
of Samuel Sewall

EDITED AND ABRIDGED
WITH AN INTRODUCTION BY

Harvey Wish

*Elbert Jay Benton Distinguished Professor
of American History
Western Reserve University*

*Capricorn Books
New York*

Contents

Preface

THE famous 56-year diary of Samuel Sewall, which contains
entries from December 3, 1673, to October 13, 1729, except
for an unexplained gap for 1677–84, is easily the most remarkable
American personal account of its time—the era of the Salem
witchcraft trials, the seizure of Captain Kidd, the brutality of King
Philip's War, and the struggles of old-line Puritans like Sewall and
the Mathers against Anglican imperial officials. There were in
contemporary England more literary and frankly sensuous diaries;
best known is that of Samuel Pepys, reflecting the bawdiness of
the Restoration, and posterity has also prized the informative, if
less intimate, diary of John Evelyn, the devout pro-Royalist Anglican. Unlike Pepys or Evelyn, Samuel Sewall liked to commune
with himself and God, jotting down briefly both daily events and
hurried impressions. Despite the scattered nature of this record,
the reader soon discovers an underlying unity depicting the mood
of the man and his times.

Cotton Mather's first diary, which he deliberately destroyed,
might conceivably have revealed greater complexity and keener
judgment than Sewall's. But Mather rejected its mere mundane
"actions" for an arid diary filled with theological speculations,
suitable as notes for sermons and the midweek religious lecture.
Diary-writing, while popular among Southern Anglicans (e.g.,
William Byrd of Westover) as well as New England Puritans,
seemed particularly appropriate for the introspective Calvinist
who sought the purpose of God through endless self-examination
and the search for meanings even in trivialities. It should be noted
that all these diaries remained hidden in manuscript, until the
nineteenth and twentieth centuries, when editors and publishers
sought them out. The text used here is the three-volume edition of

1878, 1879 and 1882, prepared by a committee of four citizens (including James Russell Lowell), and printed as the *Collections of the Massachusetts Historical Society* (Boston, volumes 5, 6, and 7, Fifth Series). While it is reported that an entirely new edition of the manuscript *Diary* of Samuel Sewall is in progress, this editor has not been able to see it. Such a project, which will of course be a major contribution to scholarship, does not obviate the convenience of a single-volume abridgment. There are innumerable names, places and miscellaneous references in the diary, but many of them are unimportant, and only essential identifications have been retained in this abridgment and the accompanying notes. No liberties have been taken with the printed text, except where editorial marks indicate needed corrections.

Samuel Sewall and His Diary:

AN INTRODUCTION

1.

THE well-to-do Sewalls of England smoothed the path for Samuel to become a rich merchant, landowner, exporter and influential Boston magistrate. His great-grandfather, Henry, was a wealthy Coventry linendraper-merchant who had served as mayor repeatedly. Another Henry, Samuel's father, migrated to New England in 1634, supplied with enough cattle and provisions to stock a plantation at Newbury. There young Henry Sewall married into the Dummer family, whose influential members figure prominently in the *Diary* as Boston officials. But when Henry's father-in-law complained of the climate, all returned to England in 1647. At their new home in Bishop-Stoke, in Hampshire, Samuel was born on March 28, 1652, later attending a local grammar school. After Henry returned to his Newbury plantation, the nine-year-old Samuel and his family followed on July 6, 1661.

Samuel continued his grammar school education under the erudite Dr. Thomas Parker, who had studied at Oxford and Leyden. It was Parker who shaped Samuel's lifelong interest in Biblical prophecies and speculations in the spirit of Biblical literalism. Fortunately, the Newbury environment also inspired Samuel's lifelong love of nature. Parker's preparatory school left Samuel well fitted for the orthodox atmosphere of Harvard under President Charles Chauncey during his student years of 1667–71. Sewall idealized this regime in later years when secularization was taking its toll. Closest to him among his classmates—quite literally since they shared the same bed—was the remarkable Edward Taylor, the future minister and poet, whose literary gifts remained a secret (except from Samuel who was to print his verses on solemn occasions). Only in the mid-twentieth century did a Harvard scholar

9

discover the Taylor manuscripts and reveal their importance for Puritan literature.

Chauncey punished severely profaneness, cardplaying, and "filthy speaking." One student, as the *Diary* tells us, was punished for blasphemy by being compelled to sit alone by himself "uncovered at meals." Still the boys enjoyed many recreations that escaped condemnation—fishing, hunting, singing, some light reading as well as devotional tracts, vacations to nearby villages, the usual college pranks and, despite everything, an occasional riot. Of special interest to Samuel were Harvard's efforts, like those of Cambridge and Oxford, to stamp out the fashion of wearing long hair and wigs in the style of Cavaliers. The clear authority of the Bible (I Corinthians XI) was invoked against these fops: "Doth not even nature itself teach you that if a man have long hair, it is a shame unto him? But if a woman have long hair, it is a glory to her." This theme suggests many an entry in the *Diary*. With all his scriptural learning, it is not surprising that Sewall chose as a Master's thesis in theory, "Is Original Sin Both Sin and Punishment?" To this he answered in the affirmative. And always he deeply admired his orthodox contemporary, Michael Wigglesworth (1631–1705), the pastor-poet of Malden whose widely read *Day of Doom* supported metrically the difficult doctrine of infant damnation.

While a resident fellow at Harvard, Sewall met Hannah Hull, the only child of the wealthy Massachusetts mintmaster and colonial treasurer John Hull. Hannah had admittedly "set her affections" on Samuel and the elaborate marriage took place on February 28, 1675. For many decades, romantics have assumed that Nathaniel Hawthorne's story of the Sewall wedding, as told in *Grandfather's Chair,* is true, with its picture of John Hull determining the dowry by weighing his eighteen-year-old girl in a scale-balance with a pile of shining pine-tree shillings. Such an advantageous marriage assured the young man not only happiness, but a long step upward financially and in prestige. There was little danger now that Samuel would become a minister, as seemed to be his "calling" at first, and it was easy to foresee his future as a merchant-exporter and a member of the Boston magisterial class.

From his father-in-law, who had long shipped wheat, furs and fish abroad, Sewall learned much about international trade. From

Hull also he acquired numerous accounts, exporting turpentine, fish and furs to the Caribbean and Europe and bringing back luxury goods, some intended for Hannah Sewall. But never did he share in the slave trade that was almost an integral part of the Triangular Trade between his fellow New England merchants, the West African slave traders, and the sugar planters of the West Indies. Like John Hull, he shared the old Puritan ethics that tempered the rising competitive capitalism, and politically he sympathized with the anti-Stuart views of the mercantile Whig dissenters in England. Among his enterprises were moneylending, banking, and the preparation of commercial documents—though he was never a lawyer—displaying a businesslike firmness toward borrowers while exercising philanthropy to many individuals and to causes such as the rights of Negroes and Indians.

He loved Harvard, which he served for many years on its Board of Overseers and aided by substantial gifts of land for the education of all youth, including Indians. He attended commencement ceremonies on numerous occasions, and accompanied his son Joseph to witness his oral examinations. When, in 1710, he feared that too much triviality had infected the College, he protested in a rather liberal vein to President Leverett, "The End of the College is that lovers of Learning may there meet; and be instructed, and have Sparks of Literature revived and enkindled. But this way of Faggoting discourages that and becomes an Extinguisher." While he was an investigator for the Board of Overseers into student morals, he refused to sustain the severe charges of the Comstockian pastor Cotton Mather, who insisted that he knew the boys to be reading plays, novels and "vicious pieces of poetry." Sewall noted only that there was too much drinking, visiting, and going to town on Sabbath mornings—altogether respectable vices. Yet he agreed with Increase and his son Cotton that the doctrinal decline of Harvard required in 1701 a conservative antidote to liberalism in a new college—Yale.

Doctrinal orthodoxy was a lifelong concern of his. He even offended his Mather circle by going over to the faction that protested Increase Mather's residence near his Boston church, instead of amid his students at Harvard, where he was president. Increase was given the ultimatum of staying with the boys—actually a small enrollment—or resigning the presidency altogether, as he did. Furthermore, as a latter-day Puritan, Sewall scrutinized suspiciously President Leverett's high-church tendencies and he insisted, despite the protests of his associates, that the president revive the custom of making weekly expositions of scripture to the students.

In 1681, while operating a Boston bookshop, Sewall was appointed by the General Court to manage the Boston printing press, but he delegated the actual printing to Samuel Green, a well-known New London printer. The Sewall list reflected his Calvinist tastes, and included the first American edition of Bunyan's *Pilgrim's Progress,* as well as numerous sermons, almanacs, and scientific essays. He provided the Mathers with an assured literary outlet, though they had others, and when he admired a Mather sermon, such as "Horrid Crime of Self-Murder," he ordered it printed. Closest to Sewall's heart was the publication of John Eliot's Bible for the Indians, which reflected the Puritan hope for Indian conversion to Christianity. Not least of his publications were his own little pamphlets, such as *The Selling of Joseph,* dealing with slavery, a discussion of Indian problems, the fulfillment of Biblical prophecies, and the mystical meanings of the Book of Revelation.

Once he became a Freeman, in 1679, and manager of the Boston Press, he advanced quickly to Westfield Deputy to the General Court (1683) and membership in the colonial Council (1684). This influence must have been compounded by the marriage of Joseph Sewall to Governor Joseph Dudley's daughter, despite the uncertain course of their connubial bliss. Samuel as a judge used his official and informal influence to aid the harassed Dudley against the hostility of the Mather faction.

After Massachusetts was deprived of her charter by the Crown, Sewall went to England to assist Increase Mather to recover it, appearing before high Parliamentary leaders as well as lesser folk to argue the case for New England and to protect his own property interests. Actually the revolutionary regime of William and Mary acted solicitously for both imperial and colonial rights. Officialdom was resolved to protect Anglicans against extreme Congregationalists and to check the Boston theocracy. Conservative as he was, Sewall was no Tory, like his kinsman Governor Dudley, and he gloried in the revolution of 1688 that expelled the hated Governor Andros, even writing a pamphlet justifying Boston's revolution.

While the new charter failed to give the orthodox Congregationalists their desired monopoly over the Massachusetts franchise, and
even perpetuated the Church of England's "Romish" practices—
which he assailed repeated in the *Diary*—the reactionary followers of Andros were replaced by more amenable friends of New
England, like Governor William Phips, who even became a convert to Congregationalism.

Some of Sewall's neighbors, as he sadly noted, were greatly
offended by what seemed to be his timidity in yielding so completely to the English demand for an official investigation and confirmation of land titles. Since in any frontier country it was obvious
that the less said about land titles the better, such an official inquisition frightened many homeowners. Sewall's concern over such
issues that involved his extensive landholdings led him to spend
most of 1688–89 in England, aside from his desire to save the old
charter.

Nothing hurt the prestige of the old Puritan theocracy—some
have challenged this term as inapplicable to a community in which
laymen carried such power—as much as the Salem witchcraft
executions of 1692. Governor Phips had appointed Sewall and
other special judges as "commissioners of the court of oyer and
terminer" to try suspected witches. Sewall, like most judges, had
no legal training and apparently he went along with the "spectral
evidence" in which the acts of devils might be cited by witnesses
as valid testimony. Though he was not as extreme as some of
his associates, yet he felt that his personal guilt was unique and
overwhelming in the decisions that sent nineteen persons to their
death.

Only men of little faith doubted the existence of witches.*
Catholics as well as Protestants in both Europe and America did
not usually question the Biblical injunction not to suffer a witch
to live. Especially heavy was the guilt of the Mathers, whose
pseudo-scientific writings about the invisible world accentuated
pietistic curiosity about the recent infusion of witches. Increase
Mather did make a belated protest against the use of spectral evidence to convict suspects, and convinced Governor Phips to sus-

---

* In the enlightened year of 1957, a Gallup Poll showed 61% of the
responders admitting that they believed in a personal devil.

pend the executions. Some New Englanders believed that these witches were a divinely sent affliction for the laxness of the Chosen People in dealing with the heretical Quakers, who frequently invaded meetinghouses with dishevelled faces or even nudity as a sign of the wickedness of the Puritan rulers. One *Diary* item of July 8, 1677, reads as follows:

Sabbath-Day. South-Meeting House. In Sermon-Time a female Quaker slipt in covered with a Canvas Frock, having her hair dishevelled and Loose, and powdered with Ashes resembling a flaxen or white Perriwigg, her face as black as Ink, being led by two Quakers and followed by two more. It occasioned a great and amazing uproar.

But the *Diary* tells all too little about the celebrated Salem trials, though it relates the tragic deaths of Sewall's two children and his great contrition and open church confession of guilt based on the assumption that his acts as judge had aroused the vengeance of God. Yet it should be added that Sewall was far from a reactionary judge by contemporary standards, for he fought a strict miscegenation law, tried to moderate extreme treason laws, opposed capital punishment for counterfeiting, and felt deep pain when he had to sentence a slave. In one notable case, Judge Sewall (he was appointed a justice of the Superior Court in 1692, a judge of Probate in 1715, and chief justice of the Superior Court in 1718) rejected a master's insistence upon the letter of his contract and freed the bondsman. Readers of the *Diary* have warmed to his words in a case of 1716, "I essayed to prevent Indians and negroes being rated with horses and hogs, but could not prevail." Frequently in court he struck this theme of human equality.

Sewall expressed this concern for Negroes and Indians in his writings as well. At a time when slavery and the slave trade were respectable and Indians appeared to be the murderous wretches of the frontier, he published emphatic pamphlets in their defense. His essay *The Selling of Joseph* (1700)* was the first antislavery tract in America. He united scriptural arguments for justice together with personal humane considerations. "It is most certain," he wrote, "that all men as they are the sons of Adam, are co-heirs;

---

* The complete text appears in this volume; see page 000.

and have equal right unto liberty and all other outward comforts of life."

As for the Indians who destroyed so many settlements during King Philip's War (1676) and killed or carried off so many people he knew, Sewall did not conceal his deep compassion for the dispossessed tribesmen, and urged practical solutions to end the flagrant abuses practiced upon them. Too often their lands had been arbitrarily seized, their hunting guns confiscated, their fisheries damaged, and, after the war, many had been sold into slavery in the West Indies. Tame Indians survived as Christians in strictly segregated "praying villages" where they imitated unenthusiastically the Puritan inhibitions that they were taught through John Eliot's Bible and other means, especially the translations into Indian readers that Sewall provided. Sewall believed, as so many contemporaries did, that the Indians were descendants of the Ten Lost Tribes of Israel, hence their conversion was most important.

One of his major activities was serving as secretary and treasurer of the Missionary Society to the American Indians. Among his projects was the printing of a Psalter and a primer for the Indians and a new edition of the Bible in an Indian tongue. He urged the establishment of good English schools to assimilate the tribesmen to English ways and to curb drunkenness. A cherished idea of his was to set aside Indian reserves, marked off by natural boundaries, to protect their lands from white absorption. This plan, he hoped, would facilitate conversion and help to perpetuate peace, and he succeeded in persuading his fellow commissioners to purchase lands for needy Indians and to support Indian schools. But in the end, colonial greed and prejudices hampered such solutions. In one of his poems on the Indians, Sewall pleaded:

> Give the poor Indians Eyes to see
> The Light of Life; and set them free;
> That they Religion may profess;
> Denying all Ungodliness.

As a Councilor, he followed a cautious traditionalism, which aligned him with the old colonial families who were staunch Congregationalists and hostile to the aristocratic Papist Anglicanism of the King's officers. He resented the encroachments of the Stuarts and their successors upon the old charter privileges of Massachusetts. Psychologically, he built a moat around the Old South Meetinghouse where Samuel Willard and son Joseph Sewall preached their orthodox tenets. Sewall and his Calvinist friends resisted the efforts of the King's men to use the meetinghouses temporarily for Church of England services. When Puritans did share a meetinghouse with Anglicans, preaching in shifts, the Anglicans groaned over the long wait—lasting perhaps three hours—while the Calvinist divines struggled over an abstruse theological sermon.

As a merchant, an official, and a convinced economic conservative, he opposed all efforts to cheapen the rather scarce colonial currency by such devices as the issuance of large quantities of bills of credit during times of emergency. The *Diary* abounds with references to the use of miscellaneous foreign coins, such as the Spanish "pieces of eight," that supplemented English currency. In addition, he fought the legal-tender acts that would make bills of credit current for all transactions. As a creditor, involved in both mercantile transactions and loans, he had no sympathy for inflation and pointed out the disasters that had always followed the depreciation of currency.

Unlike his *Letter Book,* which is mainly concerned with affairs of trade, his *Diary* gives a strong if exaggerated impression that the man was ever concerned with prayers and religious speculations. Yet there is no doubt that Sewall was outraged by the smallest evidence of alleged Papist infiltrations by England's officials or garrison soldiers, and by the practices of Boston's Anglican institutions, such as the new King's Chapel. He notes occasionally the divine mission of the Puritans and their city on a hill that had to be kept pure of popery. The *Diary* is filled with adverse references to the use of the Cross in the colors of the Royal Governor, the increasing appearance of the Book of Common Prayer brought by the Anglicans, and the taking of oaths by kissing the Bible— an idolatrous act—instead of merely laying on hands. He apparently took special satisfaction in his annual entry on December 25 to point out how completely the Bostonians were ignoring Christmas, with its pagan connotations, by carrying on their daily tasks as on weekdays. Like Governor William Bradford of Plymouth, he regarded Christmas as an idler's holiday as well as a pagan festival.

Sewall disliked the anti-Puritan revelry of the Redcoats—their bloody duels; their violation of the Sabbath by drums and other noisy instruments;* their boisterous stage spectacles; and their noisy diversions on midweek lecture days, which ranked next to Sunday as a holy day. He took a grim pleasure in recounting with disapproval the sharp increase in periwigs, the drinking of toasts, and Church of England services and rituals. He refused to sell land for Episcopalian churches, and led his fellow Congregationalists in Council in denying Governor Andros the use of the Town House for Anglican services, much to the anger of the King's men. Sewall saw the evils of the Restoration reflected in a general laxity of morals, drunkenness, cursing, street brawls, and even such old English customs as dancing around a maypole (recalling the scandal of Merrymount in Bradford's day).

Ever consistent in applying the standards of a Puritan, he criticized his own shortcomings as a Calvinist. "I pray'd this noon," he recorded on October 25, 1691, "that God would give me a pardon of my Sins under the Broad Seal of Heaven." He leaned hopefully upon the Covenant theology that conceded that God was absolute but not arbitrary since he had bound himself under a code—the Covenant of Grace—and no personal sins could outweigh the Savior's merits. His obsession with death was extreme, even by ascetic Puritan standards, suggesting neuroticism, and perhaps accounting for the hysterics that shook his children at the contemplation of death. He may have been partly motivated to record so many funerals because of their dramatic pageantry, but the contemplation of dread illnesses and man's short span was never far from his consciousnesses. Funerals also afforded him an occasion for writing a verse or two and attaching elegies to the coffin, printed copies of which were distributed by bookstores and country hawkers.

His contemporaries shared some of Sewall's fears, and would not have been surprised to learn that his diary recorded so many

---

* On the night before, not on Sunday itself. The Puritans, like the Hebrews, began the Sabbath at sundown.

cases of fatal smallpox, as well as recoveries, even far from Boston. (Cotton Mather, his younger contemporary, has won favor in the eyes of modern historians for his courageous efforts to popularize the new practice of inoculation at a time when Boston mobs condemned its high rate of fatalities as murder.)

No abridgment of the *Diary* can conceal the intensive human interest in Sewall's courtship of the middle-aged widows Winthrop, Dennison, Tilley and Gibbs, which followed the death of Hannah Sewall after forty-four years of married life. Understandably, this December courtship was based on practical considerations, such as advantageous property settlements and the style in which Sewall proposed to live: e.g., would he purchase a carriage? Yet Sewall was too tender an individual to pursue callously the aim of remarriage without affection. Some modern readers may smile at Sewall's meticulous purchase list of chocolates, dates and other gifts with which he tried to soften the mind of an undecided widow, and others may be shocked to note how realistic he could be in frankly assessing the motives of both sides. But in Sewall's day it did not seem vulgar to retail careless personal habits, ailments, symptoms, and conjugal reactions as he did when his bride displayed alarming symptoms of a serious disease on their wedding night.

In evaluating Sewall's *Diary,* especially important is the wealth of social history that can be gleaned from it. At times, it seems as if no event in that Boston of 6,000 persons escaped Sewall's attention, though the doings of his own household are best told. Evidently he greatly enjoyed the family picnics, the lavish dinners, the sleigh rides, the cheerful Harvard commencement exercises, the various Thanksgivings and days of atonement, and the semifestive activities of the militia, of which he was a distinguished officer. At times, it is true, he had the Puritan habit of magnifying trivia and accidents into signs of divine intentions. On such occasions, he was apt to insert a host of Biblical citations (which are often omitted in this abridged edition); and he speculates upon the danger of divine retribution for the real or fancied failings of the Chosen People.

But the secular side of this very human man also emerges clearly, with its remarkable freedom from rationalization concerning his own defects and his deep involvement in contemplation of the human condition. He died on January 1, 1730, on the eve of the Great Awakening, when the younger generation of Jonathan Edwards of Northampton sought to check the growth of formalism in religion by reviving the strictest tenets of Calvinism, which Sewall had prized during his lifetime. For him the issue of salvation was almost uppermost, despite his extensive worldly concerns.

The Diary

VOLUME I

(1673–1699)

Dec. 3, 1673. I read to the Junior Sophisters, the 14th Chapter of Heerboords Physick,[1] i.e. part of it, which beginnes thus, Sensus Communes &c. I went to the end, and then red it over from the beginning, which I ended the 24th of March, 1673/4.

Feb. 20, 1673/4. My Father brought down my Brother Stephen to be admitted.

March 9, 1673/4. I sent my Brother Stephen's cloaths to be washed by Mrs. Clark.

Mar. 23. I had my hair cut by G. Barret.

[Mar.] 24. In the Evening the Townsmen of Cambridge had a meeting and Mr. Gookin[2] and I being sent for went to them. They treated us very civily and agreed that the School boyes should sit no longer in the Students hinder seat. It was also consented to by us that some sober youths for the present might be seated there. *Hæc hactenus.*

April 2. Benjamin Gourd of Roxbury (being about 17 years of age) was executed for committing Bestiality * * * N. B. He committed the filthines at noon day in an open yard. He after confessed that he had lived in that sin a year. The causes he alledged were idlenes, not obeying parents, &c.[3]

June 5, 1674. Mr. Oakes gave me to understand that though he respected and loved me as formerly, yet he desired that I would refrain coming to his house, and that he did it *se defendendo,* least he should be mistrusted to discourage and dissettle me.[4]

June 15, 1674. Thomas Sargeant was examined by the [Harvard] Corporation: finally, the advice of Mr. Danforth, Mr. Stoughton, Mr. Thatcher, Mr. Mather (then present) was taken. This was his sentence.

That being convicted of speaking blasphemous words concerning the H. G. [Holy Ghost] he should be therefore publickly whipped before all the Scholars. 2. That he should be suspended as to taking his degree of Bachelour (this sentence read before him twice at the Pr.[ts] before the committee, and in the library 1 up before execution.) 3. Sit alone by himself in the Hall uncovered at meals, during the pleasure of the President and Fellows, and be in all things obedient, doing what exercise was appointed him by the President, or else be finally expelled the Colledge. The first was presently put in execution in the Library (Mr. Danforth,

Jr. being present) before the Scholars. He kneeled down and the instrument Goodman Hely attended the President's word as to the performance of his part in the work. Prayer was had before and after by the President.

July 1, 1674. Sir Thacher Commonplaced,[5] Justification was his head. He had a solid good piece: stood above an hour, and yet brake of [f] before he came to any use. By reason that there was no warning given, none (after the undergraduates) were present, save Mr. Dan Gookin, Sr. the President and myself. July 3, 1674. N. B. Mr. Gookin, Jr., was gone a fishing with his brothers.

Oct. 16. by Mr. Richardson's means I was called to speak. The sum of my Speech was that the causes of the lownes of the Colledge were external[6] as well as internal.

Tuesday, Nov. 24. My Father received a letter from Capt. Pike, of Woodbridge,[7] by which he sollicited my Father for my coming thether to be their Minister.

Friday, Dec. 25. Sam. Guile of Havarel, ravished Good-wife Nash of Amesbury, about G. Bailyes Pasture at the white Bottoms.

Mond. Jan. 25, 1674/5. Mr. Smith came to visit us, and brought with him one Mr. Bradly, who is allso a Southton[8] man, and told me that he went to old Mr. Goldwire's to school at Broadling, with 34 more. He allso told me that Thos. Warren was Apprentice to an Orange Merchant at Billingsgate, and Sam. to a Coal-seller at Cheapside.

Thurs. Feb. 13. There was a Fast held at Sam. Moody's, principally upon the occasion of his sickness: whereat were present, Mr. Woodbridge, Mr. Philips, Mr. Moody, Mr. Reinor, Mr. Richardson. The 3 first mentioned seemed to be very sensible of the state of things and of the plots of papists, Atheists: and Mr. Phillips spake how the Ministers in England, when they had their liberty, look after their own houses, quarrelled, &c. I carried my Mother to the Fast, and there we with many more, had (I hope) a feast day.

A Scotchman and Frenchman kill their Master, knocking him in the head as he was taking Tobacko. They are taken by Hew and Cry, and condemned: Hanged.

April 4, Sab. day. I holp preach for my Master, [Mr. Parker][9] in the afternoon. Being afraid to look on the glass, ignorantly and unwillingly I stood two hours and a half.

Indians

April 29 Brother John and Sister Hañah Sewall begin to keep house at the Falls.

My father having found things out of order at the Little Farm, viz, Fences down, ground Eaten and rooted up by Cattle and hogs, and wanting a good Tenant, the Season of the year now spending, resolves and goes to live there, notwithstanding the littleness and unpretines of the house.

Saturday, May 15. Brothers house was raised, at the raising of which I was.

Inds?

Friday about 3 in the afternoon, April 21, 1676, Capt. Wadsworth and Capt. Brocklebank fall. Almost an hundred, since, I hear, about fifty men, slain 3 miles off Sudbury: the said Town burned, Garrison houses except.[10]

Sabbath day, evening, 23 April, considerable thunder shower. Monday 24, about 6 afternoon, a Woman taken, and a Man knocked in the head, at Menocticot, Braintrey.

Friday, May 5. 16 Indians killed: no English hurt: near Mendham. 19 May. Capt. Turner, 200 Indians. 22 May, about 12 Indians killed by Troop.

Monday, May 9. Cold encreases mightily, all night burning Fever: next night rested indifferently.

Tuesd. [June] 6, late in the Afternoon, a violent wind, and thunder shower arose. Mr. Bendal, Mrs. Bendal, Mr. James Edmunds, and a Quaker female were drowned: their Boat (in which coming from Nodle's Iland) being overset, and sinking by reason of ballast. Mr. Charles Lidget hardly escaped by the help of an oar.

Wednesday, June 7., 5 Afternoon Mr. Bendal, Mrs, carried one after another, and laid by one another in the same grave. Eight young children. Tuesday, June 6, Hatfield fight, 5 English killed, about 14 Indians. Wednesday, June 7, Ninety Indians killed and taken by Coñecticut ferry: 30 and odd by C. Henchman.

June 16, 1676. Went with my Father to Mr. Smith's, there to see the mañer of the Merchants.[11]

June 22. Two Indians, Capt. Tom and another, executed after Lecture.

Note, at the Execution I delivered 2 Letters, one to Unckle Steph, another enclosed to unckle Nath, unto John Pike, to be by him conveyed. Last week two killed by Taunton Scouts, as they were in the river, fishing.

Note. This week Troopers, a party, killed two men, and took an Indian Boy alive. Just between the Thanksgiving,[12] June 29, and Sab. day, July, 2, Capt. Bradfords expedition 20 killed and taken, almost an 100 came in: Squaw Sachem. July 1., 9 Indians, sold for 30£. Capt. Hincksman took a little before. The night after, James the Printer and other Indians came into Cambridge. Father Sewall came Tuesday June 27. Went home Friday last of June.

Saturday, July 1, 1676. Mr. Hezekiah Willet slain by Naragansets, a little more than Gun-shot off from his house, his head taken off, body stript. Jethro, his Niger, was then taken: retaken by Capt. Bradford the Thorsday following. He saw the English and ran to them. He related Philip to be sound and well, about a 1000 Indians (all sorts) with him, but sickly: three died while he was there. Related that the Mount Hope Indians that knew Mr. Willet, were sorry for his death, mourned, kombed his head, and hung peag in his hair.

Saturday, July 8, 9 Indians, 2 English sallied out, slew 5 and took two alive. These Indians were killed not many miles from Dedham.

July 9, 10, &c. This week Indians come in at Plymouth to prove themselves faithful, fetch in others by force: among those discovered are some that murdered Mr. Clark's family: viz, two Indians: they accuse one of them that surrendered to the English. All three put to death.

Saturday, July 15. Quaker marcht through the town, crying, "Repent, &c." After, heard of an hundred twenty one Indians killed and taken. Note. One Englishman lost in the woods taken and tortured to death. Several Indians (now about) come in at Plymouth, behave themselves very well in discovering and taking others. Medfield men with volunteers, English and Indians, kill and take Canonicus with his son and 50 more.[13]

July 27. Sagamore John comes in, brings Mattoonus and his sonne prisoner. Mattoonus shot to death the same day by John's men.

Saturday Even. Aug. 12, 1676, just as prayer ended Tim. Dwight sank down in a Swoun, and for a good space was as if

our Timothy Dwight?

he perceived not what was done to him: after, kicked and sprawled, knocking his hands and feet upon the floor like a distracted man. Was carried pickpack to bed by John Alcock, there his cloaths pulled off. In the night it seems he talked of ships, his master, father, and unckle Eliot. The Sabbath following Father went to him, spake to him to know what ailed him, asked if he would be prayed for, and for what he would desire his friends to pray. He answered, for more sight of sin, and God's healing grace. I asked him, being alone with him, whether his troubles were from some outward cause or spiritual. He answered, spiritual. I asked him why then he could not tell it his master, as well as any other, since it is the honour of any man to see sin and be sorry for it. He gave no answer, as I remember. Asked him if he would goe to meeting. He said, 'twas in vain for him; his day was out. I asked, what day: he answered, of Grace. I told him 'twas sin for any one to conclude themselves Reprobate, that this was all one. He said he would speak more, but could not, &c. Notwithstanding all this semblance (and much more than is written) of compunction for Sin, 'tis to be feared that his trouble arose from a maid whom he passionately loved: for that when Mr. Dwight and his master had agreed to let him goe to her, he eftsoons grew well.

Friday, Aug. 25. I spake to Tim of this, asked him whether his convictions were off. He answered, no. I told him how dangerous it was to make the convictions wrought by God's spirit a stalking horse to any other thing. Broke off, he being called away by Sam.

Sabbath day, Aug. 20, we heard the amazing newes of sixty persons killed at Quinebeck, by barbarous Indians, of which were Capt. Lake, Mr. Collicot, Mr. Padashell.

Aug. 27. We hear of Major Talcots coming on Indians travailing towards Albany, to dwell on this side Connect. river. He slew some, tooks others with most of the plunder.

Sept. 13. The after part of the day very rainy. Note, there were eight Indians shot to death on the Common, upon Wind-mill hill.

Mr. Reyner, of Sept. 25, saith that their Indian Messengers returned the night before, and informed they saw two Indians dead, their Scalps taken off; one of them was Canonicus his Captain. 'Tis judged that Canonicus himself is also killed or taken by the same Hand, viz, of the Mohawks.

Sept. 21, '76. Stephen Goble of Concord, was executed for murder of Indians: three Indians for firing Eames his house, and murder. The wether was cloudy and rawly cold, though little or no rain. Mr. Mighil prayed: four others sate on the Gallows, two men and two impudent Women, one of which, at least, Laughed on the Gallows, as several testified.

[Sept. 23, 1676] Mr. Reynor, in a Letter dated at Salisbury, Sept. 21, '76., hath these passages: "God still is at work for us. One-ey'd John, with about 45 of your Southern Indians, have been apprehended since the Souldiers went Eastward. They we judge them All of our Southern Indians. And nothing yet lately heard of damage in the Eastern parts. A Sagamore of Quapaug is one of the Indians taken and sent. Canonicus we believe was killed by the Mohawks, when his Captain was slain. N. B. We have in our Business here great discoveries of our shameful Natures. Pray that the Sanctification and Reconciliation by Xt. [Christ] may prevail to his honour."

Sept. 26, Tuesday, Dr. Hawkins takes away from my Mother Hull about 4 ounces of blood. Sagamore Sam goes, and Daniel Goble is drawn in a Cart upon bed cloaths to Execution. One ey'd John, Maliompe, Sagamore of Quapaug, General at Lancaster, &c, Jethro, (the Father) walk to the Gallows. Note. One ey'd John accuses Sag. John to have fired the first at Quapaug, and killed Capt. Hutchison.

Oct. 9. Bro. Stephen visits me in the evening and tells me of a sad accident at Salem last Friday. A youth, when fowling, saw one by a pond with black hair, and was thereat frighted, supposing the person to be an Indian, and so shot and killed him: came home flying with the fright for fear of more Indians. The next day found to be an Englishman shot dead. The Actour in prison.

MR. EDWARD H[ULL] AND LOVING COUSIN, Although I never saw you, yet your Name, Affinity to me, and what I have heard concerning you, make me desirous of your acquaintance and Correspondence. Your Remembrance to me in my Father's I take very kindly. And I, with your Cousin, my Wife, do by these, heartily re-salute you. My Wife hath been dangerously ill, yet is now finely recovered and getting strength. It hath been generally a sick summer with us. The Autumn promiseth better. As to our enemies, God hath, in a great measure, given us to see our desire on them. Most Ring leaders in the late

Massacre have themselves had blood to drink, ending their lives by
Bullets and Halters. Yet there is some trouble and bloodshed still in
the more remote Eastern parts. What is past hath been so far from
ushering in a Famine, that all sorts of Grain are very plenty and
cheap. Sir, my Father in Law hath consigned to yourself two hh of
Peltry, to be for his and my joint Account, as you will see by the
Letter and Invoice. I shall not need to entreat your utmost care for
the best Disposal of them according to what is prescribed you: which
shall oblige the writer of these Lines, your loving friend and Kinsman,

SAMUEL SEWALL.

BOSTON, Oct. 23, 1676.

Novem. 27, 1676, about 5 M. Boston's greatest Fire[14] brake
forth at Mr. Moors, through the default of a Taylour Boy, who
rising alone and early to work, fell asleep and let his Light fire the
House, which gave fire to the next, so that about fifty Landlords
were despoyled of their Housing. N. B. The House of the Man of
God, Mr. Mather, and Gods House were burnt with fire. Yet God
mingled mercy, and sent a considerable rain, which gave check
in great measure to the (otherwise) masterless flames: lasted all
the time of the fire, though fair before and after. Mr. Mather saved
his Books and other Goods.

Dec. 14, 1676, Seth Shove was brought to our House to dwell,
i. e. Father Hull's. N. B. In the evening, seeing a shagged dogg
in the Kitchin, I spake to John Alcock, *I am afraid we shall be
troubled with the ugly dogg:* whereupon John asked which way
he went. I said out at the Street door. He presently went that way,
and meeting Seth (who went out a little before) took him for the
dogg, and smote him so hard upon the bare head with a pipe staff,
or something like it, that it grieved me that he had strook the
dogg so hard. There arose a considerable wheal in the childs head,
but it seems the weapon smote him plain, for the Rising was almost
from the forehead to the Crown, grew well quickly, wearing a Cap
that night. 'Twas God's mercy the stick and manner of the blow
was not such as to have spilled his Brains on the Ground. The
Devil, (I think) seemed to be angry at the childs coming to dwell
here.

Dec. 18, Mr. Rowlandson and Mr. Willard[15] came and visited
my Father. While they were here, Mr. Shepard also came in and
discoursed of Reformation, especially the disorderly Meetings of

Quakers and Anabaptists: thought if all did agree, i. e. Magistrates
and Ministers, the former might easily be suprest, and that then,
The Magistrates would see reason to Handle the latter. As to
what it might injure the country in respect of England, trust God
with it. Wished, (speaking of Mr. Dean's) that all the children
in the country were baptised, that religion without it come to
nothing. Before Mr. Shepards coming in, one might gather by
Mr. Willards speech that there was some Animosity in him toward
Mr. Mather: for that he said he chose the Afternoon that so he
might have a copious auditory: and that when the Town House was
offered him to preach to his Church distinct, said he would not
preach in a corner.

Jan. 30. [1676/7] Sent a letter to Cousin Quinsey, which enclosed a piece of Gold that cost me 23.ˢ Gave the Letter to Mr.
Josson. In it ordered to buy 2 pair of Silk Stockings, pink colored,
black, 1 pair Tabby Bodyes, cloath-coloured, ½ wide and long
wastied: also Turkish Alcoran, 2ᵈ Hand, Map of London. Sent
him a copy of verses made on Mr. Reynor. Jan. *ult.,* sent a letter
to Mr. Thacher, by the Bagg, in which Salutations, and some
newes. Wednesday, 31 Brother John Sewall brought down Sister
Jane to live with Mrs. Usher, but the next morn I went to her and
she gave me to understand that she thought Jane would not come,
and so had supplyed herself. Father Hull kindly invited her to stay
here till she should change her condition if she so liked.

Feb. 8. John Holyday stands in the Pillory for Counterfeiting
a Lease, making false Bargains, &c. This morn. I visited Mr. Sanford, who desired me to remember his Christian (he hoped) Love
to my Father Sewall, and mind him of Discourse had between
them at Belchers, Cambridge, which he professed pleased him as
much as more than any he had heard from any person before.

[February 10, 1676/7] In the thorsday even Mr. Smith of
Hingham speaks to me to solicit that his Son, and my former Bed-
fellow, Henry Smith, might obtain Mr. Sanfords House and authority therein to teach School. Sister Jane brought us in Beer.
Friday morn Feb. 16, I go to Mrs. Sanford and (by her hint) to
Mr. Frary, one of the overseers, who gave me some encouragement, and said that within a day or two, I should have an Answer.

Wrote a Letter to Mr. Smith that Frary had given an encouraging answer, and that I thought no Delay was to be made least the

Scholars should be lodged elsewhere. Feb. 18. The seats full of Scholars brought in by a Stranger who took Mr. Sanfords place: this I knew not of before.

Feb. 23, 1676/7. Mr. Torrey spake with my Father at Mrs. Norton's, told him that he would fain have me preach, and not leave off my studies to follow Merchandize. Note. The evening before, Feb. 22, I resolved (if I could get an opportunity) to speak with Mr. Torrey, and ask his Counsel as to coming into Church, about my estate, and the temptations that made me to fear. But he went home when I was at the Warehouse about Wood that Tho. Elkins brought.

Satterday, Mar. 3, 1676/7 went to Mr. Norton to discourse with him about coming into the Church. He told me that he waited to see whether his faith were of the operation of God's spirit, and yet often said that he had very good hope of his good Estate, and that one might be of the Church (i. e. Mystical) though not joined to a particular Congregation. I objected that of Ames, he said *vere quærentibus,* the meaning was that such sought not God's kingdom in every thing. I said it was meant of not at all. He said, was unsettled, had thoughts of going out of the country: that in coming into Church there was a covenanting to watch over one another which carried with it a strict obligation. And at last, that he was for that way which was purely Independent. I urged what that was. He said that all of the Church were a royal Priesthood, all of them Prophets, and taught of God's Spirit, and that a few words from the heart were worth a great deal: intimating the Benefit of Brethrens prophesying: for this he cited Mr. Dell.

March 12. Went to the first Town Meeting that ever I was at in Boston.

March 19, 1676/7 Dr. Alcock was buried, at whoes Funeral I was. After it, went to Mr. Thachers . . . who took us up into his Chamber; went to prayer, then told me I had liberty to tell what God had done for my soul. After I had spoken, prayed again. Before I came away told him my Temptations to him alone, and bad him acquaint me if he knew any thing by me that might hinder justly my coming into Church. He said he thought I ought to be encouraged, and that my stirring up to it was of God.

March 30, 1677. I, together with Gilbert Cole, was admitted

into Mr. Thacher's Church, making a Solemn covenant to take the L. Jehovah for our God, and to walk in Brotherly Love and watchfulness to Edification. Goodm. Cole first spake, then I, then the Relations of the Women were read: as we spake so were we admitted; then alltogether covenanted. Prayed before, and after.

Mar. 31. Old Mr. Oakes came hether, so I wrote a Letter to his Son, after this tenour:

SIR, I have been, and am, under great exercise of mind with regard to my Spiritual Estate. Wherefore I do earnestly desire that you would bear me on your heart tomorrow in Prayer, that God would give me a true Godly Sorrow for Sin, as such: Love to himself and Christ, that I may admire his goodness, grace, kindness in that way of saving man, which I greatly want. I think I shall sit down tomorrow to the Lords Table, and I fear I shall be an unworthy partaker. Those words, *If your own hearts condemn you, God is greater, and knoweth all things,* have often affrighted me.

SAMUEL SEWALL.

Note. [May Training No date] I went out this morning without private prayer and riding on the Common, thinking to escape the Souldiers (because of my fearfull Horse); notwithstanding there was a Company at a great distance which my Horse was so transported at that I could no way govern him, but was fain to let him go full speed, and hold my Hat under my Arm. The wind was Norwest, so that I suppose I took great cold in my ear thereby, and also by wearing a great thick Coat of my Fathers part of the day, because it rained, and then leaving it off. However it was, I felt my throat ill, the danger of which I thought had been now over with the winter, and so neglected it too much, relapsed, and grew very sick of it from Friday to Monday following, which was the worst day: after that it mended. Mr. Mather visited me and prayed on that day.

July 8, 1677. New Meeting House [the third, or South]: In Sermon time there came in a female Quaker, in a Canvas Frock, her hair disshevelled and loose like a Periwigg, her face as black as ink, led by two other Quakers, and two other followed. It occasioned the greatest and most amazing uproar that I ever saw.

Oct. 22. Musing at Noon and troubled at my untowardness in

worship, God, he holp me to pray, Come, Lord Jesus, come quickly
to put me into a better frame, taking possession of me. Troubled
that I could love Xt. [Christ] no more, it came into my mind that
Xt. had exhibited himself to be seen in the Sacrament, the Lords
Supper, and I conceived that my want of Love was, that I could
see Xt. no more clearly. . . . The Lord set it home efficaciously by
his Spirit, that I may have the perfect Love which casts out fear.

Jan. 22. [1677/8(?)] Went to Mr. Thachers, found him at
home, mentioned my desire of communion with his Church, re-
hearsed to him some of my discouragements, as, continuance in
Sin, wandering in prayer. He said 'twas thought that was the Sin
Paul speaks of, Rom. VII. At my coming away said he thought I
ought to be encouraged.

Feb. 15. Having been often in my mind discouraged from joining to the Church by reason of the weakness, or some such un-
desirableness in many of its members: I was much relieved by the
consideration of 1 Cor. 1. 26, 27. which came to my mind as I
was at prayer. What is spoken there was set home on me, to take
away my pride and be content with God's wisdom: thought it
might seem to unconvenanted reason foolishness.

Having often been apt to break out against God himself as if
he had made me a person that might be a fit subject of calamity,
and that he led me into difficulties and perplexing miseries; I had
my spirit calmed by considering what an absurd thing it was to
say to God—"Why hast thou made me thus?," and startled at the
daring height of such wickedness. These thoughts had reference to
Isaiah XLV. 9, 10. This was at prayer time, Feb. 19. *Mane*.
Death never looked so pleasingly on me as Feb. 18 upon the
hearing of Mr. Thachers 3 Arguments. Methought it was rather a
privilege to dye, and therein be conformed to Christ, than, remain-
ing alive at his coming, to be changed.

Mar. 1. Was somewhat relieved by what John read occasionally
out of Antipologia,[16] concerning the unwarrantable excuse that
some make for not coming to the Sacrament: viz. unworthiness.

Mar. 15, even. Was holp affectionately to argue in prayer the
promise of being heard because asking in Christ's name.

March 1678/9. Note. I have been of a long time loth to enter
into strict Bonds with God, the sinfullness and hypochrisy of
which God hath showed me by reading of a Sermon that Mr.

Do Sacrament day Sunday?

Burgess preached before the House of Commons, Nov. 17, 1640, and by the forementioned Sermons and prayers.

Remember, since I had thoughts of joining to the Church, I have been exceedingly tormented in my mind, sometimes lest the Third church [the South] should not be in God's way in breaking off from the old. (I resolved to speak with Mr. Torrey about that, but he passed home when I was called to business at the Warehouse. Another time I got Mr. Japheth Hobart to promise me a Meeting at our House after Lecture,—but she that is now his wife, being in town, prevented him.) Sometimes with my own unfitness and want of Grace: yet through importunity of friends, and hope that God might communicate himself to me in the ordinance, and because of my child (then hoped for) its being baptised, I offered myself, and was not refused. Besides what I had written, when I was speaking [at his admission to the Church] I resolved to confess what a great Sinner I had been, but going on in the method of the Paper, it came not to my mind. And now that Scruple of the Church vanished, and I began to be more afraid of myself. And on Saturday Goodman Walker came in, who used to be very familiar with me. But he said nothing of my coming into the Church, nor wished God to show me grace therein, at which I was almost overwhelmed, as thinking that he deemed me unfit for it. And I could hardly sit down to the Lord's Table. But I feared that if I went away I might be less fit next time, and thought that it would be strange for me who was just then joined to the Church, to withdraw, wherefore I stayed. But I never experienced more unbelief. I feared at least that I did not believe there was such an one as Jesus Xt., and yet was afraid that because I came to the ordinance without belief, that for the abuse of Xt. I should be stricken dead; yet I had some earnest desires that Xt. would, before the ordinance were done, though it were when he was just going away, give me some glimpse of himself; but I perceived none. Yet I seemed then to desire the coming of the next Sacrament day, that I might do better, and was stirred up hereby dreadfully to seek God who many times before had touched my heart by Mr. Thacher's praying and preaching more than now. The Lord pardon my former grieving of his Spirit, and circumcise my heart to love him with all my heart and soul.

why should another man's opinion disturb him?

For his much esteemed Friend, Mr. Cotton Mather, pr. Eliakim M.
BOSTON, Xr. 25, 84.

SIR,—Would intreat you to send me the little book you spake of to
me, which Dr. Owen writt of the Glory of Christ.

Please also, in stead of some Recreation, when you can spare the
time, to give me your Reasons why the Heart of America may not
be the seat of the New-Jerusalem. The worthy Pastor of Newbury, in
his fourth letter to Mr. Meade, (which I thank you for directing
me to,) warrants me in such an Inquiry. Your Arguments, briefly
laid down under several heads, will be refreshing to me to have them
to consider of. Desiring your Prayers, that I may be found in Christ,
not having my own Righteousness, I take leave, who am, Sir,

Yours,   SAM. SEWALL.
My son Sam: is still sick.

Wednesday, June 17th. [1685] a Quaker or two goe to the Governour and ask leave to enclose the Ground [on the Common]
the Hanged Quakers are buried in under or near the Gallows,
with Pales: Governour proposed it to the Council, who unanimously denied it as very inconvenient for persons so dead and
buried in the place to have any Monument.

Thorsday, June 18. A Quaker comes to the Governour and
speaks of a Message he had which was to shew the great Calami-
ties of Fire and Sword that would suddenly come on New-England.
Would fain have spoken in the Meetinghouse, but was prevented.
Eliakim comes home this day, brings word that Capt. Henchman
is coming away from Worcester with his Family.

Noyes this day of a French Pirat on the Coast, of 36 Guns.

Satterday, June 20th. 1685. . . . The final difference between
the Magistrates and Deputies is: The Governour and several with
him would Repeal the Proviso [regarding the makeup of the
courts], letting the rest of the Law stand as it does; the Deputies
have voted the Repeal of the Proviso; and withall that the Re-
mainder of the Law have this alteration, viz: in stead of greater
part of the Magistrates,—greater number of the Magistrates present—so to make the Law new as [it] might be construed contrary
to the Charter: the Governour, Mr. Stoughton, Dudley and several others could not consent.

Satterday, P. M. Carried my Wife to Dorchester to eat Cherries,
Rasberries, chiefly to ride and take the Air: the Time my Wife and

flesh vs.
spirit text

Mrs. Flint spent in the Orchard, I spent in Mr. Flint's Study, reading Calvin on the Psalms &c.

Sabbath, June 21, 1685. Mr. Solomon Stoddard[17] preaches in the Afternoon from Gal. 5. 17. shewing that there is a principle of Godliness in every true Believer; and how it differs from Moral Vertue, &c. Some little disturbance by a Quaker about the time of Baptism.

Wednesday, June 24, 1685. Carried my Wife to Cambridge-Lecture; Mr. Willard preached from those words, He that knows and does not his Master's will, shall be beaten with many Stripes.

Publick Fast, By the Governour and Company of the Massachusetts Bay in N. E. at a Gen! Court held at Boston May 27. 1685.

This Court having taken into their serious consideration, that in respect of afflictive Sicknesses in many Places, and some Threatenings of Scarcity as to our necessary food, and upon other Accounts also, we are under solemn Frowns of the Divine Providence; being likewise sensible, that the People of God in other parts of the World are in a low Estate,

what abt this qualy?

Do therefore appoint the Sixteenth day of July next, to be set apart as a Day of publick *Humiliation* by Fasting and Prayer throughout this Colony, exhorting all who are the Lord's Remembrancers, to give Him no rest, till Isai. 62. 7. He establish and make Jerusalem a Praise in the Earth: And do hereby prohibit the Inhabitants of this Jurisdiction all servile Labour upon the said Day.

Monday, July 6.th. I am taken with a Feverish Fit; yet go to Court in the Afternoon, the County Court, where was read Major Pynchon's[18] Letter to the Council; which is that 5 Men came to one of the Houses of Westfield (I think) about midnight 28.th June, knockt at the door, the Man bid him come in, so in they came all Armed with drawn Swords, and threatened to run the man and his wife through if they stirred: so plundered that House, and another in like manner: told they had 60 Men in their Company and that if they stirred out of door, they would kill them; so stayd in a great part of Monday, then when thought the Coast was clear told the Neighbours and some were sent to Search after them; at last found them: one of the 5 snapt and missed fire, another shot, then one of ours shot so as to shoot one of theirs dead:

another of the 5 fought one of ours with his sword, till another of
ours knockt him down. One or two that were taken are brought
to Boston, one at least is escaped. Major Pynchon his Works will
cost near an hundred Pounds.

An Indian was branded in Court and had a piece of his Ear cut
off for Burglary.

Tuesday, July 7.th Brother Moody visits us. General Court sits
in the Afternoon. Time is spent in ordering a Drum to beat up
for Volunteers about 30. Samson Waters, Capt., to go with Mr.
Patteshal's Brigenteen to fetch in two Privateers that this morn
are said to be in the Bay, a Sloop and Shalop, in the Shalop,
Graham.[19] . . .

Now about News comes to Town that Panama is taken by one
Banister an English Man; and that by the help of the Natives he
intends to hold it.

[July 10, 1685] We were speaking about Col. Kirk's coming
over.[20]

Mr. Stoughton[21] visits me and tells of the Court's Adjournment
till next Tuesday Sennight [a week] and then the Elders to meet
them and advise. Mr. Dudley and Mr. Bullivant visit me at the
same time. Mr. Stoughton also told me of George Car's Wife being
with child by another Man, tells the Father, Major Pike sends her
down to Prison. Is the Governour's Grandchild by his daughter
Cotton.

Friday, July ult. Condey arrives, hath had the Small Pocks[22]
of which Jn.o Cutts, his own Son, a youth, and one more are dead;
but 'tis said have been well a 14 night. When came a little above
the Castle, took in the Colours and cast Anchor, and a Man coming from on Board would not tell what the matter was, so began
to noise it that the new Governour was come, flocking to the wa-
terside.

Wednesday, Augt. 5. rode to Dorchester Lecture with Cous.
Nath. Dummer; was kindly entertained at Mr. Stoughton's after
Lecture. Going thither I saw a few Feet of Ground enclosed with
Boards, which is done by the Quakers out of respect to som one
or more hanged and buried by the Gallows: though the Governour
forbad them, when they asked Leave.

This day Augt. 28. is a Church Meeting at which 'tis consented
that Persons may be taken in, the Church only being present, and

not the Congregation: at the same time Mr. Benj. Davis, Mr. Nath. Oliver and Mr. Sam! Checkly were propounded.

Monday, Augt. 31. Eight Companies and the Troop Train. Dine with the South-Company, Capt. Blackwell, Mr. Brown of Barbados, Mr. Tho. Bayly, Capt. Gerrish, Capt. Jn.º Higginson, Cous. Dummer Trained. This morn Commissioners chosen, and by reason of the Training, persons came and delivering their Votes went away, and some came not at all, so that was but Nine Persons when they were proclaimed and but eleven at any time in telling. Most had 61 Votes, generally 50 odd. Mr. Nowell and my self present for 2.

Tuesday Sept. 8. A Porpus was pursued and taken within the inward Wharfs.

Wednesday, [September] 9th. . . . Mr. Hutchinson shewed me his Letter concerning his Mill at Piscataqua, wherein is sollicited to build a Fort, lest the Indians burn it. When came home heard of a Body of Indians near Chelmsford, 3 or 400. The Rumors and Fears concerning them do much increase.

The Indians are near Albany: Wonolanset brings the news to Chelmsford; and mistrusts of their mischievous Designs.

Sabbath-day Sept: 13, 1685. Mr. Benj. Davis, Nath! Oliver, Sam. Checkly and his wife are received into the Church, which is a Sabbath or 2 sooner than I expected: The Lord's Supper not being to be administered till Oct: 4th. Sam! Checkly had most in 's Relation: two wear Perriwigs: viz: Davis, Checkly.

Sept. 14, 1685. Go to Cambridge, and there hear Mr. Wigglesworth[23] preach excellently from those words, Fight the good Fight of Faith, Lay hold on eternal Life. . . . Coming home, hear of Meadfield Mill being burnt, and their confusion at Malborough last Satterday night. A suspected Indian is put in Prison. It seems were in Arms last Sabbathday at Dedham, somway knowing of Meadfield Mill being burnt. People are much perplexed.

Tuesday, Sept: 15, 1685. Mr. Barns tells me the Governour of Carolina is come to Town this day for his health: is so weak that stumbled at a pebble and fell down. Name, West. Mr. Willard speaks to the 7th. Commandment, condemns naked Brests: and seems to be against the Marriage of First-Cousins.

Thorsday, Sept: 17. News comes to Town of the rising of the Negros at Jamaica. Proves nothing answerable to the Rumor.

Generall Court having Voted that care be taken to see that all Persons are furnisht with Arms and Amunition according to Law because of Indians, that Wonolanset have £10. given him to appease [him] because he alledges some of his carried away contrary to safe Conduct, and for his late Service; that the West end of the Town-House be secured with Lead at the Country's Charge, Court is adjourned to the 2.ᵈ Wednesday in October at one of the Clock.

Tuesday, [September] 22. 1685. Jnᵒ Gardener came in late last night; this morning the News he brings runs throw the Town, viz. that James late D. of Monmouth was beheaded on Tower-Hill on the 15ᵗʰ July last. Argyle drawn, hanged and quartered.²⁴ Neigbour Fifield brought me the News, who had it from the Cryer of Fish.

Wednesday night, Septᵣ 23. Mr. Clutterbuck Arrives from New-Castle and brings word that he saw Argile's head cut off June the last; and the certain Newes of the Death of Monmouth about the middle of July. Dissenters in the North released, and Scotland is quiet.

'Tis remarkable that Clutterbuck should from Ocular Testimony contradict diametrically the Rumors that were spread in Town Friday was Sennight and strongly propagated, said to come by Clutterbuck: which was a meer Lye.

Thorsday, Octᵣ 1. 1685. Mr. Samson Stoddard arrives, who came from London the 25. July: brings the particulars of the Taking and Executing of the Late Duke of Monmouth whoes Head he saw struck off. Persons confined are now released.

Friday, Octᵣ 16. The Reverend Mr. Michael Wigglesworth is chosen by the Magistrates to Preach the next Election-Sermon.

Monday, Octᵣ 19ᵗʰ Training of Six Companies. Exercise was Taking of the Fort and advancing White Colours with Red Cross, above the Red Colours: so it stood while went to Dinner. Then Retaken. Firings on the Common: Vollies to the Governour. About Nine aclock at night News comes to Town of Capt. Henchman's Death at Worcester last Thorsday; buried on Friday. Very few at his Funeral, his own Servants, a white and a black, carried him to, and put him in his Grave. His Wife and children following and no more, or but one or two more.

Satterday, Octᵣ 31. in the even I read in course in the Family

Mr. Norton's Sermon. . . . All Engagements of Spirit, and Advantages notwithstanding; the Changes that befall Men, they come neither before nor after, but in the appointed Hour, or the precise Time, foreappointed of God.

Sometime this Week a virulent Libel was fixed on Mr. Dudley's[25] Fence, extreamly abusive, especially to Him.

Mr. Allin preached Nov! 5. 1685—finished his Text 1 Jn? 1. 9. mentioned not a word in Prayer or Preaching that I took notice of with respect to Gun-powder Treason. Although it rained hard, yet there was a Bonfire made on the Common, about 50 attended it.

Friday night being fair about two hundred hallowed about a Fire on the Common.

Friday, Nov! 6. Mr. Willard calls in and tells me of a Thanks-Giving intended by the Ministers through the Colony upon the 3ᵈ of the next Moneth: Go to the Governour to get his Approbation, which He doth not presently grant; but will speak of it in Council on Thorsday next; whether convenient for the Churches generally to attend such a Day without an Order from Authority, as usual. The difficulty of Printing an Order is, lest by putting in, or leaving out, we offend England. Having occasion this day to go to Mr. Hayward the Publick Notary's House, I speak to him about his cutting off his Hair, and wearing a Perriwig of contrary Colour: mention the words of our Saviour, Can ye not make one Hair white or black: and Mr. Alsop's Sermon. He alledges, The Doctor advised him to it.

Monday Nov! 9. Mr. Cobbet buried about 4. in the Afternoon. Flight of snow. This day about 6 or 7 at night a Male Infant pin'd up in a sorry Cloth is laid upon the Bulk of Shaw, the Tabacco-Man: Great Search made tonight and next day to find the Mother. So far as I can hear this is the first Child that ever was in such a manner exposed in Boston.

After, the Ministers of this Town Come to the Court and complain against a Dancing Master who seeks to set up here and hath mixt Dances, and his time of Meeting is Lecture-Day; and 'tis reported he should say that by one Play he could teach more Divinity than Mr. Willard or the Old Testament. Mr. Moodey said 'twas not a time for N. E. to dance. Mr. Mather struck at the Root, speaking against mixt Dances.[26]

Governour's Hat blew off and fell flat on the Ground just as [he] went to go in at 's Gate. Hath a new Border which began to wear Catechising day or Sabbath last, as I take it. Dept. Governour not in Town. New Almanack comes out this Day intituled New-England's Almanack, by Mr. Danforth.

Sabbath-day, Novr 15, 1685. In the Afternoon Mary Smith, Widow, Mr. Wheelwright's Grandchild, was taken into Church; then Mr. Willard mentioned what the Elders had done as to a Thanksgiving, and propounded to the Church that we might have one on the First Thorsday in December:[27] because had Fasted, and God had graciously answered our Prayers; so should meet Him in the same place to give Thanks for that, and any other Providence that hath passed before us. Silence gave Consent, no one speaking.

Novr 26, Thorsday. Nurse Goose[28] dyes about 2. or 3. aclock in the night; having lien sick about a Week. . . . Was helpfull to her self all along till this last sickness: washt her own Cloaths. She saw her great Grandchildren: was a good Woman.

Mary an Indian, James's Squaw, was Frozen to death upon the Neck near Roxbury Gate on Thorsday night Novr 27.th '85, being fudled.

Thorsday, Decr 17.th Mr. Mather preacheth from Mat. 16., former part of the 25.th Verse. For whosoever will save his Life shall Lose it. At County-Court nothing done in Mr. Sergeant's Business: So he makes a Speech when the Court open, that if the Court did nothing they would give him a Record of it, that he might go elsewhere for he would not be kept out of 's Money; speaking warmly.

Mr. Francis Stepney, the Dancing Master, desired a Jury, so He and Mr. Shrimpton Bound in 50£ to Jan.^{r} Court. Said Stepney is ordered not to keep a Dancing School; if he does will be taken in contempt and be proceeded with accordingly. Mr. Shrimpton muttered, saying he took it as a great favour that the Court would take his Bond for £50.

Sabbath-day, Dec. 20. Send Notes to Mr. Willard and Mr. Moodey to pray for my Child Henry.

Monday, about four in the Morn the faint and moaning noise of my child forces me up to pray for it.

21. Monday even Mr. Moodey calls. I get him to go up and Pray with my extream sick Son.

Tuesday Morn, Dec. 22. Child makes no noise save by a kind of snoaring as it breathed, and as it were slept.

Read the 16.ᵗʰ of the first Chron. in the family. Having read to my Wife and Nurse out of John: the fourteenth Chapter fell now in course, which I read and went to Prayer: By that time had done, could hear little Breathing, and so about Sun-rise, or little after, he fell asleep, I hope in Jesus, and that a Mansion was ready for him in the Father's House. Died in Nurse Hill's Lap. Nurse Hill washes and layes him out: because our private Meeting hath a day of Prayer tomorrow, Thorsday Mr. Willard's Lecture, and the Child dying after Sunrise (wether cloudy), have determined to bury on Thorsday after Lecture. The Lord sanctify his Dispensation, and prepare me and mine for the coming of our Lord, in whatsoever way it be.

Thorsday, Decᵣ 24.ᵗʰ 1685. We follow Little Henry to his Grave: Governour and Magistrates of the County here, 8 in all, beside my Self, Eight Ministers, and Several Persons of note. Mr. Phillips of Rowley here. I led Sam., then Cous. Savage led Mother, and Cousin Dummer led Cous. Quinsey's wife, he not well. Midwife Weeden and Nurse Hill carried the Corps by turns, and so by Men in its Chesnut Coffin 'twas set into a Grave (The Tomb full of water) between 4 and 5. At Lecture the 21. Psalm was Sung from 8.ᵗʰ to the end. The Lord humble me kindly in respect of all my Enmity against Him, and let his breaking my Image in my Son be a means of it. Considerable snow this night. At night little Hull had a sore Convulsion Fit.

Dec. 25. Friday. Carts come to Town and Shops open as is usual. Some somehow observe the day; but are vexed I believe that the Body of People profane it, and blessed be God no Authority yet to compell them to keep it.[29] A great Snow fell last night so this day and night very cold.

Dec. 28. Cous. Fissenden here, Saith he came for Skins last Friday, and [there] was less Christmas-keeping than last year, fewer Shops Shut up.

Dec. 30.ᵗʰ An Indian Man is found dead on the Neck with a Bottle of Rum between his Legs. Fast at Charlestown this day.

Mr. Cotton Mather Preaches forenoon, mentions the Notion Mede
has about America's Peopling.

[January 21, 1685/6] It seems Mr. Hubbard's Son of Long
Iland, presented a Gun at his Sister and it went off and killed her.
Cous. Fissenden tells me there is a Maid at Woburn who 'tis feared
is Possessed by an evil Spirit. Mr. Eliot not at Lecture Jan: 21.
which I think is the 3.ᵈ day of his absence.

Sabbath, Jan.ʳ 24. Friday night and Satterday were extream
cold, so that the Harbour frozen up, and to the Castle. This day
so cold that the Sacramental Bread is frozen pretty hard, and rat-
tles sadly as broken into the Plates.

Thorsday, January 28. Mr. Jenner having lodged at Capt.
Clap's last night, with Mr. Belcher and others, come near twenty
together to Serj.ᵗ Bull's over the Ice and bring the News of the
Rose Frigot ready to come and bring Mr. Randolph, who is to be
Deputy Governour, and Mr. Dudley Governour. Sheriff Cornish
executed [in London], and a woman burnt about the [Popish] Plot
and such like Treason. The Town much filled with this discourse.

Sabbath-day, Febr. 14. Little Hull speaks *Apple* plainly in the
hearing of his Grand-Mother and Eliza Lane; this the first word. At
the Burial of Mr. Eyr's Child, Mr. Moodey discoursed of the
grievous spreading of the Small Pocks in, and round about Portsmouth, at Exeter, &c.

Tuesday, Feb. 16. 1685/6. Generall Court meets. Dine 3 times.
Is a discourse this day of a strange Beast killed at Middletown,
or 4 miles off that place, last Dec., 10 foot long his Body, 10 foot
his Tail, as tall as a two year and vantage Horse; Had a dead
Horse and two Dear lay at 's Den, and Indians waiting for him,
at last saw him coming with another in 's Mouth, as a Cat carries
a Mouse almost. Indian shot him down. [Sewall writes in the margin—all untrue.] Great disorder in the Town by Cock-skailing:
I grant 2 warrants. Tho. Barnard has one, and James Barns the
other, whereby several Companies broke up: but for want of a
Law and Agreement shall find much ado to supress it.

Mr. Eliot at Meeting on Lecture day.

The Arrow against Dancing comes out.[30]

Sabbath-day, Feb. 28. A Jury is summoned to sit upon the
Body of Sarah, the Daughter of Henry and Mary Flood, about 13

weeks old, for that said Mary was suspected of Murder. So now
3 in Prison for suspected Murder. *an Indian, a dead baby's mother,*

Tuesday, March 2. Brother St. and Wife visit us. Mr. Chickly *2 under.*
is cast in his Attaint. Morgan, Indian and Flood put upon Tryal.

Thorsday, March 4. Mr. Moodey preaches. After Lecture,
James Morgan is condemned to dye: He said was murdered; but
spake not of Appealing, which I expected he might.

Friday 5. Joseph Indian is acquitted. James Morgan is sent to,
and acquainted that he must dye next Thorsday, and ordered that
Mr. Mather be acquainted with it who is to preach the Lecture.
Note. Mr. Stoughton and Dudley voted not in the Judgment, and
went off the Bench when Sentence was to be passed. Major Richards slid off too. Judgment was voted at George Monk's before
rose from Table, on Thorsday.

Satterday, March 6. James Morgan sends a Petition by one
Vaughan, signed with Morgan's own hand, wherein he acknowl-
edges his own sinfull Life, the justness of the Court's Sentence;
and desires longer time to live, but 'tis not granted.

Thorsday, March 11. Persons crowd much into the Old Meeting-House by reason of James Morgan;[31] and before I got thether
a crazed woman cryed the Gallery or Meetinghouse broke, which
made the People rush out with great Consternation, a great part
of them, but were seated again. However, Mr. Eliot, the Father,
speaks to me that I would go with him back to the Governour, and
speak that the Meeting might be held in our Meeting-House [the
South] for fear of the worst. Deputy Governour forwarded it, so
Governour proceeded, met Mr. Mather, paused a little and then
went to our House, the stream of People presently following and
deserting the old: first part of the 51. Ps. Sung. Mr. Mather's Text
was from Num. 35. 16. And if he smite him with an Instrument
of Iron, &c. Saw not Mr. Dudley at Meeting, nor Court; suppose
he might not be in Town. Mr. Stoughton here. Morgan was turn'd
off about ½ an hour past five.

Know not whether the mad woman said the House fell, or
whether her beating women made them scream, and so those afar
off, not knowing the cause, took it to be that; but the effect was as
before; and I was told by several as I went along, that one Gallery
in the old Meetinghouse was broken down. The mad woman was
the Daughter of Goodm. Bishop, master of Morgan. She went in

at the Southwest Dore, beat the women, they fled from her: they above supposed they fled from under the falling Gallery. Mr. Cotton Mather accompanied James Morgan to the place of Execution, and prayed with him there.

Sabbathday. [March 14] Mr. Jnº Bolt, and Jnº Nichols are received into our Church. Mr. Bolt mentioned profan Courses he had been entangled in after Conviction. Relations of both well accepted, being such as gave good hope.

Tuesday Morn [May 11]. Mr. Mather's Maid, a Member of [blank] Church is brought to Bed of a Child. Nothing suspected before that I hear of. 'Tis said He has turn'd her out of 's House.

Sabbath, May 30.ᵗʰ 1686. My Son reads to me in course the 26.ᵗʰ of Isaiah—In that day shall this Song, &c. And we sing the 141. Psalm, both exceedingly suited to this day. Wherein there is to be Worship according to the Church of England as 'tis call'd, in the Town-House, by Countenance of Authority. 'Tis deferred 'till the 6.ᵗʰ of June at what time the Pulpit is provided; The pulpit is movable, carried up and down stairs, as occasion serves; it seems many crouded thether, and the Ministers preached forenoon and Afternoon.

Friday, June 11. Waited on the Council, took the Oath of Allegiance, and rec'd my new Commission for Capt. Was before at a privat Fast at Deacon Allen's: so Capt. Hutchinson and I went about 5. oclock, and all the rest were sworn, Capt. Hutchinson at present refuses. I read the Oath myself holding the book in my Left hand, and holding up my Right Hand to Heaven.[32]

Friday, June 18. My dear Son, Hull Sewall, dyes at Newbury about one aclock. Brother Toppan gets hither to acquaint us on Satterday morn between 5 and 6. We set out about 8. I got to Newbury a little after Sun-set, where found many persons waiting for the Funeral; so very quickly went.

[June 21, 1686] On Monday I distributed some Gloves,[33] and in the Afternoon about 6 aclock came with Deacon Coffin to Salem about 10 at night. From thence early in the Morn by reason of the flaming Heat, and got to Winnisimmet before the Ferry-men up, Got home about ¾ after seven, found all well. Hullie was taken ill on Friday Morn. The Lord sanctify this Third Bereavement.

July 27, 1686. Mr. Stoughton prayes excellently, and makes a notable speech at the opening of the Court. The Foreman of the Grand-Jury, Capt. Hollbrook, swore laying his hand on the Bible, and one or two more. So Mr. Ballard, Foreman of the Petit Jury, and one or two more. Others swore lifting up their hands, as formerly. Attorneys are sworn and none must plead as Attorneys but they.

July 28. A considerable Troop from Watertown come and fetch Mr. Bayly, some of ours also accompany them. Francis Stepney the Dancing Master runs away for Debt. Several Attachments out after him.

About the same time W.[m.] Johnson Esq.[r.34] is sharply reproved by the Council for his carriage on the Fast-day, staying at home himself and having a Duzen Men at 's House. Told him must take the Oath of Allegiance; he desired an Hour's consideration, then said he could not take it; but when his *Mittimus* writing, or written, he consider'd again, and took it rather than goe to Prison. Objected against that clause of acknowledging it to be Lawfull Authority who administered; would see the Seals.

Aug.[t] 5. W.[m.] Harrison, the Bodies-maker, is buried, which is the first that I know of buried with the Common-Prayer Book in Boston. . . . One Jn[o] Gold, Chief Commander of the Military Company at Topsfield, is sent to Prison for Treasonable Words spoken about the change of Government, is to be tryed this day fortnight. Council said he was not bailable.

Sabbath-day, Aug.[t] 8. 'Tis said the Sacrament of the Lord's Supper is administered at the Town-House.[35]

Friday, Augt. 20. I was and am in great exercise about the Cross to be put into the Colours, and afraid if I should have a hand in 't whether it may not hinder my Entrance into the Holy Land.[36]

Sabbath-day, Augt. 22. In the Evening seriously discoursed with Capt. Eliot and Frary, signifying my inability to hold, and reading Mr. Cotton's Arguments to them about the Cross, and sayd that to introduce it into Boston at this time was much, seeing it had been kept out more than my Life-time, and now the Cross much set by in England and here; and it could scarce be put in but I must have a hand in it. I fetcht home the Silk Elizur Holyoke had of me, to make the Cross, last Friday morning; and went and discoursed Mr. Mather. He judged it Sin to have it put in, but the Captain not at fault; but I could hardly understand how the

Command of others could wholly excuse them, at least me who had spoken so much against it in April 1681, and that Summer and forward, upon occasion of Capt. Walley's putting the Cross in his Colours. Augt. 22.

Monday, Augt. 23. At even I wait on the President and shew him that I cannot hold because of the Cross now to be introduc'd, and offer'd him my Commission, which he refus'd, said would not take it but in Council. Receiv'd me very candidly, and told me we might expect Sir Edmund Andros, our Governour, here within six weeks; for ought I know that might make him the more placid.

Friday, Septr 3. Mr. Shrimpton, Capt. Lidget and others come in a Coach from Roxbury about 9. aclock or past, singing as they come, being inflamed with Drink: At Justice Morgan's they stop and drink Healths, curse, swear, talk profanely and baudily to the great disturbance of the town and grief of good people. Such high-handed wickedness has hardly been heard of before in Boston.

Tuesday, Septr 7th The Dartmouth Frigot comes up. I goe with my wife, Cous. Ruth, Savages and Mrs. Baker and their Children to Hog-Iland [where Sewall owned 498 acres of land]. We put off just as the Frigot and Ships and Town Salute each other mutually. Got home by 9. aclock.

I little thought of its being the day signed by the Almanack for the Court of Assistants, till coming home I accidentally spyed. It has been a great day of feasting on Board Capt. Head. Mr. Lidget and Shrimpton there. I suppose they are little concerned for being bound over in the morn for their Friday night Revel.

Satterday, Septr 25. The Queen's Birthday is celebrated by the Captains of the Frigots and sundry others at Noddles Iland. King and Council's Proclamation of Novr 6. last, was published by beat of Drum throw the Town to hinder their making Bonfires in the Town however. Went with their Boats to the Ships and Vessels and caused them to put out their Ancients. Many Guns fired. A kind of Tent set up at the Iland and a Flagg on the top on 't. Made a great Fire in the Evening, many Hussas.

Sabbath, Septr 26. Mr. Willard expresses great grief in 's Prayer for the Profanation of the Sabbath last night. Mr. Lee preaches with us in the Afternoon from Isa. 52. 7. Said that all America should be converted, Mexico overcome, England sent over to convert the Natives.

Sabbath-day, Oct.ͬ 10. By reason of the Fires the Meeting-Houses are much filled with Smoke; so 'twas a Lecture-day, one might feel it in ones eyes.

Tuesday, Dec.ͬ 21. There is a meeting at Mr. Allen's, of the Ministers and four of each Congregation, to consider what answer to give the Governour; and 'twas agreed that could not with a good conscience consent that our Meeting-Houses should be made use of for the Common-Prayer Worship.[37]

Dec.ͬ 22. In the evening Mr. Mather and Willard thorowly discoursed his Excellency about the Meeting-Houses in great plainness, showing they could not consent. This was at his Lodging at Madam Taylor's.[38] He seems to say will not impose.

Friday, Dec.ͬ 24. About 60 Red-Coats are brought to Town, landed at Mr. Pool's Wharf, where drew up and so marched to Mr. Gibbs's house at Fort-hill.

Satterday, Dec.ͬ 25. Governour goes to the Town-House to Service Forenoon and Afternoon, a Red-Coat going on his right hand and Capt. George on the left. Was not at Lecture on Thorsday. Shops open today generally and persons about their occasions. Some, but few, Carts at Town with wood, though the day exceeding fair and pleasant.

Thorsday, Dec.ͬ 30. The Council meets. Gentlemen from Plimouth and Rhode-Iland here and take their Oaths without any Ceremony, perhaps for the sake of the Quakers, who have promised to deliver up their Charter.

Satterday, January 1, [1687]. Took Capt. Elisha Hutchinson with me and went to Jnᵒ Alcocke, talked throughly with him about his ill courses. Told him by reason of our fear of the Small Pocks must fetch his chest away; would have had him done it then, but he would not, yet promis'd to do it Monday next.

Wednesday, Jan. 5. Sam. is taken ill of a Fever and we fear the Small Pocks.

Friday, Jan. 7ᵗʰ. I went to Capt. Winthrop's upon business, and the Governour happen'd to be there, Capt. Winthrop had me up to him, so I thankfully acknowledged the protection and peace we enjoyed under his Excellencie's Government. Capt. Wing waited on him at the same time about a Man slain at Worster yesterday by a Logs rolling upon and over him which he just before had cut off. Capt. Davis carries his wife out of Town for fear of the Small

Pocks, she being with Child. This day Dame Walker is taken so ill that she sends home my Daughters, not being able to teach them.

[January 18, 1687] Wednesday is snowy storm, but not much falls. Mr. Stoughton and Dudley and Capt. Eliot and Self, go to Muddy-River to Andrew Gardener's, where 'tis agreed that 12 £ only, in or as Money, be levyed on the people by a Rate towards maintaining a School to teach to write and read English. Andrew Gardener, Jn? White, Tho. Stedmand are chosen to manage their affairs. Boilston Clark, Capt. Eliot and I, formerly chosen with Stedmand, refuse.

Sabbath, January 30.ᵗʰ 1686/7. About ¾ past eight at night my wife is delivered of a Son, Eliza. Weeden, Midwife. Was fine moderate wether though had been very severe for near a week together before. My wife sent not for the Midwife till near 7. at night. But one staid at home with her, though was not well most part of the day. The child large, so my wive's safe delivery is much to be heeded, considering our former fears.

Monday, January 31. There is a Meeting at the Townhouse forenoon and afternoon, Bell rung for it, respecting the beheading Charles the First. Governour there, very bad going by reason of the watery snow. Joseph Brisco's wife gives my son suck.

Feb. 15, 1686/7. Jos. Maylem carries a Cock at his back, with a Bell in 's hand, in the Main Street; several follow him blindfold, and under pretence of striking him or 's cock, with great cart-whips strike passengers, and make great disturbance.[39]

Thorsday, March 10, 1686/7. Mr. Mather preaches the Lecture. Speaks sharply against Health-drinking, Card-playing, Drunkenness, profane Swearing, Sabbath-breaking, &c. Text [Jere. 2. 21], Degenerat Plant. Mr. Stoughton treated the Governour and Council March 9.ᵗʰ .

April 9. One Wᵐ. Sargent of Almsbury is trapand into a Tipling house about 9 at night and robbed of Money, a Gold Ring and several papers.

Friday, [April] 22. [1687] Two persons, one array'd in white, the other in red, goe through the Town with naked Swords advanced, with a Drum attending each of them and a Quarter Staff, and a great rout following as is usual. It seems 'tis a chaleng to be fought at Capt. Wing's next Thorsday.

Satterday, Ap. 23. Eight Companies Train: Many persons: some officers have red paper Crosses fastened to their Hats. The Governour rode by and among the Souldiers, accompanied by the President, Mr. Davie and others. Major Lidget the Chief Commander, Col. Shrimpton, he, and Luscomb on Horse-back. Gave a Volley or two on the Common, march'd out about one aclock to the Market place. The Rose fired and others. Companies gave three Vollyes, broke off about 3. in the afternoon. In the night a Bonfire or two were made on Fort-hill. After followed fire-works with Huzzas, ended about 11. or 12.

His Excellency on Mr. Shrimpton's House to behold the works.

Monday, Apr. 25. Another Challenge goes with his naked Sword through the Street with Hitchborn Drummer, and a person carrying a Quarter-Staff.

On Sabbath-day Old Meeting and ours much disturbed in Sermon-Time the afternoon by a distracted Fr. [French?] Man. Mr. Willard fain to leave off for some time. The same afternoon the Governour's Meeting was broken up by the Fire of Capt. Paige's chimney: and rallyed not again.

Ap. 28. After the Stage-fight, in the even, the Souldier who wounded his Antagonist, went accompanyed with a Drum and about 7. drawn Swords, Shouting through the streets in a kind of Tryumph.

Tuesday, May 17. Brother and I ride to Newbury in the rainy Dusk; this day Capt. Hamilton buried with Capt. Nicholson's Redcoats and the 8 Companies: Was a funeral-Sermon preach'd by the Fisher's Chaplain: Pulpit cover'd with black cloath upon which Scutcheons: Mr. Dudley, Stoughton and many others at the Common Prayer and Sermon. House very full, and yet the Souldiers went not in.

Wednesday, May 18. Mr. Cotton Mather preaches Newbury-Lecture, Ps. 39. I am a Stranger with Thee. This day Mr. Foye comes in and brings the Kings Declaration for Liberty of Conscience.

May 26. Marshal Green visits me, and tells that he is wholly left out of all publick employment. Sam! Gookin Sheriff for Middlesex. Said Green told me he knew not of it till today, and that he was undone for this world. It seems the May-pole at Charlestown was cut down last week, and now a bigger is set up, and a

Maypole

Garland upon it. A Souldier was buried last Wednesday and disturbance grew by reason of Joseph Phips standing with 's hat on as the Parson was reading Service. 'Tis said Mr. Sam! Phips bid or encouraged the Watch to cut down the May-pole, being a Select-Man:[40] And what about his Brother and that, the Captain of the Fisher and he came to blows, and Phips is bound to answer next December, the Governour having sent for him before Him yesterday, May 26, 1687.

Friday, May 27, between 5. and 6. Father Walker is taken with a Lethargy as was shutting up his shop to goe to their privat Meeting: His left side was chiefly struck with a kind of Palsy: His speech came to him something between 6. and 7. He told me there was plenty of Lavander in the Town where he was Prentice. He overheard some discourse about the May-Pole, and told what the manner was in England to dance about it with Musick, and that 'twas to be feared such practices would be here. Told me he had been liable to be overtaken with Sleep for threescore years, and that 'twas his Burden which he something insisted on.

May 29. Sabbath. Dame Walker desires me to pray with her Husband, which I do and write two notes, one for our House and one for the Old. Sam. carries the first. Between 12. and one Robert Walker dies, about a quarter after Twelve. He was a very good Man, and conversant among God's New-England People from the beginning. About one, several great Guns were fired.

Wednesday, June 1. A privat Fast of the South-Church was kept at our house, Mr. Willard pray'd and preach'd in the morn. Mr. Cotton Mather pray'd first in the afternoon, Mr. Moodey preach'd and pray'd. Mr. Willard dismiss'd with a Blessing. . . . Occasion of the Fast was the putting by the Sacrament the last Turn, and the difficult circumstances our Church [is] in above others, regarding the Church of England's meeting in it.

Sabbath, June 12. Lord's Supper at the South-Church. But Church of England men go not to any other House: yet little hindrance to us save as to ringing the first Bell, and straitning the Deacons in removal of the Table.

June 28, 1687. Went to Roxbury and heard Mr. Cotton Mather preach from Colos. 4. 5. Redeeming the Time. Shew'd that [we] should improve Season for doing and receiving good whatsoever it cost us. His Excellency was on the Neck, as came by, call'd Him in and gave Him a glass of Beer and Claret and deliver'd a Petition respecting the Narraganset Lands.

July 1, 1687. Went to Hog-Iland; had Eliakim thither: went to see where to make a Causey to land handsomly: brought home a Basket of Cherries: As went, saw a Surveyor with two red-coats, and another measuring and surveying Noddles-Iland. Came home about ½ hour after four aclock.

Tuesday, July 12. I go to Mr. Usher's about 5. *mane,* about 7. or eight we goe on Board, the Ship being under Sail. Go with them to Alderton's [Allerton's] Point, and with our Boat beyond, quite out of the Massachusetts Bay, and there catch'd fresh Cod. Went to Nantasket, in which way lost my hat, and for fear of running the Boat on the Rocks, left it. From Nantasket, in less than an hour and half sail'd home between 7. and eight. . . . Had an extraordinary good wind. Mr. Usher wept at taking leave of 's Wife and Daughter. Before went from Mr. Usher's, Mr. Moodey went to Prayer in behalf of those going to sea, and those staying behind, in a very heavenly mannor.

Satterday, July 16. At night a great Uproar and Lewd rout in the Main Street by reason of drunken raving Gammar Flood, came from about Wheeler's pond, and so went by our House into Town. Many were startled, thinking there had been fire, and went to their windows out of Bed between 9. and 10. to see what was the matter.

Monday, July 18. Was startled in the morn as was at prayer in the Kitchen, at a sudden unusual noise; which prov'd to be two Cows running into our little Porch; the like to which never fell out before, that I know of.

Nov. 3. Mrs. Anne Williams tells me that an English Maid was Executed last Thorsday at Bristow, for murdering her Indian Child.

Wednesday, Nov. 16. The Governour comes to Town returning from taking the Government of Connecticut. In the Even sends for the Ministers and so Schools them that the Thanksgiving is put by which was to have been the 17.th.

Sabbath, Dec. 4. Mr. Willard baptiseth his little Margaret, born about 8. last night. In the Even Capt. Eliot, Frary, Williams and Self, Treat with Brother Wing about his Setting a Room in his House for a man to shew Tricks in. He saith, seeing 'tis offensive, he will remedy it. It seems the Room is fitted with Seats. I read what Dr. [William] Ames saith of Callings, and Spake as I could, from this Principle, That the Man's Practice was unlawfull, and therefore Capt. Wing could not lawfully give him an accommodation for it.

Sabbath, 25. Have the Lord's Supper at the South Church, break up about noon, at which time I hear that Mr. Mather was, on Satterday between 1. and 2. P.M. Arrested by Larkin, to answer for a Trespass on Mr. Randolp, 500.£. damage.[41] Just as Morn-Exercise ends Mr. Cotton Mather's child dies; yet he preaches at Charlestown in the afternoon.

Friday, Jan. 13. [1688] Joshua Gee with Joseph Bridgham, Jn° Barnard and Dyar, come to agree with me what I must have for my Money disbursed in London: said Gee presents me with a pair of Jerusalem Garters which cost above 2 pieces 8/8 [Spanish dollars] in Algier; were made by a Jew.

Satterday, Jan. 21. My dear Daughter Hannah is put to bed, or rather kept in Bed, being sick of the Measles. Droop'd ever since Thorsday.

Sabbath, 22ᵈ. Hannah's Measles appear very full in her face: had a restless night, read in course the 38ᵗʰ Psalm. My Lady Andros was prayed for in Publick; who has been dangerously ill ever since the last Sabbath. Today I hear that Mr. Brown of Salem, the Father, dyed on Friday last in the afternoon. One of a Dutch Church in London is admitted to the Lord's Supper with us. About the beginning of our afternoon Exercise, the Lady Andros expires.

Monday, Jan. 23. The Measles come out pretty full on my dear Wife, which I discern before I rise. She was very ill in the night.

Tuesday, Jan. 24. Betty Sewall keeps her Bed; but is not so full as her Sister Hannah.

Tuesday, Jan. 24ᵗʰ About noon, the Physician tells me the Measles are come out in my face, and challenges me for his Patient.

Jan. 31. Mr. Randolph, in his Action against Mr. Increase Mather, is cast. Mr. Hale being subpœna'd by Mr. Randolph, pleaded he might not lay his hand on the Bible; must Swear by his Creator, not Creature. 'Twas granted that he only lift up his Hand as customary in New England. Col. Shrimpton lent Mr.

Mather his Coach to ride home: He abode there the time of the Tryal, to be at hand if need were.

March 30, 1688. Obadia Gill, John Atwood and Joseph Davis are by a Writt from the Sheriff imprisoned, because they paid not the $13^{\underline{s}}$ $4^{\underline{d}}$ which each was fined, Feb. 8., for not laying their Hand on the Bible: Judgment run thus—refusing to take the Oath as by Law is required. Though they offer'd to take the same Oath, the oath the others did, that Ceremony set aside. They pay the Fine and charges and Ly not in Prison one night. Mr. Larkin sought after Mr. Mather this week to Arrest him. Mr. Mather on Tuesday was taking Physick and so was free, and since hath purposely avoided him.

Wednesday, Apr. 4. At night Sam. Marion's wife hangs herself in the Chamber, fastening a Cord to the Rafter-Joice. Two or three swore she was distracted, and had been for some time, and so she was buried in the burying place.

Satterday, Apr. $7^{\underline{th}}$ 1688. Capt. Arthur Tannar sails about 10 aclock, a shallop follows quickly after, which 'tis said is to prevent Mr. Mather's getting on Board: 'tis certain all the Town is full of discourse about Mr. Mather.

Friday, March 30. I am told Mr. Mather left his House and the Town and went to Capt. Phillips's at Charlestown.

Apr. 13, 1688. Grafted a Stock next Jno Wait's, pretty high out of the Cows reach, with cions from Mr. Moodey's Orange Pear, and grafted Two Appletree Stocks with Mr. Gardener's Russetings; the Cow having eaten last year's Grafts all save one Twigg. Mr. Moodey, Willard, Cotton Mather, Capt. Townsend, Mr. Eyre were here last night. It seems Mr. Watter and Elisha Odlin were fined last Wednesday, 13. $4^{\underline{d}}$, apiece, for refusing to lay their hand on the Bible in Swearing.

April 18. The news about Lima's Ruine comes abroad.[42] Mr. Cotton Mather mentions it on the $19^{\underline{th}}$ at the Lecture. Above 60.000 persons perished, and now there is a Pool of Water where it stood, if the news be true.

Friday, May $4^{\underline{th}}$ 1688. Last night there was a very refreshing Rain; this $4^{\underline{th}}$ May, a Print comes out shewing the Lawfullness of Swearing according to the English mode, Laying the hand on the Bible. Taken out of Mr. Baxter's Directory, printed by Richard Pierce May the 1. 1688; were publickly known May 4.

May 10. Mr. Dudley and his Son call here. I speak to him about the mode of swearing, if no remedy might be had, of which had no encouragement, but said Lifting up the Hand was the handsomest way.

Thorsday, May 17th 1688. Capt. Leach arrives from London, brings news of the 10th of March, or Later. Col. Dongan is to be Governour of Barbados, and New-York annexed to this Government. Fears of War with Holland. Now is talk that no Parliament till October next.

May 23, Wednesday, 1688. Went to Hog-Island with Brother Stephen Sewall, Brother Toppan and Sam. Shepard: Upon the Hill we agreed that Sam. Toppan should be bound to Brother Stephen for five years from September next, to be bound to Brother only during his Life. Brother Toppan chose it rather than that he should be bound to a trade as a Taylor, or the like; Hopes by going to Sea or the like after his Time is out, may get a livelihood.

Friday, June 1, 1688. Went to Watertown Lecture. . . . By that time we got home, we heard that Sir William[43] came in his Pinace from Portsmouth this day. Many of the Town gone to complement Him.

Thorsday, June 7th. Mr. Dudley and Stoughton call here. In comes Mr. West and hath one Mr. Newton, a newcomer, sworn an Attorney. Mr. Dudley ask'd for a Bible, I ask'd if it might not better be done without. He laugh'd and seeing a Bible by accident, rose up and took it.

June 22. I goe to Hogg-Island with Mr. Newgate to see if [we] could agree about his Marsh: Father Griggs and Sam! Townsend there. When came back, went and bit Sir William welcome to Town, who landed an hour or so before me, being come with his Frigot from Portsmouth. This day Mrs. Joyliff and Mrs. Grecian goe to his Excellency, and expostulat with Him about his Design of meeting first on Sabbath-days in our Meetinghouse.

Satterday, June 23. Capt. Frary and I goe to his Excellency at the Secretaries Office, and there desired that He would not alter his time of Meeting, and that Mr. Willard consented to no such thing, neither did he count that 'twas in his power so to doe. Mr. West said he went not to ask Mr. Willard Leave. His Excellency asked who the House belong'd to; we told Him the Title to the House was on Record. His Excellency turned to Mr. Graham and said, Mr. Attorney we will have that look'd into. Governour said if Mr. Willard not the Parson, so great an Assembly must be considered. We said He was Master of the Assembly, but had no power to dispose of the House, neither had others, for the Deed expressed the Use 'twas to be put to. Governour complain'd of our long staying Sabbath-day sennight; said 'twas the Lord's Supper, and [he] had promised to go to some other House on such dayes; Mr. Randolph said he knew of no such promise, and the Governour seemed angry, and said He would not so break his word for all the Massachusetts Colony, and therefore, to avoid mistakes, must give in writing what we had to say; we answered, Mr. Randolph brought not any writing to those he spake to. Governour said we rent off from the old Church against the Government, and the Land the House stood on was bought clandestinely, and that one should say he would defend the work with his Company of Soldiers. Mention'd folks backwardness to give, and the unreasonableness; because if any stinking filthy thing were in the House we would give something to have it carried out, but would not give to build them an house: Said came from England to avoid such and such things, therefore could not give to set them up here: and the Bishops would have thought strange to have been ask'd to contribute towards setting up the New-England Churches. Governour said God willing they would begin at Eight in the Morning, and have done by Nine: we said 'twould hardly be so in the winter. Mr. Graham said if they had their Service by Candle-Light what was that to any: And that the Service appointed by the Church for morning could not be held after Noon.

Thursday, July 12. Mr. Jnᵒ Hubbard tells me there is a Writt out against me for Hog-Island, and against several other persons for Land, as being violent intruders into the Kings Possession. George Keith [a Quaker] doth this day send a Challenge to the 4 Ministers of Boston, in an open letter by Edward Shippen, to dispute with them about the false Doctrine they delivered.

Satterday, July 14ᵗʰ Jeremiah Belcher comes and brings me the Information Mr. Sherlock left with him on Thorsday last in the Afternoon, when he served on him a Writt of Intrusion. I try'd to goe to the Island yesterday but could not, wind and Tide being against me, and one Oar broke. Went from Winnisimmet to the

Point, but none fetch'd me over. Wind is out [from the east], and so Sir William comes up and Capt. Belcher.

Satterday, July 14. Writt to Mr. Wharton, Mr. Mather, Capt. Hutchinson, inclosing the state of my case and craving their help to give Check; sent the Letters under covert to Cousin Hull, ordering him to pay them Fifty pounds if they call'd for it.

Thorsday, July 19th. Eight Companies in Arms, and Sir Edmund's Commission is published, extending his Authority from the remotest eastern parts so as to take in East and West Jersey.

To Sir Edmund Andros Knight, Capt. General and Governour in Chief of His Majesties Territory and Dominion of New-England in America, the humble Petition of Samuel Sewall of Boston, Sheweth.

That whereas your Petitioner stands seized and possessed of a certain Island or Islands, commonly called and known by the name of Hogg-Island, lying seituate near Boston aforesaid, in the present tenure and occupation of one Jer. Belcher, having been peacably and quietly possessed by your Petitioner and his Predecessors for the space of fourty years or upwards by past: And whereas the said Belcher hath been lately served with a Writt of Intrusion at His Majesties Suit, And your Petitioner not being willing to stand Suit, but being desirous of His Majesties Confirmation for the said Island or Islands:

He therefore humbly prays your Excellencies favour that he may obtain His Majesties Grant and Confirmation of the said Hogg-Island, with the members and Appurtenances thereof, unto your Petitioner his Heirs and Assigns forever under the Seal of this His Majesties Territory. To be holden of His Majesty, His Heirs and Successors, upon such moderat Quit-Rent as your Excellency shall please to order.

And your Petitioner shall ever pray.

SAM SEWALL.

Presented the above written Petition to the Governour with my own hand July 24th. 1688.

July 26th. 'Twas read in the Council, and an order made upon it for a Survey.

Thorsday, Augt. 9th. This day I goe for Mrs. Weeden, my wife having been ill a week or more, and now ready to conclude her time to Travail was come. Midwife staid and went to Bed here; in the night was call'd away by another woman about 2. *mane.*

It seems the Monday the Governour went hence towards New-York, Five Indians were killed at Spectacle Pond not far from Springfield, four taken Captive, two escaped. They that did the Murder are some of our late Enemies who have since lived under the protection of the French.

Augt. 14, 1688. About ½ hour past Nine at Night Stephen Greenleaf comes in and brings my Mother Sewall; they set sail from Newbury about 10. in the morning, had a brisk Norwest Gale, turn'd up from Dear-Island and lay aground a pretty while before they could fleet in. Cous. Greenleaf sups with Mother. I give him the Catechise, Day of Doom, &c. bound together in a good Cover, in part for Mother's passage.

Wednesday, Augt. 15th. About 4. *mane,* I rise to make a fire, and to call the Midwife, Charlestowns Bell rung for 5. as came away from Mrs. Weeden's House. Very cool day. My Wife is brought to Bed of a Son between 8. 9. while the Service-Bell was ringing.

Thorsday, 16th. Put up a Bill for Thanksgiving. About 9. in the night news comes from Salem, by a Vessel from Holland, that the Queen was deliver'd of a Prince, June 10th. So from 11. to 1. or 2. is Drumming, Bonfire, Huzas, small and great Guns, Ringing of Bells, at which many startled for fear of fire or an Alarm; because the thing was so sudden, People knew not the occasion. Brother Needham was called out of 's Bed to deliver the Keys, which at first he refus'd, they not telling him the occasion [for a Church service].

Sabbath, Augt. 19th. 1688. Town is full of the news of 5. English persons killed at Northfield; So the Councillors sent for; and by that means Mr. Stoughton at our House in the afternoon to hear Mr. Willard, who after Sermon, baptized my young Son, whom I named Joseph, in hopes of the accomplishment of the Prophecy, Ezek. 37th and such like: and not out of respect to any Relation, or other person, except the first Joseph. The Lieut. Governour goes this day to Woburn to secure some Indians there, now busied in gathering Hops. It seems were met together and praying when secured, or just before.

Thorsday, Augt. 23. Fast at the old Church, respecting the Indians, at which was my dear Mother Sewall, set in Mrs. Baker's

Pue, went not out at Noon because of the Rain. Mr. Willard begun with Prayer in the morn. Mr. Mather in the Afternoon.

Sept. 10, 1688. There is a press in Boston, of 32 Men, four out of a Company, to goe to the Eastward, by reason of the fears and dispersions people there are under. It seems 10. or 11 English persons are taken away as hostages till those Indians sent to Boston be return'd.

Tuesday, Sept. 11ᵗʰ. Two and thirty Men are press'd in Boston, and 6 from Charlestown and sent away to the Eastward, and a Post dispatcht to acquaint the Governour at Albany.

Sept. 15, 1688. Corrected Sam. for breach of the 9ᵗʰ Commandment, saying he had been at the Writing School, when he had not.

Satterday, Oct. 13ᵗʰ. . . . . Came home without seeing the Governour, whom [we] went to meet. When I come home here the sad news of a family of 8 persons being cut off by the Indians.

Tuesday, Oct. 16. Little Hannah going to School in the morn, being enter'd a little within the Schoolhouse Lane, is rid over by David Lopez, fell on her back, but I hope little hurt, save that her Teeth bled a Little, was much frighted; but went to School; one Stebbin took her in, who lives next Solomon Rainsford's Shop up the Lane, on the left hand as goe up. This day the Ground-Sills of the Church [the first King's Chapel, built of wood] are laid; the stone foundation being finished. Visit Cousin Dummer sick abed.

*   *   *   *   *   *

[SEWALL IN ENGLAND]

LONDON, April 26, 1689.

HONOURED SIR, Hat in Hand, &c, Necessity puts men upon hard Shifts to find out some pretence or other for making their addresses to those from whom they may expect relief. There was Capt. John Hull, of Boston in N. E., with whom in his life-time you had some Correspondence by way of Merchandize. He died in Sept. 1683, leaving a Widow and a Daughter, who is my wife; by whom I had an Estate that might afford a competent Subsistence according to our manner of living in N. E. But since the vacating of the Charter, and erecting a Government by Commission, the Title we have to our Lands has been greatly defamed and undervalued: which has been greatly prejudicial to the Inhabitants, because their Lands, which were formerly the best part of their Estate, because of very little value, and consequently the Owners of very little Credit. Sir, I am glad that you are returned again to England, to your Country, Possessions, and dear Relations, and to a Seat in Parliament. I hope your former Distresses will help you to sympathise with others in the like condition. I, and several besides me, are here far removed from our Wives and Children, and have little heart to goe home before some comfortable settlement obtained, whereby we might be secured in the Possession of our Religion, Liberty and Property. I am informed some favorable Votes have been passed in the House of Commons, wherein N. E. was mentioned. I intreat your forwarding of such Votes as you have Opportunity, in doing which you will be a Partner with God, Who is wont to be concerned in relieving the Oppressed. I shall not take up more of your time from your momentous Employments. My hearty Service presented to you, I take leave, who am, Sir, your humble Servant,

SAM. SEWALL.

Above is Copy of my Letter to Tho: Papillon, Esq.[44]

April 29. went to Greenwich with Mr. Mather, Whiting, Brattle, Namesake: Supped at the Bear. Went through the Park to Mr. John Flamsted's, who shewed us his Instruments for Observation, and Observed before us, and let us look and view the Stars through his Glasses.

April 30. Queen's Birth-Day. Streamers, Flaggs, Guns. Writ to Mrs. Dulcibella Horsman, inclosed Mr. Cotton Mather's Sermons bound up in good Calv's Leather. Hat in Hand, &c. Spent 4.3^d apiece in going to Greenwich.

Thursday, May 9, went to H[ampton] Court, to wait on the King and Council. Mr. Mather not there:[45] said he was feverish, yet I perceive was at Change. Sir Robt Sawyer spake of the Quo Warranto in Charles the First's time, and supposed we had no Charter: asked if any had seen it. I said I had seen a Duplicate. Dr. Cox craved Day; so are to appear agen next Thorsday, and just as we were going out, by Sawyer's means were called back, and then he spake of the Quo-Warranto for Misdemeanors, and we are ordered to attend the Attorney General with our Charter. As we came home were entertained by Mr. Stephen Mason with Cider, Ale, Oysters and a Neat's Tongue, being ten of us, or 11.

Satterday, May 11ᵗʰ Declaration of War against France comes out.

Tuesday, May 14ᵗʰ, Mr. Richard Wharton dyes about 10 *post merid*. He rid to Town the Wednesday before in order to goe to Hampton-Court last Thorsday. Monday, May 6, was at Westminster pleading against Mr. Blathwayt, in behalf of N. E. Mr. Brattle and I came down by water with him. Wednesday, May 15, went and dined with Fish at Capt. Kelly's upon Mr. Partrige's Invitation. Capt. Hutchinson, Clark, Appleton, Brattle, Hull, in company. Went to a Garden at Mile End and drunk Currant and Rasberry Wine, then to the Dog and Partrige's, and plaid Nine Pins. At the house a Souldier was shot by his drunken companion the night before.

Thorsday, May 16, went to the Old Bailey, the Court was holden by Pilkinton, Mayor, Lord Chief Justice Holt, Lord Chief Justice Pollixfen, Chief Baron Atkins, and 7 more Judges. Sat till 3 o'clock, in which time the London Jury returned and brought in four Verdicts, which they were charged with at once.

May 18, goe to Hampton Court in company of Capt. Hutchinson and Jo. Appleton; Mr. Mather, Sir Sam. Tomson, Mr. Whiting, and Mr. Joseph Tomson ridd in another Coach. Cost 21ˢ apiece, besides money to the Drivers. . . . Just now about a virulent Libel comes out against N. E.

Monday, May 20. Meet to answer the Print, and in the evening another accosts us, called an abstract of our repugnant Laws, full of Untruths almost as the former. To comfort me when got home, met with a Letter from my dear Brother, by the way of Bilbao, dated the 12 March; all friends and my wife and Children well, but New England bleeding.

May 21, writt to Mr. Flavell of our N. E. Affairs. Writt of the 20ᵗʰ to Cousin Bean and Cous. Nath. Enclosed in a packet ¼ Hundred of Mr. Cotton Mather's funeral Sermons.

May 31. Went to Mr. Papillon to speak to him in behalf of N. E., who entertains me candidly, and promises to promote our Interest, and would have me take off [dissuade] those who may think contrarily. May 31. Is a Fast kept at Dr. Annesly's: they began with singing and sang 4 or 5 times. After all, had a Contribution. When came home, found a Letter from Cousin Quinsey, giving an account of the Health of my Wife, Children and friends, on the 26 March.

June 3, 1689. As came home saw one Elisabeth Nash, born at Enfield, about 25 Years old, just about Three foot high, not the breadth of my little finger under or over. Her Hands show Age more than anything else. Has no Brests. By reason of her thickness and weight can goe but very sorrily. Can speak and sing but not very conveniently, because her Tongue is bigger than can be well stowed in her Mouth. Blessed be God for my Stature, unto which neither I, nor my Dear Mother, my Nurse, could add one Cubit.

June 10th Gave the Ch. Wardens of Cree-church, for the relief of the Protestants of Ireland, four Crowns—£1.0.0. Writt to Richard Cornish copies of Mr. Tho. Read's Bonds, and the Affidavit by Bant, for fear of miscarriage, that so he might understand how his business lay and not be cheated out of his Money by his Unkle. Cousin Robert Andrews brings me a Letter from my Cousin of Swathling, his Mother-in-Law. Dines with us on a good Line of Veal and Strawberries.

June 15. Being at Mrs. Calvin's alone in a Chamber, while they were getting ready dinner, I, as I walked about, began to crave a Blessing, and when went about it remembered my Cloaths I had bought just before, and then it came into my mind that it was most material to ask a blessing on my Person: so I mentally pray'd God to bless my Flesh, Bones, Blood and Spirits, Meat, Drink and Aparrel. And at Dinner, paring the Crust of my Bread, I cut my Thumb, and spilt some of my Blood, which word I very unusually, or never before, have used in prayer to my present remembrance.

Wednesday, June 26. Mr. Mather, his Son, Cousin Hull and self, set out for Cambridge, 45 miles: got thither by 7 o'clock, with one set 4 Horses. Lay at the Red Lion in Petit Curie.

Thorsday, June 27, Mr. Littel, Fellow of Emmanuel Colledge,[46] shows us the Gardens, Walks, New Chapel, Gallery, Library of the Colledge, in it a Bible MS. of Wickliffe's Translation. Mr. John Cotton and Hooker had been Fellows, as appeared by Tables hanging up. Dr. Preston, Head of it. The Street where it stands is called Preacher's Street, from Black Friars formerly resident there. Note. Said Fellow had in 's Chamber, Sir Roger Le Strange, Jesus Salvator and K. Charles, 2ᵈ, hanging up together. Saw St.

John's Colledg, which stands by the River. Hath a good Library
and many Rarities, among which was a petrified Cheese, being
about half a Cheese. Trinity Colledge is very large, and the new
Case for the Library very magnificent, paved with marble check-
ered black and white; under, stately walk on brave stone; the
Square very large, and in midst of it a Fountain. In the Hall many
Sparrows inhabit, which is not known of any Hall beside. At meal-
Times they feed of Crums, and will approach very near Men.
King's Colledge Chapel is very stately. Went on the top of the
inward Stone Roof, and on the top of the outward Lead-Roof,
and saw the Town, and Ely about 10 miles off. Below, on the side,
under little Arches, is the Library. Mr. Littel dined with us at
our Inn: had a Legg Mutton boiled and Colly-Flowers, Carrets,
Rosted Fowls, and a dish of Pease. Three Musicians came in, two
Harps and a Violin, and gave us Musick. View the Publick Library, which is in form of an L, one part not fil'd with books, some
vacant shelves to bespeak Benefactors. Saw the Divinity School
over which the Regent House is. The School fair and large. Pub-
lic Acts are kept in St. Marie's Church, over against which the
Schools are. Just before night our Landladie's Son had us along
Bridge-Street, and shewed us Sidney-Colledg as I take it, and be
sure Magdalen Colledg on the other side of the River, on which
side there is none but that. Went to the Castle-Hill, where is a
very pleasant Prospect, the Prison and Sessions House just by,
which is very ordinary, like a Cow-House. Cattell having free
egress and regress there. Gallows just by it in a Dale, convenient
for Spectators to stand all round on the rising Ground. . . . I
saw the Chapel in the outside of which 'tis said There was a great
deal of Rome in a little Chapel: but Mr. Mompesson, Cousin's
friend, not being within, saw not the Inside. 'Tis a small Colledge.
St. Maries is a fair Church. In sum Cambridge is better than it
shows for at first; the meaness of the Town-buildings, and most of
the Colledges being Brick.

June 28. Mr. Harwood and I step'd out and saw Queen's Colledge, which is a very good one. . . . Got to Mr. Croper's about
Eleven aclock. He keeps a Coffee House. While Mr. Mather read
the Votes I took Thorsdays Letter and read the News of Boston,
and then gave it Mr. Mather to read. We were surpris'd with joy.
At Change Capt. Hutchinson shew'd me Capt. Byfield's Letter,

which comes by Toogood. They had the News on Change that day we went to Cambridge.[47]

LONDON, July, 2. 1689.

HON'D SIR, I have just now read the noble Petition of the Citizens of London, in the Common Hall assembled, the 24th past, whereby I hope the honorable Commons of England will be effectually moved to expedite the Bill for restoring Corporations to their Ancient Rights and Priviledges, in doing which I am very glad that yourself is so ready to bear a part. I have met with a Letter written to the Queen when Princess of Orange, in behalf of New England, which I intreat yourself and Lady to accept of, from, Sir, your humble Servant,

S. S.

To THO. PAPILLON, Esq.

July 4, Writt to Mrs. Hannah Tuckey, of Warwick, enclosing a Print of the Revolution in New England, four of Mr. Cotton Mather's Sermons, and Mr. Kick's Letter to the Queen.[48] Hat in hand.

July 6, '89.

To MR. THO. GOODWIN,

SIR, Capt. Brookhaven did a pretty while since signify to me a desire you had to see me at Pinor [Pinner?], which is to me very obliging, who am a Stranger in this Land. I hope before my return I may have an Opportunity to pay you a Visit. 'Tis little is here to be done, and yet for all that I find it inconvenient to be out of the way, one thing or other presenting of a sudden, wherein we that are here count it our Duty if we can in anything assist Mr. Mather. I have inclosed a printed account of what has lately happened in New England, which I would fain hope is their Resurrection, and not a precluding of it only. What is there transacted seems to be well resented [regarded] at Court, and the King promises to doe what is in His power towards restoring our Liberties. If you come to Town, I should be glad to see you on the N. E. Walk, or at my Chamber. Desiring your Prayers that all things may work together for Good, respecting N. E. and me, I take leave, who am, Sir, your obliged friend and Servant,

S. S.

July 8. Went with Mr. Brattle and swam in the Thames, went off from the Temple Stairs, . . . I went in in my Drawers. I think it hath been healthfull and refreshing to me.

Wednesday, July 10th. Between 12 and 1 it grows very dark, thunder, Lightening and Rain, much like a N. E. Thunder Shower: but the Thunder not so sharp.

July 12. This day two stood in the Pillory before the Royal Exchange for speaking against the Government. Shears was one. They were exceedingly pelted with dirt and Eggs. Another, that stood for forgery, had none thrown at him that I took notice of. Cousin Hull startled me again this day in the even, saying with a concern'd Countenance, there was bad News for me, which was, that my Suit of Cloaths was in danger of being Moth-eaten. Treated John Rawson at the Clubb to day. He belongs to the Pearl Frigot, a 5th Rate, 30 odd Guns.

Monday, July 15th. I rid to Tyburn, and saw Eighteen Persons, 16 Men and 2 Women, fall. They were unruly in the Prison, which hasten'd the Execution. Din'd in Great Russell Street, view'd the House and Walks of Lord Montague: then ridd to Hemsted. Montague House makes a goodly Shew that way. Hempsted is a most sweet and pleasant place for Air and shady Groves. Bought the Gazett there. From thence ridd to Highgate, which is about a Mile. There drank at the Crown, and then came home by Islington.

July 17. Mr. Mather, on Change, told Capt. Hutchinson and Sam. Appleton that he had put in their Names as Witnesses to Sir Edmund's [Andros] raising Money without an Assembly. Aske'd where was Capt. Hutchinson. I shewed and went with him to him, and Mr. Mather ask'd him to be at Westminster at such a time, but said not a word to me. Afterwards I went home, and then went to Mr. Whiting's and told him that I could testify, and Mr. Walker that collected the Money was in Town. He seem'd little to heed it, and said I might be there: he knew not that I could testify: but he seems plainly to be offended, and for my part I can't tell for what. A Moneth or two agoe Mr. Mather spake something about it, and I said I could not tell whether 'twere so convenient then, because we hop'd every day for the Parliament Act to come forth, and thought Sir Edmund might have friends there, and such a thing as this might make them more desperately eger to hinder the Bill. But now the Bill is even despair'd of, and our friends in N. E. are in for Cakes and Ale, and we must doe all we may and swim or sink with them. . . . Capt. Hutchinson, Mr. Sam. Appleton and I went to Westminster to give an Evidence for

N. E., but there was not an opportunity. So must wait on Mr. Mather again another time.

July 19. I was in the Shop to read a Print Cousin Hull had took in about Ireland, and Madam Owen and Madam Usher passed by, so I invited them and they kindly came up to my Chamber. I treated them with a Glass of good Cider. Gave Madam Owen one of Mr. Cotton Mather's Sermons, the Revolution of N. E., and Mr. Kick's Letter. Advis'd with Mr. Mather about Mrs. Pool's Legacy. He would remit the Money by Bill of Exchange, if it were to Him.

Wednesday, July 24. Dine at Cous. Brattles. . . . Had a Dish of Bacon with Pidgeons, Sauce, Beans and Cabbage. Then roast Veal. Tarts. . . . View'd Sir Henry Johnson's Dock, where the Ships ly afloat at Low water, the Gates keeping in the Water. A very great Ship building there now. From thence went on board the Mehetabel, and then on board the America, at Bugsby hole. So to Blackwall again, which has two little Streets like a Carpenters Square. Walk'd home. I fell down and hurt my right hand and left Legg on the Gravel. Standard out and Bells ringing for joy the Princes Anne is brought to Bed of a Son.

Aug. 1. News Letter. A Ship is arriv'd at Penzans in Cornwall, from New England, and reports that that Government has in all their Towns and Cities proclaimed William and Mary their rightfull Soveraigns, and caused all Processes of Law, and otherwise, to run in their Majesties Names, and are sending over two persons in the nature of Envoys, to have their Liberties confirmed and to pay fealty for the same. I read the above-written at Temple-Bar, at Cheapside and Algate, in the very same words.

[SEWALL LEAVES ENGLAND]

[ARRIVES HOME DECEMBER 2, 1689]

* * * * * *

Jan. 9th. [1690] Tho. Hawkins, Pirat, was Tried and found guilty.

Sabbath, Jan. 12. Richard Dumer, a flourishing youth of 9 years old, dies of the Small Pocks. I tell Sam. of it and what need he had to prepare for Death, and therefore to endeavor really to pray when he said over the Lord's Prayer: He seem'd not much to mind, eating an Apple; but when he came to say, Our father, he burst out into a bitter Cry, and when I askt what was the matter and he could speak, he burst out into a bitter Cry and said he was afraid he should die. I pray'd with him, and read Scriptures comforting against death, as, O death where is thy sting, &c. All things yours. Life and Immortality brought to light by Christ, &c. 'Twas at noon.

Friday, 17. Went after dinner to the Town-House, to Mr. Addington, from thence to Mr. Browning's, from thence with Mr. Cotton Mather to the Prisoners who were condemned on Friday. Spoke to, and pray'd with Pounds and others; then with Coward, Johnson and others.[49] Gave him [Mr. Mather] two Duzen Books bound, viz. Right thoughts. &c. Sermons to his Father Philips, and on the Ark.

Monday, Jan. 27. Five were order'd to be executed, but chiefly through Mr. Winthrop's earnestness in Reprieving, only Tho. Johnson dies. Had join'd in reprieving Pounds and Buck at the Governour's, and then got away; but Mr. Winthrop, Addington, Shrimpton followed me to my house with another Writing for Hawkins, which Winthrop and Shrimpton had signed, and got me to sign: He was ready to be turn'd off before it took effect, which gave great disgust to the People: I fear it was ill done. Governour, Winthrop, Shrimpton, Addington, Phillips, repriev'd Coward, and most seem'd to desire that he and his 3 companions might be spar'd. Some in the Council thought Hawkins, because he got out of the Combination before Pease was kill'd, might live as well as Coward; so I rashly sign'd, hoping so great an inconvenience would not have followed. Let not God impute Sin.

Feb. 8. and 9th Schenectady, a village 20 miles above Albany, destroy'd by the French. 60 Men, Women and Children murder'd. Women with Child ripp'd up, Children had their Brains dash'd out. Were surpris'd about 11. or 12 aclock Satterday night, being divided, and secure.

[February 24, 1690] Just about dinner time Mr. Nelson comes in and gets me to subscribe 100. to the Proposals against the French. I thought 'twas time to doe something, now were thus destroy'd by Land too. Mr. Danfoth looks very sorrowfully. Mr. Stoughton thinks best to prosecute vigorously the business against the Eastern French.

TO THE CONSTABLES OF BOSTON,
AND EVERY OF THEM.

You are Required in their Majesties Names to Walk through the several parts of the Town this day, and take effectual care to suppress and dissipate all unlawfull Assemblies, or tumultuous gathering together of people for the Shailing or throwing at Cocks, and such like Disorders, tending to the disturbance of their Majesties Liege People, and breach of the Peace, contrary to the wholsom Laws on that behalf made and provided, particularly, those entituled Cruelty, and Prescriptions. Hereof you may not fail. Dated in Boston the fourth day of March 1689/90. Annoque Reg. and Reginæ Willielms and Mariæ—Secundo.

SIMON BRADSTREET *Gov*.
WAIT WINTHROP
ELISHA HUTCHINSON
SAM SEWALL
ISAAC ADDINGTON
*Assist*ᵗˢ

BOSTON; March 5 1689/90.

HONOURED SIR,—The Governour and Council have this day ordered us to advise with your self about disposing of the Friend-Indians in such place and manner as may be most expedient for the safety of the English and themselves. The Condition they are in requires some speedy Consideration; We therefore intreat your Company next Friday morning at either of our Houses; except you rather choose our waiting on you at Dorchester. The affording your Counsel in this momentous and difficult Concern, will be a means to succour your distressed Country, and very much oblige your friends and humble Servants.

WAIT WINTHROP.
SAM SEWALL.

Above is a Copy of a Letter to Mr. Stoughton by Eliakim.

March 10ᵗʰ 1689/90. Mr. Stoughton, Major Generall and my self met at my house . . . Enquired what might be most expedient for the present settlement of the Friend-Indians, so as may be for the safety of themselves and English; in order to passing a Law for them in the Generall Court.

Friday, March 21, 1689/90. It should have been on Wednesday, when the news came indistinctly in the afternoon of the Surprisal of Salmon Falls. This Friday morn before they went to Mr.

Stoughton's, the dolefull news came that between 80. and 100. persons were kill'd and carried away, were taken by surprise about break of day: no Watch kept: are about half French, half Indians. Hopewood Capt. of the Indians, Artel [François Hertel] of the French. Hampshire General got 100. Men and came up with the Enemy about Sun-set and fought them till night took away the sight of them. One Frenchman taken making up his pack who gives an account as above.

This day Capt. Townsend is appointed Commander in Chief.

Satterday, March 22. Sir William Phips offers himself to go in person; the Governour sends for me, and tells me of it, I tell the Court; they send for Sir William who accepts to goe, and is appointed to Command the Forces; Major Townsend relinquishes with Thanks. Sir William had been sent to at first; but some feared he would not goe; others thought his Lady could not consent. Court makes Sir William free, and Swear him Major Generall, and several others.

March 24, 1689/90. Eight Companies and Troops Train. I goe into the field, pray with the South Company, Exercise them in a few Distances, Facings, Doublings; before which Thanked them for their Respect in mentioning me when in England, warning the Company in my Name; and told them the place I was in required more Time and Strength than I had, so took leave of them.

March 25. Drums are beat through the Town for Volunteers.

April 4, 1690. Major Richards, Hutchinson, Col. Shrimpton, Mr. Addington and my self went to the Castle to view what Capt. Fayerwether had done, and what was proper for him further to doe in making Batteries, and putting the place into yet a more defensible posture. Went to Dear-Island, and saw how the sea wash'd it away. Then went to Apple-Island, to the Castle again, and there din'd; suffer'd no Guns to be fired; but the Captain caus'd the Flagg to be hoisted all the while we were there, in token of Respect. Cost us 5^s 8^d apiec.

April 15. Capt. Willard's Letter comes to Town of the 9th Instant, giving an account of the danger they were in at Casco of an Assault from the Enemy, 30 Indian Canoes being seen, and Several Fires on the Land.

Sabbath-day, August the four and twentieth, 1690. I publish my little Daughter's name to be Judith, held her up for Mr. Willard to baptize her. She cried not at all, though a pretty deal of water was poured on her by Mr. Willard when He baptized her: . . . I named my Daughter Judith for the sake of her Grandmother and great Grandmother, who both wore that Name, and the Signification of it very good: The Lord grant that we may have great cause to praise Him on her account and help her to speak the Jews Language and to forget that of Ashdod. Nehem. 13. 24. And that she may follow her Grandmother Hull, as she follows Christ, being not slothfull in Business, fervent in Spirit, serving the Lord. Her Prayers and Painstaking for all my Children are incessant, voluntary, with condescension to the meanest Services night and day: that I judg'd I could in justice doe no less than endeavour her remembrance by putting her Name on one of her Grand-Daughters. I have now had my health and opportunity to offer up Nine Children to God in Baptisme. Mr. Tho. Thacher baptized the two eldest; John and Samuel; Mr. Samuel Willard baptized the Seven younger. Lord grant that I who have thus solemnly and frequently named the name of the Lord Jesus, may depart from Iniquity; and that mine may be more His than Mine, or their own.

Augt. 28. Publick Fast. Letters are brought to the Governour informing that the Maquaws [Mohawks] failing to join the Christians at Wooden [Wood] Creek about 100 miles above Albany, they were coming back again, which puts a great damp upon us here, to think that our fleet should be disappointed of their expected Aid.

Sept. 1, 1690. Eight Companies Train. Governour dines at Mr. Pain's with the South Company. Capt. Frary exercises the Company. Joseph is carried into the Common to take the air and see the men.

Thorsday Sept. 11ᵗʰ. Being crowded in the Pue, by reason Mr. Hutchinson and Sergeant constantly sit there and claim Propriety, so Mr. Usher is forced to take my place; having also found that sitting so near the out-side of the House causeth me in Wintertime to take cold in my head, I removed into Gallery, and sat with Dept. Governour, Mr. Russel, Major Hutchinson, where had very convenient sitting.

Sept. 13ᵗʰ. . This Week we hear of a sore fight between the English and French Fleets.

Sept. 14ᵗʰ I Watch, Word was Salmon-Falls, had a very comfortable night; only between 3. and 4. were disquieted by Guns
fired at Charlestown, and Drum beat: But I did not observe a
continual Beat of the Drum, so caus'd not an Alarm; and about
day a Messenger was sent over who told us the occasion was some
Indians seen in their back fields. Run-away Servants they appear
to be; by which means the Town was generally rais'd: But throw
God's goodness Trouble at Boston prevented.

Tuesday, Sept. 16ᵗʰ. About eleven at night a Fire breaks out
at the House of Jnᵒ Allen, Worsted Comber, in which his Apprentice, Sam. Worster, was burned, with the House of Lieut. Reynolds,
Mr. Bligh, Langden and a great part of Savil Simson's. The wind
being Sou-west the South-Meeting-House was preserv'd with very
much difficulty, being in a flame in diverse places of it.

Sept. 22. In the even, Mr. Moodey, Allen, Mather come from
Mrs. Clark's Funeral to see us. Mr. Moodey and I went before
the other came, to neighbor Hord, who lay dying; where also
Mr. Allen came in. Nurse Hord told her Husband who was there,
and what he had to say; whether he desir'd them to pray with him:
He said with some earnestness, Hold your tongue, which was
repeated three times to his wive's repeated intreaties; once he
said, Let me alone, or, be quiet, (whether that made a fourth or
was one of the three do not remember) and, My Spirits are gon.
At last Mr. Moodey took him up pretty roundly and told him he
might with the same labour have given a pertinent answer. When
were ready to come away Mr. Moodey bid him put forth a little
Breath to ask prayer, and said twas the last time had to speak to
him; At last ask'd him, doe you desire prayer, shall I pray with
you, He answer'd, Ay for the Lord's sake, and thank'd Mr. Moodey
when had done. His former carriage was very startling and amazing to us. About One at night he died. About 11. aclock I supposed
to hear neighbour Mason at prayer with him, just as I and my wife
were going to bed. Mr. Allen prayed with us when came from
said Hord's.

March 19, 1690/1. Mr. C. Mather preaches the Lecture from
Mat. 24., and appoint his portion with the Hypocrites: . . . To be
zealous against an innocent fashion, taken up and used by the
best of men; and yet make no Conscience of being guilty of great
Immoralities. Tis supposed [he] means wearing of Perriwigs: said

would deny themselves in anything but parting with an opportunity to do God service; that so might not offend good Christians. Meaning, I suppose, was fain to wear a Perriwig for his health. I expected not to hear a vindication of Perriwigs in Boston Pulpit by Mr. Mather.

March 25, 1691. I walk on foot to Roxbury, and visit Mr. Bowls, who lies very sick of the Small Pocks, this the 7ᵗʰ day. Mr. Walter pray'd with him before I came away.

Apr. 20ᵗʰ 1691. Being pressed with the sense of my doing much harm and little good, and breach of Vows at my return from New York, this time twelvemonth, that is, not heedfully regarding to go at God's Call, I kept a Fast to pray that God would not take away but uphold me by his free Spirit.

Sept. 25ᵗʰ 1691. Elisabeth Clements of Havarill is tried for murdering her two female bastard children.

Sept. 26. She is brought in guilty by the Jury, Mr. Crisp Foreman. Mr. Stoughton was not in Court on Friday afternoon when the Trial was; and went off the Bench on Satterday morn when the Jury were call'd to give in their verdict.

April 11ᵗʰ 1692. Went to Salem, where, in the Meeting-house, the persons accused of Witchcraft were examined; was a very great Assembly; 'twas awfull to see how the afflicted persons were agitated. Mr. Noyes pray'd at the beginning, and Mr. Higginson concluded. [In the margin], *Vœ, Vœ, Vœ,* Witchcraft.[50]

Apr. 25, 1692. Eight Companies Train for the first time; considerable heat, and hurt done in skirmishing just at night. Mr. Lawson concluded with prayer; saluted one another with a general volley, gave the South Company a Piece of 8/8 [a Spanish dollar] to drink.

May 2. No Artillery Training, so near the Election.

May 4. Election-Day. Major Hutchinson and Capt. Greenough's Companies attend, Mr. Moodey preaches. Dine at Wing's. At the Election Capt. Johnson of Wooburn is left out, and Major Richards chosen again. Sir William Phips had the most votes, viz: 969. No Treat at the Governour's but Beer, Cider, Wine.

May 14ᵗʰ 1692. Sir William arrives in the Nonsuch Frigat: Candles are lighted before He gets into Townhouse. Eight Companies wait on Him to his house, and then on Mr. [Increase] Mather to his. Made no volleys because 'twas Satterday night.

Monday, May 16. Eight Companies and two from Charlestown guard Sir William and his Councillors to the Townhouse, where the Commissions were read and Oaths taken. I waited on the Dept. Governour to Town, and then was met by Brother Short and Northend, who inform'd me of the dangerous illness of my father, so I went with them, and was not present at the Solemnity; found my father much better. At Ipswich, as we were going, saw a Rainbow just about Sunset, in Company of Brother Northend.

July 13, 1692. Eight Companies in Arms on the Common, Right-hand File of each Company drawn off for the Service.

July 30, 1692. Mrs. Cary makes her escape out of Cambridge-Prison, who was Committed for Witchcraft.

Augt. 19th 1692. This day the Lieut. Governour, Major Phillips, Mr. Russel, Capt. Lynde and my self went to Watertown. Advis'd the Inhabitants at their Town-Meeting to settle a Minister; and if could not otherwise agree, should first have a Town-Meeting to decide where the Meetinghouse should be set.

This day [in the margin, Dolefull Witchcraft!] George Burrough, John Willard, Jn° Procter, Martha Carrier and George Jacobs were executed at Salem, a very great number of Spectators being present. Mr. Cotton Mather was there, Mr. Sims, Hale, Noyes, Chiever, &c. All of them said they were innocent, Carrier and all. Mr. Mather says they all died by a Righteous Sentence. Mr. Burrough by his Speech, Prayer, protestation of his Innocence, did much move unthinking persons, which occasions their speaking hardly concerning his being executed.

Augt. 25. Fast at the old [First] Church, respecting the Witchcraft, Drought, &c.

Monday, Sept. 19, 1692. About noon, at Salem, Giles Corey was press'd to death for standing Mute;[51] much pains was used with him two days, one after another, by the Court and Capt. Gardner of Nantucket who had been of his acquaintance: but all in vain.

Sept. 20. Now I hear from Salem that about 18 years agoe, he was suspected to have stampd and press'd a man to death, but was cleared. Twas not remembered till Anne Putnam was told of it by said Corey's Spectre the Sabbath-day night before the Execution.

Sept. 21. A petition is sent to Town in behalf of Dorcas Hoar, who now confesses:[52] Accordingly an order is sent to the Sheriff to forbear her Execution, notwithstanding her being in the Warrant to die to morrow. This is the first condemned person who has confess'd.

Thorsday, Sept. 22, 1692. William Stoughton, Esqr., John Hathorne, Esqr., Mr. Cotton Mather, and Capt. John Higginson, with my Brother St., were at our house, speaking about publishing some Trials of the Witches. Mr. Stoughton went away and left us, it began to rain and was very dark, so that getting some way beyond the fortification, was fain to come back again, and lodged here in Capt. Henchman's Room. Has been a plentifull Rain, blessed be God.

[October 11, 1692] Read Mr. Willard's Epistle to Mr. Mather's book, as to Cases of Conscience touching Witchcraft.[53]

Satterday, Oct. 15th Went to Cambridge and visited Mr. Danforth, and discoursed with Him about the Witchcraft; thinks there cannot be a procedure in the Court except there be some better consent of Ministers and People. Told me of the woman's coming into his house last Sabbath-day sennight at Even.

Oct. 26, 1692. A Bill is sent in about calling a Fast, and Convocation of Ministers, that may be led in the right way as to the Witchcrafts. The season and manner of doing it, is such, that the Court of Oyer and Terminer count themselves thereby dismissed. 29 Nos. and 33 yeas to the Bill. Capt. Bradstreet and Lieut. True, Wm. Huchins and several other interested persons there, in the affirmative.

Oct. 29. Mr. Russel asked whether the Court of Oyer and Terminer should sit, expressing some fear of Inconvenience by its fall. Governour said it must fall. Lieut. Governour not in Town today.

Nov. 4, 1692. Law passes for Justices and Ministers Marrying persons. By order of the Committee, I had drawn up a Bill for Justices and such others as the Assembly should appoint to marry: but came new-drawn and thus alter'd from the Deputies. It seems they count the respect of it too much to be left any longer with the Magistrate. And Salaries are not spoken of; as if one sort of Men might live on the Aer. They are treated like a kind of useless, worthless folk.

Nov. 6. Joseph threw a knop of Brass and hit his Sister Betty on the forhead so as to make it bleed and swell; upon which, and for his playing at Prayer-time, and eating when Return Thanks, I whipd him pretty smartly. When I first went in (call'd by his Grandmother) he sought to shadow and hide himself from me behind the head of the Cradle: which gave me the sorrowfull remembrance of Adam's carriage.

Nov. 22, 1692. I prayd that God would pardon all my Sinfull Wanderings, and direct me for the future. That God would bless the Assembly in their debates, and that would chuse and assist our Judges, &c., and save New England as to Enemies and Witchcrafts, and vindicate the late Judges, consisting with his Justice and Holiness, &c., with Fasting.

Jan. 19, 1693/4. Kitchen floor is finished. This day Mrs. Prout dies after sore conflicts of mind, not without suspicion of Witchcraft.

March 27, 1694. Governour, Mr. Danforth, Winthrop, Russell, Sewall, Addington, Foster, Sergeant, Walley, Lieut. Alford, Goodwin, Mason, and Atkins, Carpenter, went to the Castle to view the works in order to Reparation. Mr. Secretary read there the dialogue between Whig and Tory,[54] while it rained. As came up, Capt. Clark saluted us with 3 Huzâs and Guns from his Briganteen.

April 2, 1694. Monday. Artillery Training; Bastian and I set seeds of White-Thorn at Saunders's Pasture, north end. In the Afternoon, all the Town is filled with the discourse of Major Richards's Death, which was very extraordinarily suddain; was abroad on the Sabbath, din'd very well on Monday, and after that falling into an angry passion with his Servant Richard Frame, presently after, fell probably into a Fit of Apoplexy, and died. On Tuesday night was opened and no cause found of his death; noble Parts being fair and sound.

Wednesday, July 18, 1694. Oyster-River is surprised and 90 odd persons kill'd and captivated, 13 Houses burnd, much Cattel killed and Corn stroy'd.

Friday, July 27. Groton set upon by the Indians, 21 persons kill'd, 13 captivated, 3 badly wounded. About 9. night, Mr. Lodowick comes to Boston. Between 10. and 11. there is an Alarm through the Town kept up till near day-break. Mr. Brattle was arriv'd at Col. Shrimpton's, there he told me of Mr. Lodowicks unhappiness in coming just then.

[December 4, 1694] I mov'd Mr. Willard and Mr. Cotton Mather, that, seeing the Old and South Church fell short in their singing on the Thanksgiving-day, might make it up now, if they saw meet: Mr. Willard said would sing what He intended then, prevented by the night: Ask'd Lieut. Governour and read the 47. Ps. Clap hands.—Spake to me and I set it.

Tuesday, Dec. 25. Shops are open, men at work; Carts of Pork, Hay, Coal, Wood come to Town as on other days. Mr. Maccarty's shop is open.

April 1, 1695. Joseph speaking about my sending two Frenchmen to prison upon the Act relating to them, said, If this Country stand when I am a Man, I'll drive them all out.

April 1. Three of Watertown came to me and gave an account of their Town-Meeting; which was Wednesday last, but could do nothing: so adjourned to the 28.th Inst. and then chose Select-Men; Though the Farmers voted with the East-End; yet the Middle outvoted them and have chosen Select-men to their mind, and Capt. Garfield Town-Clerk, in stead of Capt. Prout, who has endeavour'd much to obstruct their proceedings about the New-meetinghouse. Parties were so combin'd on either side that 'twas a continued Duel in each, One to One; and Four Score and odd Votes apiece. The Lord give a peacable Settlement to that Church and Town, so as may be most for the advantage of His Interest and Glory.

April 3, 1695. I planted Two Locusts, two Elms at Wheelers pond, and one in Elm-Pasture near the Line over against the Middle-Elm. The middle Locust-Tree at Wheelers pond was set there the last year.

Apr. 5. There is pretty much Thunder and Lightening about break of day. Thunder seem'd to me like Great Guns at first.

Tuesday, Apr. 9, 1695. Piam Blower and others from Virginia and Barbados bring a Confirmation of the Queens death: and Report that the French King is dead; and his Gen! Luxemburg; that two other [s] duelled for the honour of his place, one fell, and the other went over to the Confederats.

Apr. 10. When I rise in the morn I find the Ground and houses covered with Snow. Be it that Lewis the 14th. be indeed dead &c. yet we may have a sharp, though short winter in New England still. God defend.

Monday, April 29, 1695. The morning is very warm and Sunshiny; in the Afternoon there is Thunder and Lightening, and about 2. P.M. a very extraordinary Storm of Hail, so that the ground was made white with it, as with the blossoms when fallen; 'twas as bigg as pistoll and Musquet Bullets; It broke of [f] the Glass of the new House about 480 Quarrels [Squares] of the Front; of Mr. Sergeant's about as much; Col. Shrimpton, Major General, Gov.r Bradstreet, New Meetinghouse, Mr. Willard, &c. Mr. Cotton Mather dined with us, and was with me in the new Kitchen when this was; He had just been mentioning that more Ministers Houses than others proportionably had been smitten with Lightening; enquiring what the meaning of God should be in it. Many Hail-Stones broke throw the Glass and flew to the middle of the Room, or farther: People afterward Gazed upon the House to see its Ruins. I got Mr. Mather to pray with us after this awfull Providence; He told God He had broken the brittle part of our house, and prayd that we might be ready for the time when our Clay-Tabernacles should be broken. Twas a sorrowfull thing to me to see the house so far undon again before twas finsh'd. . . .

I mentiond to Mr. Mather that Monmouth made his discent into England about the time of the Hail in '85, Summer, that much cracked our South-west windows.

Friday, June 14. The Bill against Incest was passed with the Deputies, four and twenty Nos, and seven and twenty Yeas. The Ministers gave in their Arguments yesterday in Writing; else it had hardly gon, because several have married their wives sisters, and the Deputies thought it hard to part them. 'Twas concluded on the other hand, that not to part them, were to make the Law abortive, by begetting in people a conceipt that such Marriages were not against the Law of God.

Augt. 6, 1695. Mr. Obinson's wife comes to me and complains of her Husband's ill usage of her; kick'd her out of bed last night; lets her have nothing but water to drink, won't let her have Cloths or victuals.

Feb. 1. 1695/6. Sam. Haugh came to speak about Frank's burial: I sent Atherton away before and spake to Sam as to his

Mistress' Maid being with child, and that she Laid it to him, and told him if she were with child by him, it concerned him seriously to consider what were best to be done; and that a Father was obliged to look after Mother and child. Christ would one day call him to an account and demand of him what was become of the child: and if [he] married not the woman, he would always keep at a distance from those whose temporal and spiritual good he was bound to promote to the uttermost of his power. Could not discern that any impression was made on him. I remark'd to him the unsuitableness of his frame under a business of so great and solemn Concern.

Sixth-day, Feb. 7th. Last night Sam. could not sleep because of my Brother's speaking to him of removing to some other place, mentioning Mr. Usher's. I put him to get up a little wood, and he even fainted, at which Brother was much startled, and advis'd to remove him forthwith and place him somewhere else, or send him to Salem and he would doe the best he could for him. Since, I have express'd doubtfullness to Sam. as to his staying there.

He mention'd to me Mr. Wadsworth's Sermon against Idleness, which was an Affliction to him. He said his was an idle Calling, and that he did more at home than there, take one day with another. And he mention'd Mr. Stoddard's words to me, that should place him with a good Master, and where had fullness of Imployment. It seems Sam. overhead him, and now alleged these words against his being where he was because of his idleness. Mention'd also the difficulty of the imployment by reason of the numerousness of Goods and hard to distinguish them, many not being marked; whereas Books, the price of them was set down, and so could sell them readily. I spake to Capt. Checkly again and again, and he gave me no encouragement that his being there would be to Sam's profit; and Mrs. Checkly always discouraging.

Mr. Willard's Sermon from those Words, What doest thou here Elijah? was an Occasion to hasten the Removal.

Feb. 10. Secund-day. I went to Mr. Willard to ask whether had best keep him at home to day. He said, No: but tell Capt. Checkly first; but when I came back, Sam was weeping and much discompos'd, and loth to goe because it was a little later than usual, so I thought twas hardly fit for him to go in that Case, and went to Capt. Checkly and told him how it was, and thank'd him for his

Patient obt. Don Sam not having found his calling yet.

78   THE DIARY OF SAMUEL SEWALL

kindness to Sam. Capt. Checkly desired Sam. might come to their house and not be strange there, for which I thank'd him very kindly. He presented his Service to my wife, and I to his who was in her Chamber. Capt. Checkly gave me Sam's Copy-book that lay in a drawer.

Just before I got thether, I met Mr. Grafford who told me that Mumford said I was a knave. The good Lord give me Truth in the inward parts, and finally give Rest unto my dear Son, and put him into some Calling wherein He will accept of him to Serve Him.

Feb. 22. 1695/6. Betty comes into me almost as soon as I was up and tells me the disquiet she had when waked; told me was afraid should go to Hell, was like Spira, not Elected. Ask'd her what I should pray for, she said, that God would pardon her Sin and give her a new heart. I answer'd her Fears as well as I could, and pray'd with many Tears on either part; hope God heard us. I gave her solemnly to God.

Feb. 26. 1695/6. I pray'd with Sam. alone, that God would direct our way as to a Calling for him.

Sabbath, May 3, 1696. Betty can hardly read her chapter for weeping; tells me she is afraid she is gon back, does not taste that sweetness in reading the Word which once she did; fears that what was once upon her is worn off. I said what I could to her, and in the evening pray'd with her alone.

June 11, 1696. I strove with my might that in stead of Tuesday, Thursday, and Satterday in every Week, it might be said, Third, fifth and seventh day in every week: but could not prevail, hardly one in the Council would secund me, and many spake against it very earnestly; although I asked not to have it chang'd in the Fairs. Some said twas the speech of the English Nation; mend it in the Fasts; mend it every where or no where, others said persons would scarce know what days were intended; and in England would call us Quakers. I urg'd that the Week only, of all parcells of time, was of Divine Institution, erected by God as a monumental pillar for a memorial of the Creation perfected in so many distinct days.

June 20th Wm Veisy is bound over for plowing on the day of Thanksgiving &c. News comes that the embargo is kept strictly in England.

[July] 27th [1696] At the Council the Lt. Govr reads the Letters that give notice from the Lords of a French Squadron intending for America: they will afford us what Assistance they can under the present Circumstance of Affairs. . . . This day also receiv'd an Express from Col. Pynchon, of Count Frontenac's coming ag.ᵗ the 5 Nations, or Albany, or N. E., or all, with 2000 French and 1000 Indians: Casteen with 4 or 500 to hold us in play the mean while. The wind coming North last night ships arrive at Nantasket this morning. Mr. Myles and Bullivant come to Town.

Third day Augt 4. Pemmaquid Fort is summond by the French: the two ships which took the Newport Gally, and said Gally; besides many hundreds by Land.

Fourth day of Aug.ᵗ 5.ᵗʰ summond them again, and for fear of their Guns, Bombs and numbers, Capt Chub surrendred, and then they blew up the Fort. This News came to Town Aug.ᵗ 10. Capt. Paxton brought it; just after publishing the Act referring to Navigation. Fourth-day Augt. 12, 1696. Mr. Melyen, upon a slight occasion, spoke to me very smartly about the Salem Witch-craft: in discourse he said, if a man should take Beacon hill on 's back, carry it away; and then bring it and set it in its place again, he should not make any thing of that.[55]

Seventh-day, Aug.ᵗ 15.ᵗʰ Bro.ʳ St. Sewall comes to Town; Gets an order to Col. Hathorne for erecting a Beacon on Pigeon hill on Cape-Anne, and for pressing 20. men at Marble-head. This day vessels arrive from Barbados, bring news of 10. great ships at Petit Quavers, of between 60 and 90 Guns. Mr. Williams, the physician, and his wife are both dead. Mrs. Hatch and her children in Tears for the death of her husband, which was brought to her about an hour by Sun. We are in pain for Saco fort. Guns were heard thrice on fifth day all day long. One Peters and Hoyt scalp'd at Andover this week; were not shot, but knock'd on the head.

Sept.ʳ 8. Mr. Benj.ᵃ Wadsworth is ordain'd pastor of the first Church. Mr. Allin gave the charge, Mr. I. Mather gave the Right Hand of Fellowship: Spake notably of some young men who had apostatized from New England principles, contrary to the Light of their education: was glad that he [Mr. Wadsworth] was of an-other spirit. Mr. Willard was one who joined in laying on of hands.

[September 10, 1696] Letter. Mrs. Martha Oakes. Not finding opportunity to speak with you at your house, nor at my own, I write, to persuade you to be sensible that your striking your daughter-in-law before me, in my house, is not justifiable: though twas but a small blow, twas not a small fault: especially considering your promise to refrain from speech it self; or at least any that might give disturbance. As for New England, It is a cleaner Country than ever you were in before, and, therefore, with disdain to term it *filthy,* is a sort of Blasphemie, which, by proceeding out of your mouth, hath defiled you. I write not this to upbraid, but to admonish you, with whom I sympathize under your extraordinary provocations and pressures; and pray God command you freedom from them. S. S.

S.ᵣ 16. Keep a day of Prayer in the East end of the Town-House, Gov.ᵣ, Council and Assembly. Mr. Morton begun with Prayer, Mr. Allin pray'd, Mr. Willard preached—If God be with us who can be against us?—Spake smartly at last about the Salem Witchcrafts, and that no order had been suffer'd to come forth by Authority to ask Gods pardon.

[January 1, 1696/7] On the 22ᵗʰ of May I buried my abortive son; so neither of us were then admitted of God to be there, and now the Owners of the family admit us not: It may be I must never more hear a Sermon there. The Lord pardon all my Sins of Omission and Commission: and by his Almighty power make me meet to be partaker of the Inheritance with the Sᵗˢ in Light. Second-day Jan.ʸ 11, 1696/7 God helped me to pray more than ordinarily, that He would make up our Loss in the burial of our little daughter and other children, and that would give us a Child to Serve Him, pleading with Him as the Institutor of Marriage, and the Author of every good work.

[January 15, 1696/7] Copy of the Bill I put up on the Fast day; giving it to Mr. Willard as he pass'd by, and standing up at the reading of it, and bowing when finished; in the Afternoon.

Samuel Sewall, sensible of the reiterated strokes of God upon himself and family; and being sensible, that as to the Guilt contracted upon the opening of the late Commission of Oyer and Terminer at Salem (to which the order for this Day relates) he is, upon many accounts, more concerned than any that he knows of, Desires to take the Blame and shame of it, Asking pardon of men, And especially desiring prayers that God, who has an Unlimited Authority, would pardon that sin and all other his sins; personal and Relative: And according to his infinite Benignity,

and Sovereignty, Not Visit the sin of him, or of any other, upon
himself or any of his, nor upon the Land: But that He would
powerfully defend him against all Temptations to Sin, for the
future; and vouchsafe him the efficacious, saving Conduct of his
Word and Spirit.[56]

[May 1, 1697] Hannah Dustan came to see us; I gave her part
of Connecticut Flax. She saith her Master, whom she kill'd, did
formerly live with Mr. Roulandson at Lancaster: He told her, that
when he pray'd the English way, he thought that was good: but
now he found the French way was better. The single man shewed
the night before, to Sam! Lennarson, how he used to knock Eng-
lishmen on the head and take off their Scalps; little thinking that
the Captives would make some of their first experiment upon himself. Sam. Lennarson kill'd him.

Oct! 1. 1697. Jer. Balchar's sons came for us to go to the
Island. My Wife, through Indisposition, could not goe: But I
carried Sam, Hannah, Elisa, Joseph, Mary and Jane Tapan: I
prevail'd with Mr. Willard to goe, He carried Simon, Elisabeth,
William, Margaret, and Elisa Tyng: Had a very comfortable Passage thither and home again; though against Tide: Had first Butter, Honey, Curds and Cream. For Dinner, very good Rost Lamb,
Turkey, Fowls, Applepy. After Dinner sung the 121 Psalm. Note.
A Glass of spirits my Wife sent stood upon a Joint-Stool which,
Simon W. jogging, it fell down and broke all to shivers: I said
twas a lively Emblem of our Fragility and Mortality.

Sept 29, 1697, A Council met at Plimouth:

Sept 30. They published their Advice, that Mr. Cotton[57] should
make an orderly secession from the Church. Advis'd the Church
to dismiss him with as much Charity as the Rule would admit of;
and provide for themselvs. This was for his Notorious Breaches
of the Seventh Commandmt, and Undue Carriage in chusing
Elders. Thus Christs words are fullfilled, Unsavoury Salt is cast
to the Dunghill. A most awfull Instance!

Fourth day Oct! 6. 1697. A Church is gathered at Watertown,
East-end, and Mr. Gibbs Ordained. Mr. Fox ordains, Mr. Sher-
man gives the Right Hand of Fellowship. This was done in the
Afternoon in the open Aer though a cold day. The Western party,
having the Select-Men on their side, got possession of the Meetinghouse, and would not suffer the Assembly to enter there. The Lord

be mercifull to his people, pardon our sins and heal our gaping wounds. Mr. Torrey tells me that Mr. Mather declar'd among the Ministers Octr 7. that they had dealt too favourably with Mr. Cotton.

Decr 22. 1697. A Law against Exportation of Money is published, and the Court prorogued to March 16. at one in the Afternoon. No Prayer this Court that I hear of in the Council. It hath been extream cold. Decemb^r 25. 97. Snowy day: Shops are open, and Carts and sleds come to Town with Wood and Fagots as formerly, save what abatement may be allowed on account of the wether. This morning we read in course the 14, 15, and 16th Psalms. From the 4th v. of the 16thth Ps I took occasion to dehort mine from Christmas-keeping, and charged them to forbear. Hannah reads Daniel, 6. and Betty, Luke, 12. Joseph tells me that though most of the Boys went to the Church yet he went not. By the Intercession of his Mother, and his brothers Concession, he begins to read the Psalm.

March, 8. [1697/8] Get to Plimouth about Noon, Are entertain'd at Cole's. Send two mile for Mr. Little, who prays at the opening of the Court: invite him to Dinner: Speak not to Mr. Cotton. I lodge at Cole's, the house was built by Govr Winslow and is the oldest in Plimouth.

[March 10, 1697/8] Had large discourse in the even with Mrs. Cotton, Mr. Cotton, Mr. Rowland. I told Mr. Cotton, a free confession was the best way; spake of Davids roaring all the day long and bones waxing old whilest he kept silence. I spake with Deacon Fance today, sent for him to Mr. Cotton's: It seems upon the 5th of October, The Church, by speaking one by one, declared their Mind was to Release Mr. Cotton from his office-bond as Pastor; sent to Mr. Cotton to meet them (they were at Shirtly's, 25 in number, some that could not come sent their minds to the same effect: and New Society ready to do it). Mr. Cotton to come to the Meeting-house, thither they goe, and there Deacon Fance declares what the church had done. Mr. Cotton was at Cole's: when ready to come away March, 11. I said his danger was lest catching at shadows, he should neglect the cords thrown out to him by Christ and so be drown'd. Some of my last words to him was, Kisse the Son, lest he be angry! This was in the house between him and me alone. Just as was mounting, He desired me to pray for him till I heard he was dead.

Tuesday, June, 28. 1698. Court at Salem, Major Brown praesident; were remov'd to the Ship Tavern and candles lighted; a cry of Fire was made. A Girl drawing Rum in a little Warehouse of Mr. Lyndon's, or looking after a cask that leak'd, the candle fired it, which took the cask and broke it up with a Report, so catch'd Cotton and fired Mr. Willoughbys house in the Garret of which was a Barrel of Powder, that taking fire blew off the Roof and very much dispersed the flaming partickles; much of which was thrown on Major Brown's house over the way, the wind carrying it thither so that and his warehouse were quickly burnt down, and much Money and Goods lost with the Buildings. Five houses in all burnt, Mr. Hirst's for one. This is the first considerable Fire that ever was in Salem. It seems the stroke makes a deep impression on Maj^r Brown. Has lost 3 or four Thousand pounds.

July, 15. 1698. Mr. Edward Taylor[58] comes to our house from Westfield. Monday July 18. I walk'd with Mr. Edward Taylor upon Cotton Hill, thence to Becon Hill, the Pasture, along the Stone-wall: As came back, we sat down on the great Rock, and Mr. Taylor told me his courting his first wife, and Mr. Fitch his story of Mr. Dod's prayer to God to bring his Affection to close with a person pious, but hard-favoured. Has God answered me in finding out one Godly and fit for me, and shall I part for fancy? When came home, my wife gave me Mr. Tappan's Letter concerning Eliza, which caus'd me to reflect on Mr. Taylor's Discourse. And his Prayer was for pardon of error in our ways—which made me think whether it were not best to overlook all, and go on. This day John Ive, fishing in great Spie-pond, is arrested with mortal sickness which renders him in a manner speechless and senseless; dies next day; buried at Charlestown on the Wednesday. Was a very debauched, atheistical man. I was not at his Funeral. Had Gloves sent me, but the knowledge of his notoriously wicked life made me sick of going; and Mr. Mather, the president, came in just as I was ready to step out, and so I staid at home, and by that means lost a Ring: but hope had no loss. Follow thou Me, was I suppose more complied with, than if had left Mr. Mather's company to go to such a Funeral.

Augt. 16. To Quaboag, with a guard of 20 Men under Cornet Brown. Between Worcester and Quaboag we were greatly wet with Rain; wet to the skin. Got thither before twas dark. A Guard of 20 from Springfield met us there, and saluted us with their trumpets as we alighted. Augt. 17. very fair day in which we went to Springfield. Augt. 18. Open'd the Court, present Winthrop, Cooke, Sewall. Gave a Bill to the Grand-Jury, Mr. John Holyoke, Foreman. They found the Bill. Inpanel'd a Jury of Trial; upon her [?] Arraignment, she having at last pleaded Not guilty, Adjourn'd to the morning, when court Open'd, Mr. Taylor of Westfield prayed. Augt. 19. Jury, Mr. Parsons foreman, brought in Sarah Smith Guilty of murdering her Bastard daughter. Adjourn'd till Noon. Court met and the Maj^r Generall pronounced the sentence. She had been kept at Derefield about a Moneth's time, by reason of the extremity of the Winter, was brought down to Springfield Jail Febr. 18.

Augt 22. Return'd to Springfield; Mr. Tailor [Taylor] with me. Rain'd hard in the Afternoon and night, and part of the morn. Augt. 23. By which means were not able to reach Quaboag; and twas thought could not pass the Rivers. So went to Northampton, a very Paradise. Lodg'd at the ordinary, getting to town in the night. Augt. 24. very fair day, Mr. Cook and I went with Mr. Stoddard and heard Mr. I. Chauncy preach his first Lecture at Hadley. Made a very good sermon. Invited us to dinner. Went over to Hatfield. Mr. Cook being importun'd to see Benj Wait's wife; it was late and lodg'd all night with Mr. Williams.

Oct. 23^r [1699] The amazing news of the dismal Mortality at Charlestown in Carolina comes to Town and is spread all over it: 150 dead in 6 days time: Draw the dead to the Grave in Carts. Mr. Cotton is dead among the rest. Infection was brought from Providence. This made us the rather put Plantations in the plural number in the Bill this day order'd for Thanksgiving.

Octob^r 26. 1699. Joseph Bradish, Tee Witherly, and Kate Price are brought to Town and sent to Prison, from whence they escaped June, 24. Fast is warned to be next Thorsday for the Afflicted church abroad.

The Diary

VOLUME II
(1699–1714)

Tuesday, Febr. 6 [1699/1700] A Council is held at my Lord's. The Advice of Councillors asked about sending the Pirats on Board. I motioned that by that time the Prisoners could be got from N. York, Connecticut, Rode-Island: the Assembly might sit if his L^dship saw meet, and they would willingly rid themselves of them. Govr seem'd displeas'd. I had ask'd before, What Pirats, and the Govr said them and their Associates. Govr mention'd Kid, Gillam, Bradish, Witherly, to be sent aboard presently for better security. Council voted to leave it to the Govrs. Discretion whom to send aboard: only the Govr had said to some that enquired, He intended not [to let] them out upon Bail. I think only I, Col. Townsend and Capt. Byfield were in the Negative. I said I was not clear in it. The grounds I went upon were because I knew of no power I had to send Men out of the Province. Capt. Byfield said, He was for their going aboard: but reckon'd twas not so safe to send them presently as to keep them in Goal. Voted also the Treasure to be deliver'd to such as the Govr should appoint.[1]

Febr. 22. I had thoughts of sitting up to see the eclipse: but the cloudy thick sky discouraged me: yet kept a candle burning, and went to the Window at two of the clock; the wether was still thick with clouds, that I could see nothing: only seem'd very dark for a full Moon.

In the evening I visited Mrs. Williams in her Languishing. Am invited to a Fast there on Friday.

Wednesday, Febr. 28. We ship off the Iron chest of Gold, Pearls &c., 40 Bails of East-India Goods, 13 hogsheads, chests and case, one Negro Man, and Venturo Resail, an East-Indian born at Ceilon. Wether was doubtfull in the morning, which made us irresolute: but at last we set about it, and accomplish'd it very happily. I look upon it as a great Mercy of God, that the Storehouse has not been broken up, no fire has happened. Agreed in the Weight of the Gold with our former Weight, and had so comfortable a day at last to finish our work. Mr. Bradstreet, and Capt. Winn's Clerk took an account at the Crane; but Capt. Winn would not give a Rec^t till had them on board the sloop Antonio, which ridd off just without the Outward Wharf. Gave a Rec^t for the Gold at Capt Belchar's as soon as it was weighed.

March, 4. 1699. Capt. Gullock is sent to Prison for his contempt of the Governm^t in giving in to the Govr and Council an Insolent writing under his hand, and justifying it.

March 5, Tuesday, 1699/1700. Mr. Sergeant, Capt. Frary, Capt. Hill, Capt Checkly and my self goe to Cambridge over the Ferry, and acquaint Mr. Pemberton with the Church's Call, and their desire of his Acceptance. He makes a very sensible Answer as to the Weight of the Work, his own inability; hôp'd God would hear his earnest Prayer, and help him to make a right Answer.

Monday, April, 1. I was in a great quandary whether I had best to avoid the wind, come home by water and leave my Horse, or no. At last I went on board Elisha Hedge's decked sloop laden with Oyle. He put in there in the storm from Yarmouth and lay till now for a wind. Came aboard about 2 hours by Sun, and landed at Mrs. Butlers Wharf before 3 p.m. Having had a very speedy and pleasant Passage, wherein I have experienced much of God's parental pity towards me, and care over me. I could not have got home to day by Land: and I fear my health would have been much impair'd, if I had come but part of the way. Jonathan Wheeler ridd in the Rain from Milton. I have now kept one Sabbath with those who first kept Sabbaths in New England.[2]

Sabbath, Apr. 14. I saw and heard the Swallows proclaim the Spring.

Monday, Apr. 29, 1700. Sam. Sewall, Joseph Willard, Jno Bayly, Sam. Gaskill, and —— Mountfort goe into the Harbour a fishing in a small Boat. Seeing Rich'd Fifield coming in, some would needs meet the ship and see who it was: Ship had fresh way with a fair wind; when came neare, Capt. call'd to them to beware, order'd what they should doe. But they did the clear contrary, fell foul on the ship, which broke their Mast short off, fill'd the Boat with water, threw Willard and Gaskill into the River. Both which were very near drown'd; especially Gaskill, who could not swim. It pleas'd God Fifield's Boat was out, so he presently man'd it and took them in. Gaskill was under water, but discover'd by his Hat that swam atop as a Buoy. Sam, Jno Bayly and Mountfort caught hold of the Ship and climbed on board in a miserable fright as having stared death in the face. This is the second time Sam has been near drown'd with Josiah Willard. Mother was against his going, and prevented Joseph, who pleaded earnestly to

Slavery

go. He sensibly acknowledged the Good Providence in his staying at home, when he saw the issue.

May 14. Get to Newbury a little before sunset, visit my sick Father in bed, call in the Major Gen[l] whom Father salutes. Kiss'd my hand, and I his again.

May, 15. Walks into the west end of the house with his staff, breakfasts there. I read the 17th Luke, and went to Prayer. My father would have stood up but I persuaded him to sit still in his chair. Took leave and went on to Portsmouth.

Fourth-day, June, 19. 1700. Mr. Jn[o] Eyre is entomed in the new burying place. Nine of his children are laid there to handsel the new Tomb: Bearers, Sewall, Addington, Townsend, Byfield, Dummer, Davis: Scarvs and Rings. L[t] Gov[r] and many of the Council there. Mr. Thomas Brattle led his mourning widowed Sister. When I parted, I pray'd God to be favourably present with her, and comfort her in the absence of so near and dear a Relation.

Having been long and much dissatisfied with the Trade of fetching Negros from Guinea; at last I had a strong Inclination to Write something about it; but it wore off. At last reading Bayne, Ephes. about servants, who mentions Blackamoors; I began to be uneasy that I had so long neglected doing any thing. When I was thus thinking, in came Bro[r] Belknap to shew me a Petition he intended to present to the Gen[l] Court for the freeing a Negro and his wife, who were unjustly held in Bondage. And there is a Motion by a Boston Committee to get a Law that all Importers of Negros shall pay 40[s] p̄ head, to discourage the bringing of them. And Mr. C. Mather resolves to publish a sheet to exhort Masters to labour their Conversion. Which makes me hope that I was call'd of God to Write this Apology for them;[3] Let his Blessing accompany the same.

"The Selling of Joseph.
A MEMORIAL.

"Forasmuch as Liberty *is in real value next unto* Life: *None ought to part with it themselves, or deprive others of it, but upon most mature Consideration.*

"The Numerousness of Slaves at this day in the Province, and the Uneasiness of them under their Slavery, hath put many upon thinking whether the Foundation of it be firmly and well laid; so as to sustain the Vast Weight that is built upon it. It is most certain that all Men, as they are the Sons of *Adam,* are Coheirs; and have equal Right unto Liberty, and all other outward Comforts of Life. *GOD hath given the Earth* (with all its Commodities) *unto the Sons of* Adam, *Psal* 115. 16. *And hath made of One Blood, all Nations of Men, for to dwell on all the face of the Earth, and hath determined the Times before appointed, and the bounds of their habitation: That they should seek the Lord. Forasmuch then as we are the Offspring of GOD* &c. *Act* 17. 26, 27, 29. Now although the Title given by the last ADAM, doth infinitely better Mens Estates, respecting GOD and themselves; and grants them a most beneficial and inviolable Lease under the Broad Seal of Heaven, who were before only Tenants at Will: Yet through the Indulgence of GOD to our First Parents after the Fall, the outward Estate of all and every of their Children, remains the same, as to one another. So that Originally, and Naturally, there is no such thing as Slavery. *Joseph* was rightfully no more a Slave to his Brethren, than they were to him: and they had no more Authority to *Sell* him, than they had to *Slay* him. And if *they* had nothing to do to Sell him; the *Ishmaelites* bargaining with them, and paying down Twenty pieces of Silver, could not make a Title. Neither could *Potiphar* have any better Interest in him than the *Ishmaelites* had. *Gen.* 37. 20, 27, 28. For he that shall in this case plead *Alteration of Property,* seems to have forfeited a great part of his own claim to Humanity. There is no proportion between Twenty Pieces of Silver, and LIBERTY. The Commodity it self is the Claimer. If *Arabian* Gold be imported in any quantities, most are afraid to meddle with it, though they might have it at easy rates; lest if it should have been wrongfully taken from the Owners, it should kindle a fire to the Consumption of their whole Estate. 'Tis pity there should be more Caution used in buying a Horse, or a little lifeless dust; than there is in purchasing Men and Women: Whenas they are the Offspring of GOD, and their Liberty is,

" ' . . . . *Auro pretiosior Omni.*'

"And seeing GOD hath said, *He that Stealeth a Man and Selleth him, or if he be found in his hand, he shall surely be put to Death.* Exod. 21. 16. This Law being of Everlasting Equity, wherein Man

Stealing is ranked amongst the most atrocious of Capital Crimes:
What louder Cry can there be made of that Celebrated Warning,

" 'Caveat Emptor!'

"And all things considered, it would conduce more to the Welfare of the Province, to have White Servants for a Term of Years,
than to have Slaves for Life. Few can endure to hear of a Negro's
being made free; and indeed they can seldom use their freedom
well; yet their continual aspiring after their forbidden Liberty,
renders them Unwilling Servants. And there is such a disparity
in their Conditions, Colour & Hair, that they can never embody
with us, and grow up into orderly Families, to the Peopling of the
Land: but still remain in our Body Politick as a kind of extravasat
Blood. As many Negro men as there are among us, so many empty
places there are in our Train Bands, and the places taken up of
Men that might make Husbands for our Daughters. And the Sons
and Daughters of *New England* would become more like *Jacob,*
and *Rachel,* if this Slavery were thrust quite out of doors. More-
over it is too well known what Temptations Masters are under,
to connive at the Fornication of their Slaves; lest they should be
obliged to find them Wives, or pay their Fines. It seems to be
practically pleaded that they might be Lawless; 'tis thought much
of, that the Law should have Satisfaction for their Thefts, and
other Immoralities; by which means, *Holiness to the Lord,* is more
rarely engraven upon this sort of Servitude. It is likewise most
lamentable to think, how in taking Negros out of *Africa,* and Selling of them here, That which GOD has joyned together men do
boldly rend asunder; Men from their Country, Husbands from
their Wives, Parents from their Children. How horrible is the
Uncleanness, Mortality, if not Murder, that the Ships are guilty
of that bring great crouds of these miserable Men, and Women.
Methinks, when we are bemoaning the barbarous Usage of our
Friends and Kinsfolk in *Africa:* it might not be unseasonable to
enquire whether we are not culpable in forcing the *Africans* to
become Slaves amongst our selves. And it may be a question
whether all the Benefit received by *Negro* Slaves, will balance the
Accompt of Cash laid out upon them; and for the Redemption of
our own enslaved Friends out of *Africa.* Besides all the Persons
and Estates that have perished there.

"Obj. 1. *These Blackamores are of the Posterity of* Cham, *and therefore are under the Curse of Slavery.* Gen. 9. 25, 26, 27.

"*Answ.* Of all Offices, one would not begg this; *viz.* Uncall'd for, to be an Executioner of the Vindictive Wrath of God; the extent and duration of which is to us uncertain. If this ever was a Commission; How do we know but that it is long since out of Date? Many have found it to their Cost, that a Prophetical Denunciation of Judgment against a Person or People, would not warrant them to inflict that evil. If it would, *Hazael* might justify himself in all he did against his Master, and the *Israelites,* from 2 *Kings* 8. 10, 12.

"But it is possible that by cursory reading, this Text may have been mistaken. For *Canaan* is the Person Cursed three times over, without the mentioning of *Cham.* Good Expositors suppose the Curse entaild on him, and that this Prophesie was accomplished in the Extirpation of the *Canaanites,* and in the Servitude of the *Gibeonites. Vide Pareum.* Whereas the Blackmores are not descended of *Canaan,* but of *Cush.* Psal. 68. 31. *Princes shall come out of Egypt* [Mizraim], *Ethiopia* [Cush] *shall soon stretch out her hands unto God.* Under which Names, all *Africa* may be comprehended; and their Promised Conversion ought to be prayed for. *Jer.* 13. 23. *Can the Ethiopian change his skin?* This shows that Black men are the Posterity of *Cush:* Who time out of mind have been distinguished by their Colour. And for want of the true, *Ovid* assigns a fabulous cause of it.

> " 'Sanguine tum credunt in corpora summa vocato
> Æthiopum populus nigrum traxisse colorem.'
>
> Metamorph. lib. 2.

"Obj. 2. *The* Nigers *are brought out of a Pagan Country, into places where the Gospel is Preached.*

"*Answ.* Evil must not be done, that good may come of it. The extraordinary and comprehensive Benefit accruing to the Church of God, and to *Joseph* personally, did not rectify his brethrens Sale of him.

"Obj. 3. *The* Africans *have Wars one with another: Our Ships bring lawful Captives taken in those Wars.*

"*Answ.* For ought is known, their Wars are much such as were between *Jacob's* Sons and their Brother *Joseph.* If they be between Town and Town; Provincial, or National: Every War is upon one

side Unjust. An Unlawful War can't make lawful Captives. And
by Receiving, we are in danger to promote, and partake in their
Barbarous Cruelties. I am sure, if some Gentlemen should go down
to the *Brewsters* to take the Air, and Fish: And a stronger party
from *Hull* should Surprise them, and Sell them for Slaves to a
Ship outward bound: they would think themselves unjustly dealt
with; both by Sellers and Buyers. And yet 'tis to be feared, we
have no other kind of Title to our *Nigers. Therefore all things
whatsoever ye would that men should do to you, do ye even so to
them: for this is the Law and the Prophets.* Matt. 7. 12.

"Obj. 4. Abraham *had Servants bought with his Money, and
born in his House.*

"*Answ.* Until the Circumstances of *Abraham's* purchase be recorded, no Argument can be drawn from it. In the mean time,
Charity obliges us to conclude, that He knew it was lawful and
good.

"It is Observable that the *Israelites* were strictly forbidden the
buying, or selling one another for Slaves. *Levit.* 25. 39. 46. *Jer.*
34 8. ...... 22. And GOD gaged His Blessing in lieu of any loss
they might conceipt they suffered thereby. *Deut.* 15. 18. And since
the partition Wall is broken down, inordinate Self love should
likewise be demolished. GOD expects that Christians should be
of a more Ingenuous and benign frame of spirit. Christians should
carry it to all the World, as the *Israelites* were to carry it one
towards another. And for men obstinately to persist in holding
their Neighbours and Brethren under the Rigor of perpetual Bondage, seems to be no proper way of gaining Assurance that God
ha's given them Spiritual Freedom. Our Blessed Saviour has altered
the Measures of the ancient Love-Song, and set it to a most Excellent New Tune, which all ought to be ambitious of Learning.
Matt. 5. 43, 44. *John* 13. 34. These *Ethiopians,* as black as they
are; seeing they are the Sons and Daughters of the First *Adam,*
the Brethren and Sisters of the Last ADAM, and the Offspring of
GOD; They ought to be treated with a Respect agreeable.

"*BOSTON of the Massachusetts;*
Printed by *Bartholomew Green,* and *John Allen,* June, 24*th.* 1700."

July 25th 1700. Went to the Funeral of Mrs. Sprague, being
invited by a good pair of Gloves.

Thorsday Sept: 26ᵗʰ 1700. Mr. John Wait and Eunice his wife, and Mrs. Debora Thair come to Speak to me about the Marriage of Sebastian, Negro servᵗ of said Wait, with Jane, Negro servant of said Thair. Mr. Wait desired they might be published in order to marriage. Mrs. Thair insisted that Sebastian might have one day in six allow'd him for the support of Jane, his intended wife and her children, if it should please God to give her any. Mr. Wait now wholly declin'd that, but freely offer'd to allow Bastian Five pounds, in Money p̄ annum towards the support of his children [and of] said Jane (besides Sebastians cloathing and Diet). I persuaded Jane and Mrs. Thair to agree to it, and so it was concluded.

Nov: 21. 1700. Day of publick Thanksgiving. At 3. *post meridᵐ* Mr. Willard comes abroad and Prays to the great Refreshment of the Congregation. This the first time since his sickness. In the evening I made these verses on it, viz,

> As Joseph let his brethren see
> Simeon both alive, and free:
> So JESUS brings forth Samuel,
> To tune our hearts to praise Him well.
> Thus He with beams of cheerful light,
> Corrects the darkness of our night.
> His Grace assists us in this wise
> To seise, and bind the Sacrifice.

Janʸ 1. 1700/701 Just about Break-a-day Jacob Amsden and 3 other Trumpeters gave a Blast with the Trumpets on the common near Mr. Alford's [in Margin—Entrance of the 18ᵗʰ Century]. Then went to the Green Chamber, and sounded there till about sunrise. Bell-man said these verses a little before Break-a-day, which I printed and gave them. [in Margin—My Verses upon New Century.]

> Once more our God vouchsafe to shine:
> Correct the Coldness of our Clime.
> Make haste with thy Impartial Light,
> And terminate this long dark night.
> Give the poor Indians Eyes to see
> The Light of Life: and set them free.

So Men shall God in Christ adore,
And worship Idols vain, no more.
So Asia, and Africa,
Eurôpa, with America;
All Four, in Consort join'd, shall Sing
New Songs of Praise to Christ our King.

The Trumpeters cost me five pieces 8/8. Gave to the College-Library Dr. Owens two last Volumes on the Hebrews.

Friday, Jan.ʸ 10. 1700/1701. Mr. John Wait came to me, and earnestly desired me to hasten consummating the Marriage between his Bastian and Jane, Mrs. Thair's Negro.⁴ This day I waited upon the Lᵗ Governour at Dorchester and spent about two hours in looking over and ordering Corporation Bonds, but brought none away with me.

BOSTON, Jan.ʸ 13 1700/1701.

MADAM,—The inclosed piece of Silver, by its bowing, humble form, bespeaks your Favor for a certain young Man in Town. The Name [Real] the Motto [Plus ultra] seem to plead its suitableness for a Present of this Nature. Neither need you to except against the quantity: for you have the Mends in your own hand; And by your generous Acceptance, you may make both it and the Giver Great.

Madam, I am

Your Affectᵗ Friend   S. S.

Jan.ʸ 14ᵗʰ Having been certified last night about 10. oclock of the death of my dear Mother at Newbury, Sam. and I set out with John Sewall, the Messenger, for that place. Hired Horses at Charlestown: set out about 10. aclock in a great Fogg.

[January 15, 1700/01] Went abᵗ 4. p.m. Nathan¹ Bricket taking in hand to fill the Grave [of Sewall's mother], I said, Forbear a little, and suffer me to say That amidst our bereaving sorrows We have the Comfort of beholding this Saint put into the rightfull possession of that Happiness of Living desir'd and dying Lamented. She liv'd commendably Four and Fifty years with her dear Husband, and my dear Father: And she could not well brook the being divided from him at her death; which is the cause of our taking leave of her in this place. She was a true and constant Lover of Gods Word, Worship, and Saints: And she always,

with a patient cheerfullness, submitted to the divine Decree of
providing Bread for her self and others in the sweat of her Brows.
And now her infinitely Gracious and Bountiful Master has pro-
moted her to the Honor of higher Employments, fully and abso-
lutely discharged from all manner of Toil, and Sweat. My honoured
and beloved Friends and Neighbours! My dear Mother never
thought much of doing the most frequent and homely offices of
Love for me; and lavish'd away many Thousands of Words upon
me, before I could return one word in Answer: And therefore I
ask and hope that none will be offended that I have now ventured
to speak one word in her behalf; when shee her self is become
speechless. Made a Motion with my hand for the filling of the
Grave. Note, I could hardly speak for passion and Tears.

Tuesday, June, 10th [1701] Having last night heard that Josiah
Willard had cut off his hair (a very full head of hair) and put on
a Wigg, I went to him this morning. Told his Mother what I came
about, and she call'd him. I enquired of him what Extremity had
forced him to put off his own hair, and put on a Wigg? He answered, none at all. But said that his Hair was streight, and that
it parted behinde. Seem'd to argue that men might as well shave
their hair off their head, as off their face. I answered men were
men before they had hair on their faces, (half of mankind have
never any). God seems to have ordain'd our Hair as a Test, to
see whether we can bring our minds to be content to be at his
finding: or whether we would be our own Carvers, Lords, and
come no more at Him. If disliked our Skin, or Nails; 'tis no Thanks
to us, that for all that, we cut them not off: Pain and danger
restrain us. Your Calling is to teach men self Denial. Twill be
displeasing and burdensom to good men: And they that care not
what men think of them care not what God thinks of them. . . .
Allow me to be so far a *Censor Morum* for this end of the Town.
Pray'd him to read the Tenth Chapter of the Third book of Cal-
vins Institutions. I read it this morning in course, not of choice.
Told him that it was condemn'd by a Meeting of Ministers at
Northampton in Mr. Stoddards house, when the said Josiah was
there. Told him of the Solemnity of the Covenant which he and
I had lately enterd into, which put me upon discoursing to him.
He seem'd to say would leave off his Wigg when his hair was
grown. I spake to his Father of it a day or two after: He thank'd

me that had discoursed his Son, and told me that when his hair was grown to cover his ears, he promis'd to leave off his Wigg. If he had known of it, would have forbidden him. His Mother heard him talk of it; but was afraid positively to forbid him; lest he should do it, and so be more faulty.[5]

July, 15th Funeral-day of Lt Govr To Ipswich; Try Esther Rogers. Jury next morn ask'd advice, then after, brought her in Guilty of murdering her Bastard daughter. July, 17. Mr. Cooke pronounc'd the sentence. She hardly said a word. I told her God had put two Children to her to nurse: Her Mother did not serve her so. Esther was a great saviour; she, a great destroyer. Said [I] did not do this to insult over her, but to make her sensible.

Monday, Octr 6. 1701. Very pleasant fair Wether; Artillery trains in the Afternoon [Sewall in command]. March with the Company to the Elms; Go to prayer, March down and Shoot at a Mark. Mr. Cushing I think was the first that hit it, Mr. Gerrish twice, Mr. Fitch, Chauncy, and the Ensign of the Officers. By far the most missed, as I did for the first. Were much contented with the exercise. Led them to the Trees agen, perform'd some facings and Doublings. Drew them together; propounded the question about the Colours; twas voted very freely and fully. I inform'd the Company I was told the Company's Halberds &c. were borrowed; I understood the Leading staff was so, and therefore ask'd their Acceptance of a Half-Pike, which they very kindly did; I deliver'd it to Mr. Gibbs for their Use.

They would needs give me a Volley, in token of their Respect on this occasion. The Pike will, I suppose, stand me in fourty shillings, being headed and shod with Silver: . . . Were treated by the Ensign in a fair chamber. Gave a very handsome Volley at Lodging the Colours. The Training in Septr was a very fair day, so was this.

Octr 9. I sent Mr. Increase Mather a Hanch of very good Venison; I hope in that I did not treat him as a Negro.

Octr 10th Send my wife and me Gloves and Cake. Col. Hutchinson, Mr. Addington, Foster, Townsend, Bromfield, Stoddard, Burroughs, visit the Bridegroom and Bride, and sup there with Roast-Beef, Venison Pasty, Cake and cheese. Betty came yesterday to see us. Bror and his daughter came, and go home to day.

Octr 20. [In Margin—Opprobrium. Mr. Cotton Mather speaks

hard words of me. Mr. Cotton Mather came to Mr. Wilkins's shop, and there talked very sharply against me as if I had used his father worse than a Neger; spake so loud that people in the street might hear him. Then went and told Sam, That one pleaded much for Negros, and he had used his father worse than a Negro, and told him that was his Father.[6]

Octobr 22. 1701. I, with Major Walley and Capt. Sam¹ Checkly, speak with Mr. Cotton Mather at Mr. Wilkins's. I expostulated with him from 1 Tim. 5. 1. Rebuke not an elder. He said he had consider'd that: I told him of his book of the Law of Kindness for the Tongue, whether this were correspondent with that. Whether correspondent with Christ's Rule: He said, having spoken to me before there was no need to speak to me again; and so justified his reviling me behind my back. Charg'd the Council with Lying, Hypocrisy, Tricks, and I know not what all [in Margin—Surreptitious]. I ask'd him if it were done with that Meekness as it should; answer'd, yes. Charg'd the Council in general, and then shew'd my share, which was my speech in Council; viz. If Mr. Mather should goe to Cambridge again to reside there with a Resolution not to read the Scriptures, and expound in the Hall: I fear the example of it will do more hurt than his going thither will doe good. This speech I owned. Said Mr. Corwin at Reading, upbraided him, saying, This is the man you dedicat your books to! I ask'd him If I should suppose he had done somthing amiss in his Church as an Officer; whether it would be well for me to exclaim against him in the street for it. (Mr. Wilkin would fain have had him gon into the inner room, but he would not.) I told him I conceiv'd he had done much unbecoming a Minister of the Gospel, and being call'd by Maxwell to the Council, Major Wally and I went thither, leaving Capt. Checkly there. . . . Went to the Council, Sign'd Mr. Mather's order for £25. Hammer'd out an Order for a Day of Thanksgiving.

Thorsday, Octr 23. Mr. Increase Mather said at Mr. Wilkins's, If I am a Servant of Jesus Christ, some great Judgment will fall on Capt. Sewall, or his family.

Octr 24. Rainy Day, yet Judge Atwood comes from Rehoboth to Boston. 25. Visits several, and me among the rest. This day in the morn. I got Mr. Moody to copy out my Speech, and gave it to Mr. Wilkins that all might see what was the ground of Mr Mather's Anger.

Nov.ʳ 1. 1701. Bastian has a Daughter born, he being at the Castle; He calls her Jane. Nov.ʳ 2. She is baptised by Mr. Allen; Bastian holds her up.

[November 11, 1701] A complaint was prefer'd against Wood-bridge at Newbury Court, Jury cleer'd him. James Wise, the Complainant, Appeals. Action was dismiss'd; because a man being Acquitted by a Jury, ought not to be Try'd again. Rioters that were fined Ten pounds apiece, were now fined twenty shillings, great pains having been used to bring them quite off; but the Jury confirm'd their former Judgment and were directed by the Court only to say Guilty. The Salem Justices were much disgusted at this management and sentence: I dissented from it as too small a Plaister for so great a Sore.

[November 30, 1701] Pray'd, sung—Contribution. Gave the Blessing. I spent this Sabbath at Mr. Colman's, partly out of dislike to Mr. Josiah Willard's cutting off his Hair, and wearing a Wigg: He preach'd for Mr. Pemberton in the morning; He that contemns the Law of Nature, is not fit to be a publisher of the Law of Grace: Partly to give an Example of my holding Communion with that Church who renounce the Cross in Baptisme, Humane Holydays &c. as other New-english Churches doe. And I had spent a Sabbath at the Old Church, and at Mr. Mathers. And I thought if I should have absented my self in the *forenoon* only, it might have been more gravaminous to Mr. Willards friends than keeping there *all day*. I perceive by several, that Mr. Coleman's people were much gratified by my giving them my Company, Several considerable persons express'd themselves so.

Jan.ʸ 2. 1701/2. My Wife had some thoughts the Time of her Travail might be come, before she went to bed: But it went over. Between 4 and 5 m. I go to prayer, Rise, make a Fire, call Mrs. Ellis, Hawkins, Mary Hawkins calls Midwife Greenlef. I go to Mr. Willard and desire him to call God. The Women call me into chamber, and I pray there.

Jan.ʸ 2. 1701/2. My Wife is well brought to Bed of a Daughter just about two p.m., a very cold day: Was got into Bed without a fainting Fit.

Sabbath-day night my wife is very ill and something delirious.

Pulse swift and high. I call Mr. Oakes about Two aclock or before. Grows a little better.

Jan.ʸ 6. 1701/2 Nurse Hill watch'd last night. Wife had a comfortable night.

MEMORANDUM.

Sarah Sewall was born Novʳ 21. 1694. Baptised [by] Mr. Willard Nov.ʳ 25. Died Dec.ʳ 23. Was buried xr. 25. 1696. A dear amiable Son of Samuel Sewall and Hannah his wife, was Stillborn May, 21. 1696.

Judith Sewall was born upon Friday, Jan.ʸ 2. at two in the Afternoon, Hannah Greenlef Midwife, Judd Nurse. Lords-Day, Jan.ʸ 4. p.m., Was baptised by the Reverᵈ Mr. Ebenezer Pemberton. It being his Turn: because The Revᵈ Mr. Willard administered the Lord's supper just before. So is a New Midwife, and a New Baptiser. What through my wives many Illnesses, more than ordinary, her fall upon the stairs about 5 weeks before; from which time she kept her chamber; her thoughtfullness between whiles whether she were with child or no; her Fears what the issue would be, and the misgiving of our Unbelieving hearts, GOD hath been wonderfully Mercifull to us in her comfortable Delivery; which I desire to have Recorded.

Note. This is the Thirteenth Child that I have offered up to God in Baptisme; my wife having born me Seven Sons and Seven Daughters. I have named this little Daughter Judith, in Remembrance of her honoured and beloved Grandmother Mrs. *Judith Hull*. And it may be my dear wife may now leave off bearing. *you can help, Sam*

Thorsday, Febr. 19. Mr. I. Mather preached from Rev. 22. 16 —bright and morning Star. Mention'd Sign in the Heaven, and in the Evening following I saw a large Cometical Blaze, something fine and dim, pointing from the Westward, a little below Orion.

Febr. 21. Capt. Tim.ᵒ Clark tells me that a Line drawn to the Comet strikes just upon Mexico, spake of a Revolution there, how great a Thing it would be. Said one Whitehead told him of the magnificence of the City, that there were in it 1500 Coaches drawn with Mules. This Blaze had much put me in mind of Mexico; because we must look toward Mexico to view it. Capt. Clark drew a Line on his Globe. Our Thoughts being thus confer'd, and found to jump, makes it to me remarkable. I have long pray'd for Mexico, and of late in those Words, that God would open the Mexican Fountain.

March, 11. 1/1702 In the Afternoon, there are great Southerly Gusts and Showers; Considerable Thunder and Lightening. Last night between 10 and 11, A great Fire brake out in Mr. Thomson's Warehouse upon the Dock: Seven or Eight of the chief Warehouses were burnt and blown up. 'Tis said the Fire began in that part which Monsr. Bushee hires. About half a Ship's Loading was lately taken into it.

May, 28, [1702] Burrington from New-found-Land brings Prints of the King's death March, 8. at 8 m. Queen's Speech to her Lords at St James's. Lords Spiritual and Temporal, their Address; Queen's Speech to the Parliament; Several Addresses; and at last the Gazette containing the Proclaiming the Queen, came to Hand: Then we resolv'd to proclaim her Majesty here: Which was done accordingly below the Town-house. Regiment drawn up, and Life-Guard of Horse; Council, Representatives, Ministers, Justices, Gentlemen taken within the Guard; Mr Secretary on foot read the order of the Council, the Proclamation, and Queen's Proclamation for continuing Commissions. Mr. Sheriff Gookin gave it to the people. Volleys, Guns.

Went into chamber to drink, and there had the sad news of the Taking of 3 Salem Catches by the Cape-Sable Indians; one of them Col. Higginson's: David Hills, and one of the Masters kill'd. This arrived at Salem this day, and was sent per Express, one of the men swore it before the Council. Proclamation was made between 3 and 4.

[June 11, 1702] I was startled at 2 or 3 things; viz. The L^t. Governour [Thomas Povey] a stranger, sent, whom we knew nor heard anything of before. . . . Governour has a very large Wigg. Drink Healths, About one and Twenty Guns fired at our leaving the Centurion; and Cheers, then Capt Scot and another Ship fired. Castle fired many Guns; Landed at Scarlet's Wharf, where the Council and Regiment waited for us; just before came at the North-Meetinghouse Clock struck five. Was the Troop of Guards, and Col. Paige's Troop. March'd to the Townhouse. There before the Court; Ministers, and as many else as could crowd in, the Governour's and Lt Gov^{rs}. Commissions were published; they took their Oaths laying their hands on the Bible, and after Kissing it.

Had a large Treat. Just about dark Troops Guarded the Govr to Roxbury. He rode in Major Hobby's Coach Drawn with six Horses richly harnessed. By mistake, my coachman stayed in the yard, and so Joseph and I went alone. Foot gave 3 very good Volleys after the publication of the Commissions, and were dismiss'd. Mr. Mather crav'd a Blessing and Mr. Cotton Mather Return'd Thanks.

June 12. as Governour came to Town, he alighted and call'd at my House, Thank'd me for my Kindness to his family. I was much indispos'd by my Throat being sore, and I feverish.

[September] 11th Went to Billinges in the Cart-way; Had a very good Dinner, Venison &c. Got home in good time. Capt Williams with his Red-Coats met us between Dedham and the Turning to Fowl-Meadow. Capt Belchar and sundry Boston Gentlemen met us at Dedham. Note. Wednesday, at Osburn's, about Break-a-day, I heard one riding as I lay awake. (Mrs. Sparhawk having miscarried, I lodg'd there.) Thought I, I fear there may be some bad News from Boston. The man knock'd, and when he could make any hear, he ask'd if Capt. —— were there: I took it he said me. They answer'd yes. He said must come away presently: for his daughter was very bad. Then I said to my self, I must undertake a sorrowfull Journey, as from Salem to Boston, upon the advice of my Still-born son: But God dismiss'd me from the burden of that sorrowfull Surprise, having laid it on Capt Brown of Swansey. We saw the Funeral as went over the Ferry on Thorsday.

[September] 13. Lords-Day, Mr. Bradstreet baptiseth Simon, the Jew, at Charlestown, a young man whom he was Instrumental to convert.

Septr 15. Mr. Nehemiah Walter marries Mr. Saml Sewall and Mrs. Rebekah Dudley,^{7} in the Dining Room Chamber about 8 aclock. Mr. Willard concluded with prayer, Sung the last part of the 103 Psalm. Mr. Tho. Dudley reading and setting of it out of my Turkey-Leather Psalm book. Present Govr, Lady, family (all save Mr. Paul, who was call'd away just then with the news of Capt. Larimore's prises, Brothers Letter of it the Govr read to us). I and my family, all save Betty and Judith. . . . Got home about 11 aclock.

Thorsday, Octr 1. 1702. The Govr and Council agree that Thorsday Octr 22. be a Fast-Day. Governour moved that it might be Friday, saying, Let us be English-men. I spake against making any distinction in the Days of the week; Desired the same Day of the Week might be for Fasts and Thanksgiving. Boston and Ipswich Lecture Led us to Thorsday. Our Brethren at Connecticut had Wednesday; which we applauded. Governour, it seems, told the Secretary, He himself would draw up the Order, which he did at Cousin Dummers by Candle-Light. Some of the Council were there, but the Govr did not ask their voice. I suggested to Maj^r Genl that the Drought might be mention'd; Mr. Winthrop spake, but the Govr refused: I think at our house where the Govr Dined with Mr. Increase Mather, and Mr. Tim? Woodbridge; the Govr said was a better Harvest than had been these Twenty years.

Monday, Octr 26. 1702. Waited on the Govr to Wooburn, dined there: From thence to Billericay, Visited languishing Mr. Saml Whiting, I gave him 2 Balls of Chockalett and a pound Figgs, which very kindly accepted. Saw the Company in Arms led by Capt. Tomson. Went to Chelmsford, by that time got there twas almost dark. Saw Capt. Bowler and his Company; Gave a Volley and Huzza's. Sup'd at Mr. Clark's; I and Col. Pierce in his study. Some went on to Dunstable by Moonshine.

Octr 27. Went to Dunstable in the Rain, Din'd and lodg'd at Col. Tyng's. Saw and drunk of Merrimack. No Indians come in.

Novr 2. 1702. John Adams, a very good man, and John Drury, a desirable young man, dye of the small pocks.

Anthony Checkley dyed last week of the same disease.

Novr 10. Mr. Leverett comes from Cambridge; open the Court in the Meetinghouse, because the Townhouse is very near a house that has the Small Pocks; so that people are afraid to goe there; and Sharp is not willing to let us have his chamber. Sat in the Deacon's seat, Col. Hathorne on my Right Hand, and Mr. Leverett on my Left. After the Reading of the Queen's Proclamation, I spake to the Grand-Jury, having written it down beforehand in my Daughter's chamber.

xr. [December] 16. I went out early with David to carry two of Mr. Mathers History[8] to my Bro^r to Charlestown: Heard the church [Kings Chapel] Bell ring for Capt. Crofts. He dyed last night.

xr. 19. Is buried in the New burying place in Capt. Hamilton's Tomb. Corps was first had into the church and a Funeral Sermon preach'd. For Debauchery and Irreligion he was one of the vilest Men that has set foot in Boston. Tis said he refused to have any Minister call'd to pray with him during his Sickness, which was above a fortnight.

Feb.ʳ 5.ᵗʰ 1702/3 Went on purpose [to Roxbury] to speak to the Governour against having Illuminations, especially in the Town house; That so the profanation of the Sabbath might be prevented. I said twould be most for the Honor of God; and that would be most for the Honor and Safety of Queen Anne. Governour said twould be hard for him to forbid it, considering how good the Queen was, what successes God had given her. I answered, It could not be introduced into the Town-house without his Excellency's Order, for under his Excellency the Government of the Town was (partly) committed to us. Govʳ answer'd not a word. Others urged our Law, the Grief of Good People, his best Friends. And I think all was said between us, that could be said. Got well home about 9 at night, and had a very comfortable Journey, and sufficient Light Notwithstanding the Fogg, and absence of the very New Moon.

Feb.ʳ 6. between 8 and 9. m. The Bells begin to Ring, to celebrate Queen Anne's Birth-Day, being the last of the Week.

Feb.ʳ 11ᵗʰ 1702/3 The Govʳ under his hand remits the Fines of several sentenced to pay 5s apiece for drinking at Mrs. Monk's on Satterday night last about 9 aclock. Had warn'd Mrs. Monk an hour before. Said Monk also remitted her 25s, and the writing given to the Sheriff to Notifie Col. Townsend and Mr. Bromfield.

Friday, June, 18. 1703. My sons House was Raised at Muddy-River; The day very comfortable because dry, cloudy, windy, cool. I sent for Mr. Wigglesworth and his Wife from Deacon Barnard's in the Coach; to discourse with my Wife about her and Judith's Maladies. After they were sent back, being late in the Afternoon, I went alone in the Hackney-Coach to Roxbury, took Mr. Walter with me. By that Time got there, had just done their Work, and were going to Dinner in the new House. Mr. Walter crav'd a Blessing, Return'd Thanks. Many were there from Muddy-River, Dedham, Roxbury. I drove a [bowling] Pin before Dinner.

Thorsday June, 24. I am kept from Mr. C. Mather's Lecture by my swoln face.

June 28. 1703. I have my son Joseph to Cambridge in Austin's

Calash, where he is examined by Mr. Jonathan Remington in presence of the President and Mr. Flynt. He Answer'd well to Mr. Remingtons Critical Examination—Mr. Willard gave him for his Theme.

Second-day of the Week July 5th 1703. I had my son to Cambridge again in Austin's Calash. Paid Andrew Bordman his Cautionary Three pounds, in order to my Son Joseph's being Admitted. Went to Mr. Flynt's Chamber, where Col. Wainright's Son and others were upon Examination. When that was doing, and over, Mr. Willard call'd for Joseph's Theme. Read it, and gave it to Mr. Flynt, Then in Mr. Flynt's Study, The President and Fellows sign'd his Laws; President said, your Son is now one of us, and he is wellcom. I thanked him; and took Leave. Coming home I order'd Mr. Sheriff to take up a Scurvy post out of the middle of the High way, that had been a Nusance for many years. Gave his Son a shilling for his pains. Got home well. *Laus Deo*. Was pretty much Rain at Charlestown; yet we went almost quite dry, being but a small Sprinkling where we were.

Commencement day July, 7th 1703. Mr. Secretary, Major Walley, Major Brenton and I went by Charlestown to the hether edge of Maldon, and so met the Govr in his Return homeward from Casco-Bay. Note; in the afternoon Mr. Wells of Almsbury, is made a Master of Art. Mr. Belcher of Newbury Testified his Education under Mr. Andros at Ipswich, that he was a good Latin and Greek Scholar.

July, 24. 1703. Joseph takes leave of his Master and Scholars in a short Oration.

Augt 7. 1703. News comes from N. York that my Lord Cornbury has rec'd his commissions, and that the Militia of Connecticut and the Jersies is granted him.

From the Eastward, Fear of the French and Indians, some being seen.[9]

Augt 11. News comes of the Onset of the Enemy.

I went to Cambridge Augt 11. to make sure a study for Joseph in Mr. Remington's Chamber: came home with Mr. Torrey, call'd at the Gov^{rs}, where a Master that came by water from Black-point, gave account of the Fires kindled by the Indians in several places; brought a little youth that narrowly escaped the enemies hands.

Augt 12. at night, News comes from Wells that have buried

Drd.

15. durst not go to bury their uttermost [outermost]: Lost as they fear 60. Enemy numerous.

Augt 9. I read the Transaction of the Govr with the Indians, at the coffee house. . . . Abstract of it follows:

CASCO-BAY, June, 30. 1703.

The Queen of England in six months time of War with French King and Spanish King, has Taken more Towns and done more Exploits, than the great and valiant King William did in Twelve years. And besides all this which she hath don by Land, her Fleet by Sea hath taken 40. Sails; Taken much Money, the Royal Crown sent the Spanish King from N. Spain. Notwithstanding all this I offer peace. Twas once very dark here about 20 or 30 years ago; was great Troubles, and also great Troubles among our selves. New Hundred now, new Century, and would have the Old Hundred to be forgotten, and never talk'd of any more; New Hundred, new Queen, new Governour now will be all in new friendship. When any French March through the Country, Stop them or give notice to the Fort: For it is easy if there be but Ten Indians in some parts of the Country to fetch away whole familyes, and they not able to defend them selves. I have very particular Intelligence from Kebeck and Port Royal, they have two partys out at this time, would have you keep back those partyes according to the Treaty of peace made two years agoe. I do it not to boast of my self, but I Trust in God. I have Twelve Hundred and fifty men impress'd in N. England, ready to march at Six hours warning: they are enough to disturb all the Indians in the Country. Indians are able like wolves to disturb men, but not to do them any damage; they are not able to hurt us in the least, and I value them not, no more than the paring of my nails. And the great Queen of England has order'd me 17. sail of Men of War, all superior to the Gosport; which I may improve to do any thing upon the French or any of our Enemies. And I am confident that time will come that nothing, nor no one will remain but English here and Indians. For the Indians part they may remain a happy people if they will themselves.—I have the Assistance of the Noble Govr of N. York, who is a Kinsman of the great Queen of England.—I acknowledge have kept their promise in not passing Saco River.—If arrest and stop French partys will give them a good Reward for it. And methinks I see among you some that I know that are fit to be made Officers to bear Commission for the Queen of England, to bear Rule among you, who shall be my Officers, and shall be Rewarded from time to time, as my other officers at Boston, or any where else are; every month they shall be paid off as our own people:—have nothing more in the world to say but to persuade them that I am an honest man and their Brother:—our boys and youth will go and do beyond their prudence or strength; but these old men these Sachems here present, they and I are old men and should be discreet and wise, so as that when we dye we might be carried to our Graves with honor. Let them consider two hours and give me their Answer—Gave them a good Ox and 20— bushels corn for dinner: They return'd Thanks for their noble dinner and all other Kindnesses offer'd to them. Then, said his Excellency here is a Peace, and Satisfaction to the two Nations.

INDIANS ANSWER.

First breach was at Penobscut, which was the first thing in the morning. The 2d was the Frenchmen and Indians, they broke the peace in doing that mischief at Casco: but we do affirm that we did not know of their coming, but of their going back we knew of it: but we calling to remembrance what was don at Penobscut before, and so we thought fit not to meddle of neither side.

TWO BEVERS.

Again they say that what his Excellency was pleased to tell them, was not the same as their French was, i. e. to make war as the French would have them. His Excellency's desire is that we should be peaceably on both sides, for which we return him many a hearty Thanks and tell him we resolve to doe it.

TWO BEVERS.

His Excellency was pleas'd to desire them in the next place that if any of the English should be Taken by the French and carried over their Ground or through their Country, that we should bring them back again, and not suffer them to be carried through as Captives; but that we should do well to bring them back again. But if we should do so, such a thing as that would make us seem guilty, and so thereby we might be thought to be concern'd, when we are not.

TWO BEVERS.

There is about the Mohawks a great many ready to fight, not certain of the number, but hope to know in a day or two, for have sent scouts to Albany.

TWO BEVERS.

Again they wonder that his Excellency would be pleas'd to tell them, or desire any of them to come upon wages upon any account. For they desire it not. But their desire is to be as Neuters; not to medle nor make, nor to stir or act in any thing one way or other.

THREE BEVERS.

Now they desire to come and pay their Respects to the Govr, since [they] have said all they have to say.

Govr will have them stay and hear his Answer a little—Action at Penabscot and Casco much alike: But Govr N. E. hated the Action as to the Frenchmans death: Govr French nourished and imbraced the Casco breach; sent them to do the thing. If resolve to sit still and be quiet, I shall remain perfectly satisfied in all things and desire to remain as an entire and dear Brother unto them.

May stop the French from Marching through their Country and yet remain Neuters still; they mistake if think otherwise: Be call'd Captains and Officers; why this is pure honor meant to them not that they should be expos'd to march or fight, but to be as my Brother, as I am to them. And if I would honor them so far as to make them Captains and to send them a present now and then, why it is honor: not that I desire they should be expos'd to fight upon any occasion. Tell Moxes I am willing to honor Moxes' son that was with me, with the place of a Captain here: not that I expect him to be expos'd to fight; no not so much as to fire a piece: but that we may live as Brothers and that I may send him a piece of Cloth once a year.—— Penecook Indians not return till after Harvest.

Then the Govr and Sachems repaired to the heaps of stones, and put up each man a stone again.

Novr 26. Harrison the Controller, and Mr. Wm Pain are examined before the Govr and Council by Mr. Russell's Motion. When mention was made of putting them to their Oath, Harrison said he was ready to swear, but then it must be by laying his hand on the Bible: Govr said, So he ought, and order'd Mr. Secretary to fetch the Bible. Mr. Pain also slip'd on his hand. Mr. Harrison first look'd into it to see that 'twas the Bible. When had sworn, seem'd to applaud himself, and said he would have this forwarded

and upheld. When Questions were asked him, he answer'd, By that
Booke it is True.

Jany 31. [1703/4] George Pierce brings the News, of a Girl
being kill'd at Nichawannuck; [Berwick, Me.] 30 Indians assaulted
a Garrison there; were received bravely by the English, one of
them kill'd, and the rest by Capt. Brown with a small party of
men 10 or 12, put to flight, sundry of them wounded; left many
of their own Accoutrements, for haste, and carried nothing away
of ours.

Febr. 5. I fasted and pray'd to God that Satan might not be
commissioned any longer to buffet me and my wife; for my self and
family in the advancing year: and Province &c. for Daughter Hirst,
and little Mary to be dedicated to Him the next day.

Lt Tristram Coffin dyed Febr. 4th 1703/4. Joseph Frazon, the
Jew, dyes at Mr. Major's, Mr. Joyliff's old house; Febr. 5th Sat-
terday, is carried in Simson's coach to Bristow; from thence by
Water to Newport, where there is a Jews-burying place.[10]

Febr. 8th a Garrison-house is surpris'd at Haverhill by 6 or 7
Indians.

March, 5. The dismal News of the Slaughter made at Deerfield
is certainly and generally known, Mr. Secretary came to me in the
morning, and told me of it: I told Mr. Willard; by which means
our Congregation was made a Bochim. [Judges, II. 1–5.] Tis to
be observ'd that the great slaughters have been on the Third day
of the week; our Court day. This was Febr. 29th 1703/4. My Tenant Kibbee was arrested this day.

Lord's-Day, Apr. 23. There is great Firing at the Town, Ships,
Castle upon account of its being the Coronation-day, which gives
offence to many; See the Lord's day so profan'd. Down Sabbath,
Up St George.

Wednesday, June 7th. 1704. Col. Nathan^l Byfield, Mr. Palmer
and my self have rec'd an Order from the Govr to search for and
seize Pirats and their Treasure, and to hold a court of Enquiry
for this end at Marblehead; because Capt. Quelch in the Charles
Galley arrived there:[11] we set forward this day for Salem, having
James Noyes and Joseph Gerrish to wait on us. We got to Salem
about 8 aclock There Sam. Wakefield, the Water Baily, inform'd
Col. Byfield of a Rumor there was that Capt. Larrimore was now
with the Larramore Gally at Cape-Anne; and that two of Quelch's

company designed to go off in her. Upon this we made out a Warrant to the said Wakefield to goe and see into this matter and seize the Men if true. Despatch'd him about mid-night.

Thorsday, June 8. We went to Marblehead in the Rain, and held our Court at Capt. Brown's by the Fireside; took Major Sewall with us, who return'd to Salem the same night.

Friday, June, 9.th about 6. m. An Express from Cape-Anne, gives an Account of 9. or 11. Pirats, double arm'd, seen in a Lone-house there. This Express found us a-bed. We rose immediately, Sent for Col. Legg, and directed him to send warrants to the Northward Companies within his Regiment; to send such parties as they could raise, to Cape-Anne upon this Extraordinary occasion. And writt to Col. Wainright to do the Like in his Regiment, intimating that we were moving thither our selves to be Witness of their forwardness for Her Majesties Service. . . . Col. Byfield and I rode to Salem; there met Dr. Gatchman, took his Affidavit for some better foundation for our Actions. Sent him post to the Govr Bro^r got a shallop, the Trial, and his Pinace, and about a score of his Comp^a to go by water. Mr. Dudley went by water from Marblehead with Col. Legg. Col. Byfield and I proceeded with Sheriff Gedney and Capt. Turner and part of his Troop by Land: call'd on Lt Brisco at Beverly; that Troop resolv'd to go by Jabacko [Chebacco]. Manchester Company was mustering upon the top of a Rock; shook hand with Mr. Webster. When drew nigh the Town of Glocester a Letter from Mr. Dudley and Legg met us, to acquaint us that Larramore Sail'd in the morning and took in the Pirats at the head of the Cape. Messenger seem'd to discourage our going forward. However, we sent back the Sheriff to post their Letter to the Govr, and as many of Salem Troops as would go back, persuading them to return. Mr. Dudley had sent to stay Ipswich Regiment and direct their Return. When came to Capt. Davis's, waited Brother's arrival with his Shallop Trial, and Pinace: When they were come and had Din'd, Resolv'd to send after Larramore. Abbot was first pitch'd on as Captain. But matters went on heavily, 'twas difficult to get Men. Capt. Herrick pleaded earnestly his Troopers might be excus'd. At last Brother offer'd to go himself: then Capt. Turner offer'd to goe, Lieut Brisco, and many good Men; so that quickly made up Fourty two; though we knew not the exact number till came home, the hurry was so great, and vessel so small for 43. Men gave us three very handsom cheers; Row'd out of the Harbour after sun-set, for want of wind. Mr. Dudley return'd to Salem with Beverly Troop. Col. Byfield and I lodg'd at Cape-Ann all night; Mr. White pray'd very well for the Expedition Evening and morning; as Mr. Chiever had done at Marblehead, whom we sent for to pray with us before we set out for Glocester. We rose early, got to Salem quickly after Nine. Din'd with Sister, who was very thoughtfull what would become of her Husband. The Wickedness and despair of the company they pursued, their Great Guns and other war-like Preparations, were a terror to her and to most of the Town; concluded they would not be Taken without Blood. Comforted our selves and them as well as we could. Call'd at Lewis's. Col. Byfield went to Cambridge; Mr. Dudley and I to Boston, Joseph Gerrish waiting on us. June. 12.ᵗʰ Joseph Gerrish comes to my Bed-Chamber-door and Tells of Brother's good success. He dispatched Chapman in the night to the Govʳ. He came to the Isles Sholes about 7. m. June 10, kept his men rank'd with their Arms on both sides the shallop in covert; only the four Fishermen were in view: as drew near saw the Boat goe ashoar with six Hands, which was a singular good Providence of God. Wormwall and three of the Pirats were of the six. When were so near that were descryd, Larramores Men began to run to and fro and pull off the Aprons from the Guns, draw out the Tomkins [Tompions], Brother shew'd his men. Ask'd Larramore to aboard. He said he could not, his Boat was gon ashore. Broʳ told him he would come to him: immediately man'd the Pinace, and did it as soon almost as said it, He, Capt. Turner, Abbot step'd aboard. Brisco attempted; but one swore no more armed Men should come there. Broʳ got the Capt ashore to discourse him, got him there to sign two orders; one to send the Lᵗ and one of the Pirats ashore; the other for Abbot to command the Galley till they return'd; and so quickly finish'd his business thorowly without striking a stroke, or firing a Gun. See the News-Letter. Twas all order'd and Tim'd and effected by the Singular all-powerfull gracious Providence of God.

Feria Sexta, Junij, 30, 1704. After Dinner, about 3. p.m. I went to see the Execution. . . . Many were the people that saw upon Broughton's Hill. But when I came to see how the River was cover'd with People, I was amazed: Some say there were 100

Inds. ✗ ✗ —— why did Sewall incl. this knowy info as part of his personal diary?

THE DIARY, *Volume II: 1704–1705* 111

Boats. 150 Boats and Canoes, saith Cousin Moody of York. He told them. Mr. Cotton Mather came with Capt. Quelch and six others for Execution from the Prison to Scarlet's Wharf, and from thence in the Boat to the place of Execution about the midway between Hanson's point and Broughton's Warehouse. Mr. Bridge was there also. When the scaffold was hoisted to a due height, the seven Malefactors went up; Mr. Mather pray'd for them standing upon the Boat. Ropes were all fasten'd to the Gallows (save King, who was Repriev'd). When the Scaffold was let to sink, there was such a Screech of the Women that my wife heard it sitting in our Entry next the Orchard, and was much surprised at it; yet the wind was sou-west. Our house is a full mile from the place.

July 31, 1704. Call at Capt. Mors's about an hour in night; and he tells us of the Indians assaulting Lancaster. This was very heavy News to us now in a Fronteer Town; yet we went on, lodg'd at cousin Gookin's, and were kept safe.

Monday, Jany 1. 1704/5 Col. Hobbey's Negro comes about 8 or 9 *mane* and sends in by David to have leave to give me a Levit [a trumpet blast] and wish me a merry new year. I admitted it: gave him 3 Reals. Sounded very well.

Lord's Day, June, 10. 1705. The Learned and pious Mr. Michael Wigglesworth dies at Malden about 9. m. Had been sick about 10. days of a Fever; 73 years and 8 moneths old. He was the Author of the Poem entituled The Day of Doom, which has been so often printed: and was very useful as a Physician.

Augt. 22. Eliezer Moodey comes to us. Augt. 23. Judith is once thrown into the dirt above the stonebridge; and the same day run over by a Horse; yet through God's Goodness receives little hurt.

Augt. 24. 1705. Mr. Samuel Myles[12] comes with his Bro^r before me; I bid him, Sam., sit down: but he quickly fell upon Nichols [the constable], the complainant against his Bro^r, and said by his Looks one might see the Gallows groan'd for him; I check'd him, and said it did not become a Minister so to speak. The constable ask'd me what weight the Money must be, 15. or 17. I answered there was no Money but 17^d w^t; but if Capt. Myles offer'd Bills of Credit he must take them. Mr. Saml Myles told me he complain'd of Nichols, but withall told me he was not ready to pursue it.

Sept.ʳ 10. In the Afternoon I went to speak to Mr. Allen that
the Lord's Supper might be celebrated once in four weeks, as it
was in Mr. Cotton's Time and Mr. Wilson's: He was just come
out of his house with Elder Bridgham, Elder Copp, Deacon
Marion and Deacon Hubbard: I pray'd them to go back again,
and open'd my mind to them. All save Mr. Hubbard plainly remember'd how it was in Mr. Wilson's days; and the Alteration
upon the coming in of Mr. Davenport, upon his desire because he
had it so at Newhaven: and seem'd inclinable enough to alter it.
Then I went to Mr. Cooke, both he and Madam Cooke remember'd the change, and seem'd not displeas'd with my proposal. I
discours'd with Mr. Pemberton, and told him it would be a Honor
to Christ, and a great Privilege and Honor to Boston, to have
the Lord's Supper administerd in it every Lords Day: we having
nothing to do with moneths now; Their Respect now ceases with
the Mosaical Pedagogy. [Gal. III. 24.] It seems odd, not to have
this Sacrament administred but upon the first day of each Moneth;
and the rest of the Sabbaths always stand by.

Dec.ʳ 1. Deputies send in a Bill against fornication, or Marriage of White men with Negros or Indians; with extraordinary
penalties; directing the Secretary to draw a Bill accordingly. If
it be pass'd, I fear twill be an Oppression provoking to God, and
that which will promote Murders and other Abominations. I have
got the Indians out of the Bill, and some mitigation for them
[the Negroes] left in it, and the clause about their Masters not
denying their Marriage.[13]

Tuesday, Apr. 23, [1706] Govr. comes to Town guarded by
the Troops with their Swords drawn; dines at the Dragon, from
thence proceeds to the Townhouse, Illuminations at night. Capt.
Pelham tells me several wore crosses in their Hats; which makes
me resolve to stay at home; (though Maxwell was at my House
and spake to me to be at the Council-Chamber at 4. p. m.) Because to drinking Healths, now the Keeping of a Day to fictitious
St. George, is plainly set on foot. It seems Capt. Dudley's Men
wore Crosses. Somebody had fasten'd a cross to a Dog's head;
Capt. Dudley's Boatswain seeing him, struck the Dog, and then
went into the shop, next where the Dog was, and struck down a
Carpenter, one Davis, as he was at work not thinking anything:
Boatswain and the other with him were fined 10s each for breach

of the peace, by Jer. Dummer Esqr: pretty much blood was shed by means of this bloody Cross, and the poor Dog a sufferer.

Thorsday, [October] 24. Mr. Wadsworth appears at Lecture in his Perriwigg. Mr. Chiever is griev'd at it. . . . This day I am told of Mr. Torrey's kinswoman, Betty Symmes, being brought to Bed of a Bastard in his house last Monday night.

Mid-week. Dec.ʳ 25. Shops open, carts come to Town with Wood, Fagots, Hay, and Horses with Provisions, as usually.

Feria septima, Dec.ʳ 28, 1706. A large fair Rainbow is seen in the Morning in the Norwest. Madam Walley call'd her Husband into the Shop to see it. The Govʳ being indispos'd with the Gout, call'd a Council to meet at Roxbury; and by that means I gain'd an Opportunity to see my friend Bayley once again: He is now brought very low by his Stone, Fever, Sore Tongue and Mouth; could hardly speak a word to me. But he said, sit down. His wife ask'd him if he knew me? He answer'd, with some quickness, He should be distracted, if he should not know me. He Thank'd me when I came away. I said Christ would change his vile body, and make it like his glorious body. And when the Coachman call'd, saying the Company staid for me, I took leave, telling him God would abide with him; Those that Christ loves, he loves to the end. He bow'd with his head. His wife and sister weep over him. He call'd for Mouth-Water once while I was there, and then for his little pot to void it into: I suppos'd it was to enable him to speak. Though he doth not eat at present; yet I left the Banbury cake I carried for him, with his wife: And when came away, call'd her into next chamber, and gave her two Five-Shilling Bills: She very modestly and kindly accepted them and said I had done too much already: I told her No, if the state of my family would have born it, I ought to have watch'd with Mr. Bayley, as much as that came to. I left her weeping.

Friday, March, 7. 1707. Several Ministers prayed at the desire of the Court; began a little after Ten; Mr. Willard, Wadsworth, Bridge, Colman, Pemberton, C. Mather, Dr. I. Mather. Prayers were made with great Pertinency and Variety; I hope God will hear. Several pray'd that God would speedily, by some Providence, or one way other, let us know what might doe as to going against Port-Royal. Gave Thanks for the News of the 18. Indians kill'd, and one Taken last Tuesday; which heard of just after the Appointment of this Day. Sung the two first staves of the 20th Psalm, York Tune, which I set, Mr. Willard used my Psalm-Booke. Left off about ½ hour past Two. Council gave the Govr and Ministers a Dinner at Homes's.

[March 8, 1707] In the Afternoon Mr. [John] Williams visits us, tells me he goes to Dearfield 14 nights hence, next Tuesday. I gave him a copy of the foremention'd verses. He tells me Quebeck Seminary was burnt the 20th of 7^r 1705. our Style, Library burnt. His Narrative is now in the Press.[14] Feria tertia, March, 18th Mr. Pemberton removes into the Churches House. March 20. I visit him, and wish him and her joy. March, 21. I give him a 20s Bill to help towards his House-warming, which he accepts kindly. Joseph comes to Town. March, 20. feria quinta, Mrs. Gibbs's Warehouse was burnt down in Lecture time. Meeting was disturb'd just as was coming to the particulars of Fighting against our Enemies and praying against them. March, 27. I go into the Meetinghouse. Hannah Parker is found guilty of Adultery. I spake with two of the Middlebury Men at Mr. Little's about Mr. Palmer, who is impos'd upon them as their Minister. Gave Mr. Little a pound of Chockalat.

April, 5. Eclipse of the Moon: is seen in a serene Aer, Moon is of a Ruddy Colour when Eclipsed. April, 8. I go to Cambridge and carry Joseph a small piece of Plate to present his Tutor with, Bottom mark'd, March, 5, 1706/7 which was the day his Tutor took Leave of them; price 39^s 2^d View'd his Chamber in the President's House, which I like. Came home and went to the Funeral of little Mary Bastian.

Lord's Day, June, 15th I felt my self dull and heavy and Listless as to Spiritual Good; Carnal, Lifeless; I sigh'd to God, that he would quicken me.

June, 16. My House was broken open in two places, and about Twenty pounds worth of Plate stolen away, and some Linen; My Spoon, and Knife, and Neckcloth was taken: I said, Is not this an Answer of Prayer? Jane came up, and gave us the Alarm betime in the morn. I was helped to submit to Christ's stroke, and say, Wellcome CHRIST!

June, 19th The measuring Bason is found with Margaret Barton just carrying of it to Sea, to Hingham; said she had it of James

Hews, he gave it her to sell for him. Mr. Secretary sent her to Prison.

June, 21. Billy Cowell's shop is entered by the Chimney, and a considerable quantity of Plate stolen. I give him a Warrant to the Constable, they find James Hews hid in the Hay in Cabal's Barn, on the Back side of the Common; while they was seising of him under the Hay, he strip'd off his Pocket, which was quickly after found, and Cowell's silver in it. At night I read out of Caryl on Job, 5. 2. The humble submission to the *stroke* of God, turns into a *Kiss*—which I thank God, I have in this Instance experienced. *Laus Deo.*

July, 1. A Rainbow is seen just before night, which comforts us against our Distresses as to the affairs of the Expedition, and the Unquietness of the Souldiers at Casco [Bay], of which Gideon Lowel brings word, who came thence yesterday.[15]

[September] 9th at Dinner had the good News brought of the French privateer being Taken. Mr. Leverett came from Billinges just as were going to Dinner. [September] 10th Midweek, sentenced a woman that whip'd a Man, to be whip'd; said a woman that had lost her Modesty, was like Salt that had lost its savor; good for nothing but to be cast to the Dunghill: 7 or 8 join'd together, call'd the Man out of his Bed, guilefully praying him to shew them the way; then by help of a Negro youth, tore off his Cloaths and whip'd him with Rods; to chastise him for carrying it harshly to his wife.

[September] 12. Mehetabel Thurston tells me Mr. Willard was taken very sick. I hop'd it might go off, and went to Dinner; when I came there, Mr. Pemberton was at Prayer, near concluding, a pretty many in the Chamber. After Prayer, many went out, I staid and sat down: and in a few minutes saw my dear Pastor Expire: it was a little after Two, just about two hours from his being taken. It was very surprising: The Doctors were in another room Consulting what to doe. He administered the Lord's Supper, and Baptiz'd a child last Lord's Day; Did it with suitable voice, Affection, Fluency. Did not preach:

Tuesday, Oct.r 28. 1707. The Fellows of Harvard College meet, and chuse Mr. Leverett President.[16] He had eight votes, Dr. Increase Mather three, Mr. Cotton Mather, one, and Mr.

Brattle of Cambridge, one. Mr. White did not vote, and Mr. Gibbs
came when voting was over.

Novr 1. just about Noon the Govr produces the Petition sign'd
by Mr. Higginson and others for his Removal: And urges the
Council to vote an Abhorrence of it. I pray'd that it might be consider'd of till Monday, which the Governour would not hear of,
but order'd Mr. Secretary to draw up a Vote: which with some
alteration was pass'd. Said He had no Gall. After coming from
Council I read the Book printed against the Governour in London. I had not seen it before.

Friday, Novr 28. 1707. The Govr puts forward to have the
vote of July 9. 1706. of the Representatives, the vote of the Coun-
cil of Novr 1., the vote of the Representatives Novr 21., Printed,
to prevent spreading false Reports: I said I could not vote to it
because I had withdrawn my vote. The Govr said, I pray God judge
between me and you! Col. Townsend told me I was a Temporiser;
I hôp'd Mr. Higginson would be Govr, and endeavour'd to procure
his favor. Prayer. Lord, do not depart from me, but pardon my
sin; and fly to me in a way of favourable Protection! Capt. Phips
brings in Mr. Leverett Non-Concurr'd. Moves from the House
that a suitable person be thought of to take care of the College till
May Sessions. Col. Townsend tells me that my purpose to withdraw my Vote was known a week ago; Mr. Oaks mention'd it in
the House; He was my Counsellor. Whereas he really knew
nothing of it; and now tells me, he never mentioned my Name.

Jany 2, [1707/8] Bro^r goes home in very cold windy wether,
lyes at Lewes's, then home 3. Jany 8. 1707/8. The Govr appoints a Council to meet at Cambridge the 14th Inst for the Installment of Mr. Leverett: warns the Ministers of the Six Towns
mention'd to be overseers of the College. Midweek, Jany 14.
1707/8. Went to Cambridge in Mr. Brigg's Coach. . . . In the
Library the Governour found a Meeting of the Overseers of the
College according to the old Charter of 1650, and reduced the
Number to seven; viz. Mr. Leverett President, Mr. Neh. Hobart,
Mr. Wm Brattle, Mr. Ebenezer Pemberton, Mr. Henry Flint, Mr.
Jonathan Remington, Fellows; Mr. Tho. Brattle, Treasurer. The
Govr prepar'd a Latin Speech for Installment of the President.
Then took the President by the hand and led him down into the
Hall; The Books of the College Records, Charter, Seal and Keys

were laid upon a Table running parallel with that next the Entry. The Gov[r] sat with his back against a Noble Fire; Mr. Russel on his Left Hand innermost, I on his Right Hand; President sat on the other side of the Table over against him. Mr. Neh. Hobart was called, and made an excellent Prayer; Then Joseph Sewall made a Latin Oration. Then the Gov[r] read his Speech, and (as he told me) mov'd the Books in token of their Delivery. Then President made a short Latin Speech, importing the difficulties discouraging, and yet that he did Accept: Gov[r] spake further, assuring him of the Assistance of the Overseers. Then Mr Edward Holyoke made a Latin Oration, standing where Joseph did at a Desk on the Table next the Entry at the inside of it, facing the Govr Mr. Danforth of Dorchester pray'd. Mr. Paul Dudley read part of the 132 ps. in Tate and Bradey's version, Windsor Tune, clôs'd with the Hymn to the Trinity. Had a very good Dinner upon 3 or 4 Tables: Mr. Wadsworth crav'd a Blessing, Mr. Angier Return'd Thanks. Got home very well. *Laus Deo*.

Jany 23. I go to the Funeral of Anne Needham, who died in Child-bed: her former Husband was Lawson: her first, Airs, to whom I married her Nov[r] 5. 1690. At first I walk'd next the women with Mr. Wentworth: when had gon a little way Mr. Cotton Mather came up and went with me. Funeral was from Conney's Lane, to the new Burying-place. There Mr. Mather ask'd me to go with him to Madam Usher's, where we staid till past six. Speaking of death, I said twas a Happiness to be so Conform'd to Christ, And it was a pleasure to take part with God in executing a righteous Sentence upon one's self, to applaud his Justice ——— Mr. Mather said that was high-flying; he would have such High-flyers to be at his Funeral.

Jan[y] 30. 1707/8 John Neesnummin [Indian Preacher] comes to me with Mr. R. Cotton's Letters; I shew him to Dr. Mather. Bespeak a Lodging for him at Matthias Smith's: but after they sent me word they could not doe it. So I was fain to lodg him in my Study.[17] Jan[y] 31 p. m. I send him on his way towards Natick, with a Letter to John Trowbridge to take him in if there should be occasion. About half an hour by sun I went to the Funeral of my neighbour Sam Engs: I went first with Mr. Meers, and then with Mr. Pemberton, who talk'd to me very warmly about Mr. Cotton Mather's Letter to the Gov[r], seem'd to resent it, and expect the Govr should animadvert upon him. Said if he were as the Govr he would humble him though it cost him his head; Speaking with great vehemency just as I parted with him at his Gate.

March, 25, 1708. Intending to set out for Plimouth the 27th I went to the Major Gen^ls and to Mrs. Sergeant's to Receive their Bills if they pleas'd to pay them: found neither at home, and so went not in. Coming back, in the prison-Lane I met Mr. Sergeant. He ask'd me where I had been, I told him at his house: He said, What for, Money? I said Yes. At which he was angry, and said I was very hasty, I knew very little of that nature. He would enquire how others paid me &c. I told him I was going out of Town, this was the day, and I thought it convenient to offer the Bills; he said he should not break; and at last call'd out aloud, he should not break before I came back again! I know no reason for this Anger; the Lord sanctify it to me, and help me to seek more his Grace and favour. This day was very stormy with Rain, and then with Snow; a pretty deal of Thunder.

Feria Sexta, April, 2. Last night I dream'd that I had my daughter Hirst in a little Closet to pray with her; and of a sudden she was gon, I could not tell how; although the Closet was so small, and not Cumber'd with Chairs or Shelves. I was much affected with it when I waked.

Feria septima, Apr. 3. I went to Cous. Dummer's to see his News-Letter: while I was there Mr. Nathl Henchman came in with his Flaxen Wigg; I wish'd him Joy, i. e. of his Wedding. I could not observe that he said a Word to me; and generally he turn'd his back upon me, when none were in the room but he and I. This is the Second time I have spoken to him, in vain, as to any Answer from him. First was upon the death of his Wife, I cross'd the way near our house, and ask'd him how he did: He only shew'd his Teeth.

May, 31. The Govr call'd a Council in the Morning, and had Capt. Chandler's Letter from Woodstock concerning Nenemeno, an Indian that went away ten years ago; He said the Govr has a Crooked heart, he has taken away our Land, and now would send us to Salt Water. He first enquired after Ninequabben, who it seems was sent to sea upon Wages with his own Consent, and Taken. Govr and Mr. Secretary writ what was convenient.

In the afternoon the Govr went home indispos'd.

About the 23 or 24ᵗʰ of June Mr. Bromfield Rec'd a Letter without a name, putting him upon enquiring after Debaucheries at North's the Exchange Tavern, and that he should ask my Advice. At last, June, 28. he got in writing what North's Wife and Maid had to complain of. I went to Mr. Sim. Stoddard's; he put it into my hand, and I read it first, being surpris'd to find my self unaccountably abused in it: I told Mr. Bromfield, I should not meddle in it, I must not be a Judge in my own Cause. At last when the matter was heard before Mr. Bromfield, Townsend, Dummer, by Mr. Banister's procurement, sundry Gentlemen were present, Capt. Tho. Hutchinson, Capt. Edᵂ Winslow, and others, at Mr. Bromfield's; They gave Mrs. North and her Maid their Oaths, fin'd Mr. Tho. Banister junʳ 20ˢ for Lying; 5ˢ Curse, 10ˢ Breach of the peace for throwing the pots and Scale-box at the maid, and bound him to his good behaviour till October sessions. At the latter end of the Court, I think about the first of July, the Dept's sent in for the Govʳ £200.; for Mr. Treasurer £225: at which the Govʳ was very angry, and said he would pass none of them, they would starve together. Sent for Mr. Taylor, Govʳ told him his Salary would not be pass'd, enquir'd whether he were ready to serve.

Augᵗ 21. Mr. Edward Oakes tells me Mr. Chiever died this last night.

Note. He was born January, 25. 1614. Came over to N–E. 1637. to Boston: To New-Haven 1638. Married in the Fall and began to teach School; which Work he was constant in till now. First, at New-Haven, then at Ipswich; then at Charlestown; then at Boston, whether he came 1670. So that he has Labour'd in that Calling Skillfully, diligently, constantly, Religiously, Seventy years. A rare Instance of Piety, Health, Strength, Serviceableness. The Wellfare of the Province was much upon his Spirit. He abominated Perriwigs.

Augᵗ 23. 1708. Mr. Chiever was buried from the School-house. The Govʳ, Councillors, Ministers, Justices, Gentlemen there. Mr. Williams made a handsom Latin Oration in his Honour. . . . After the Funeral, Elder Bridgham, Mr. Jackson, Hubbard, Dyer, Tim. Wadsworth, Edᵂ Procter, Griggs and two more came to me, and earnestly solicited me to speak to a place of Scripture at their privat Quarter-Meeting in the room of Mr. Chiever. I said, 'twas a great Surprise to me; pleaded my inability for want of memory, Invention: Said, doubted not of my ability; would pray for me. I pleaded the Unsuitableness, because I was not of that Meeting. They almost took a denial. But said one would come to me next night.

Aug⁺ 28. 1708. Mrs. Taylor is buried in Mr. Stoughton's Tomb. . . . Govʳ and his Lady, Majʳ Genˡ Winthrop and his Lady, Mr. Secretary, Sewall, Mr. Eᵐ Hutchinson, Belchar, Mr. Bromfield there; and many others. There was no Prayer at the House; and at the Grave Mr. Myles Read Common-Prayer; which I reckon an Indignity and affront done to Mr. Stoughton and his Friends: There appears much Ingratitude and Baseness in it because twas Mr. Danforth's Parish, and Mr. Danforth's wife is Cousin German to Col. Taylor: and Col. Byfield and his deceased daughter dissenters as I suppose. I was much surpris'd and grieved at it, and went not into the burying place. Majʳ Genˡ said, Mr. Stoughton heard them not. Mr. Leverett went not in.

Lords-day, Aug⁺ 29. 1708. about 4 p. m. An Express brings the News, the dolefull News, of the Surprise of Haverhill by 150. French and Indians. Mr. Rolf and his wife and family slain. About Break of Day, Those Words run much in my mind, I will smite the Shepherd, and the Sheep shall be scattered: What a dreadfull Scattering is here of poor Havarill Flock, upon the very day they used to have their solemn Assemblies.

Wednesday, [October] 27, 1708. My wife is taken very sick as she was last April; taken with Shaking and intolerable pain in her Brest. Majʳ Genˡ visits her and she takes some of his powder; but is cast up so soon, that it works little. Great Rain. Dr. Noyes visits and administers: on Friday grows better, *Laus Deo*.

Monday, Novʳ 1. Govʳˢ best Horse dyes in his Pasture at Roxbury as goe to Dedham. Bouroughs, a worsted-comber, was at Mr. Colman's Meeting on the L. day p.m̄., went homeward towards Roxbury in the night; got beyond the Salt-ponds, and fell down across the Cart path in the Mud, and there perished; was found dead on Monday morn, Novʳ 1. And thô the Coroner did his Office in the Morning; yet the Corps lay as a sad spectacle, gazed on till late in the Afternoon.

Govʳ calls and smokes a pipe with my wife at night.

Dec.ʳ 5. 1708. Mr. Nathanael Gookin preaches in the forenoon;

I think every time he mention'd *James,* twas with prefixing *Saint:* about 4 or 5 times that I took notice of. I suppose he did it to confront me, and to assert his own Liberty.

[December 15, 1708] Privat-Meeting at our House. The Condition of my Grandson was commended to God.

Dec.ʳ 16. very Cold and Lecture day, that I could not tell how to travail over the Neck so soon after my former Journey. Dec.ʳ 17. Court sits and only 3 Justices, which hindered my going to Brooklin. And Alas! Alas! seventh-day Dec.ʳ 18, News is brought that the poor Child is Dead about an hour by sun *mane*. Alas! that I should fail seeing him alive! Now I went too late, save to weep with my Children, and kiss, and mourn over my dear Grandson. My son desired me to pray with his family; which I did. Madam Dudley, the Govʳˢ Lady, Mrs. Katharin, and Mrs. Mary came in while I was there; and brought my little Rebekah with them. Call'd at the Governour's as came home. Seem to agree to bury the child next fourth day. I mention'd its being best to bury at Roxbury, for my son to keep to his own parish. Govʳ said I might put the Child in his father's Grave if I pleas'd. Got home well in my Slay, had much adoe to avoid Slews. *Laus Deo.*

My son perceiving the Governour's aversion to have the child buried at Roxbury, writes to me of it. I go to the Governour's on Tuesday, and speak about Bearers, He leaves it to me; so does my son. Wednesday, Decʳ 22, 1708. My dear Grandson, Sam¹ Sewall, is buried; Son and daughter went first: Then Govʳ and I; then Madam Dudley led by Paul Dudley esqr; Then Joseph and Hannah; . . . Gave Mr. Walter a Lutestring scarf, Bearers, Capt. Noyes, Mrs. Bayley, scarves. Dec.ʳ 30. Daughter Hirst is much oppress'd with a Fear of Death; desires to speak with me: I go to her presently after Lecture, and discourse with her, and she seems better compos'd. Seventh-day, Janʸ 1 [1708/9] Is a very pleasant day. Janʸ 2. Cloudy cold day. Mr. Bromfield is pray'd for, who is in much pain by reason of his disorder'd great Toe; was very ill last Lecture-day. Elder Bridgham lyes sick. Dr. Mather is kept in by the Gout.

Friday, Apr. 29. 1709. about 4. *post m.* the Dragon Frigat arrives at Nantasket, . . . First Mr. Dier tells me that Mr. Higginson was dead of the Small Pocks; but as to the time incongruously. Though it was now about 9. at night, I got to Mr. Belchar, who

Confirms this Melancholy News. Saith he died in November, was
buried in the night in Bow-Church: He was at his Funeral. Alas
alas! that he should escape 1000. deaths in going to the East-
Indies, dwelling there, and returning; and now to die so soon in
London of the Small Pocks! The Lord help me not to Trust in
Man; but in GOD. They tell us St. John's in New-found-Land was
Taken by the French last Dec.ʳ which is like to prove a great and
surprising Evil to this place.

May, 2. Being Artillery day, and Mr. Higginson dead, I put on
my Mourning Rapier; and put a black Ribband into my little
cane. When I enter'd the Council-Chamber, the Govʳ with an Air
of displeasure said, You are Chidden! pretending my late coming;
though I think I was there before eleven, and am, I think, the most
constant attender of Councils.

I dined with the Artillery at Powells, whether Maxwell came
and warn'd me to Council at 3. There I waited all alone, as
many times I doe. At length the Govʳ came. When Col. [John]
Hathorne had his Quota 76. given him, he expostulated a little;
upon which the Govʳ was very angry, and took him up with very
smart words. I was on the same side of the board, and saw his
Warrant. Then I went to my own, and seeing a number of Letters
ly under the Secretaryes hand, I made a motion to see one which
the Secretary declin'd: and the Govʳ taking notice of it with a very
angry Air said to me, I will not be Govern'd by You!

Midweek, July, 13. 1709. N.B. Last night, between 2 or 3 hours
after midnight, my wife complain'd of Smoak; I presently went
out of Bed, and saw and felt the Chamber very full of Smoak to my
great Consternation. I slipt on my Cloaths except Stockings, and
run out of one Room into another above, and below Stairs, and
still found all well but my own Bed-chamber. I went into Garret
and rouz'd up David, who fetch'd me a Candle. My wife fear'd
the Brick side was a-fire, and the children endangered. She fled
thither, and call'd all up there. While she was doing this, I felt
the partition of my Bed-Chamber Closet warm; which made me
with fear to unlock it, and going in I found the Deal-Box of Wafers
all afire, burning livelily; yet not blazing. I drew away the papers
nearest to it, and call'd for a Bucket of Water. By that time it
came, I had much adoe to recover the Closet agen: But I did, and
threw my Water on it, and so more, and quench'd it thorowly.

Thus with great Indulgence GOD saved our House and Substance, and the Company's Paper. This night, as I lay down in my Bed, I said to my Wife, that the Goodness of God appeared, in that we had a Chamber, a Bed, and Company. If my Wife had not waked me, we might have been consumed. And it seems admirable, that the opening the Closet-Door did not cause the Fire to burst forth into an Unquenchable Flame. The Box was 18 inches over, Closet full of loose papers, boxes, Cases, some Powder. The Window-Curtain was of Stubborn Woolen and refus'd to burn though the Iron-Bars were hot with the fire. Had that burnt it would have fired the pine-shelves and files of Papers and Flask and Bandaliers of powder. The Pine-Floor on which the Box stood, was burnt deep, but being well plaister'd between the Joysts, it was not burnt through. The Closet under it had Hundreds of Reams of the Company's Paper in it. The plaistered Wall is mark'd by the Fire so as to resemble a Chimney back. Although I forbad mine to cry Fire; yet quickly after I had quench'd it; the Chamber was full of Neighbours and Water. The smell of Fire pass'd on me very much; which lasted some days. We imagine a Mouse might take our lighted Candle out of the Candle-stick on the hearth and dragg it under my closet-door behind the Box of Wafers. The good Lord sanctify this Threatening; and his Parental Pity in improving our selves for the Discovery of the fire, and Quenching it. The Lord teach me what I know not; and wherein I have done amiss help me to do so no more!

July, 21. A Council is warn'd to meet presently after Lecture before Dinner. The Govr took up Col. Vetch with him, who sat at the end of the Table leaning his Elbow on the Arm of the Gov^rs Chair; They both urg'd the sending a Flagg of Truce to Port-Royal, to fetch off Capt. Myles and others. Mr. Secretary and I opposed it as that that would expose us to be ridicul'd by our Enemies; they would detain our Flagg during their pleasure; the Canada Expedition being known to them. I mention'd the Suddenness of the Council. So the Govr adjourn'd it to Friday at 2. p. m.

Friday, July, 22. Maxwell warns me again to attend the Govr at 11. *mane* in Council. Govr and Col. Vetch sat as yesterday, and vehemently urged the sending a Flagg of Truce for poor Myles, as the Govr often spake. Mr. Secretary and I opos'd it. Mr. E^m Hutchinson said would doe no good. I mention'd that it might be

laid before the Gen¹ Court that was to sit on Tuesday. But the
Govʳ first order'd that to be prorogued to the next week; however
that was not so far gon but it might have been stay'd; for nothing
was entred. I considered also the daily Expectation of the Fleet's
arrival, where we might have further direction. I mention'd the
parting with Men, Sloops, Provisions in vain. Col. Foster, with
some Heat, said, He was ashâm'd to hear any mention Charge!
Mr. Secretary hinted they would by our Flagg have notice the
Fleet was not come. But all was rejected with disdain. Col. Vetch
urg'd once and again, that if Capt. Myles were not sent for, it
might tempt him to turn to the French, as Du Bart did. Twas
urg'd that the Flagg was going when Col. Vetch, arrived; and
that caused us unanimously to surcease, and to dismiss Col. Taylor.
That was blown off as nothing. I spake against sending the Strong
Beer to Supercass, he had dealt basely at New-found-Land and
at Port Royal. Col. Vetch urg'd, that if they deny'd to send our
Captives, they should know how to Treat the French Prisoners:
I answer'd, we knew already: The French had broke their Faith
in not sending the Captives.

Augᵗ 12. At Council 'twas enquired whether Blew should go
to Edgartown to convoy vessels there loaden with Bread: Col.
Foster much opposed it, and some others; pleading we had Bread
enough. I argued the Benefit of having Bread in time of War; and
the great Hurt twould be to us, if it should fall into the Enemies
Hands. At last it was agreed, that if at the foot of the Shoals,
whether his cruise led him, he had a fair wind, he might goe. I had
urg'd the Certainty of doing good if Blew went.

'Twas mention'd in Council, that 300 Eastern Indians, Men
Women and Children, were gon to the 5 Nations to pray leave
to dwell with them; and that others refusing them, they were gon
to the Senecas: The Govʳ mention'd that the Gentlemen of Albany
might be written to that they might be with the Maquas where
they might [be] under Inspection. But the Council were of the
mind, The further off the better; would more easily be apt to forget
their own Country, and Less ready at so great a distance to annoy.
And that twas best for us (they being Rebels) to say nothing
about it.

[October 3, 1709] Govʳ calls a Council. I acquainted the Govʳ
with the Condemnation of the two Indian Men at Bristol for

Murder, and the time intended for their Execution. Col. Vetch
mutter'd somthing as if there was no malice prepense: I told him
of the man's kicking his wife into the fire. He said he heard not
of that.

Capt. Blackmore arrives this day and brings the Wellcom Orders
for going on to print the Bible [Indian] and countermanding the
selling any more of the Genoa Paper, with a considerable Remit-
tance.

Nov.ʳ 6ᵗʰ Lord's day; Mr. Pemberton had propounded Hannah
Butler to renew her Baptismal Covenant; and now mention'd it,
and said she had sin'd scandulously against the 7ᵗʰ Commandment; read her Confession immediatly, and by the silential vote
restored her. I think it is inconvenient, when persons have so
fallen, not to give the Church some previous notice of it; that the
Brethren may have Opportunity to enquire into the Repentance.
An ignorant Consent is no Consent. And I understood Mr. Pemberton that he would not go in that way again. Once before he
did it, saying he knew not of it when the party was propounded.

Feb.ʳ 6. [1709/10] the Queen's Birth-day. The Council Treat
the Govʳ at the Green Dragon. . . . Cost us 5ˢ apiece. After our
Return to the Council-Chamber, Burnt near Six Thousand pounds
of decay'd Bills. When the Candles began to be lighted, I grew
weary and uneasy, and even slip'd away without drinking. When
I came home, it was a singular Refreshment to me to read 2 Cor. 6.
especially from the 14ᵗʰ to the end.

[April 30, 1710] Last night the Rudder of Capt. Rose's Ship
was cut; The reason was Capt. Belchar's sending of her away
Laden with Wheat in this time when Wheat is so dear.

May, 1, 1710. Fourty or fifty Men get together and seek some
body to head them to hale Capt. Roses Ship ashoar: but they were
dissuaded by several sober Men to desist, which they did. This
was about 5. m. I heard of it as I was going to Hog-Island to see
my Tenant's Loss of Sheep. Went off about Nine, and return'd
between 2 and 3.

May, 2. Mr. Pemberton prays; 5 Judges there. First Lieut
Sam. Johnson was made Foreman of the Jury. May, 3. He pray'd
to be dismiss'd by reason of sickness, which was granted while I
was withdrawn into the Council-Chamber, and writing to Mr. C.
Mather to dine with us; and Mr. Cumby was made Fore-man. At

Noon Mr. Attorney objected against Cumby that he should say, Sure they cut the Rudder themselves, that is, Capt. Roses Men. Upon this Mr. Cumby was spoken to by the Court, and he in open Court desired dismission, or at least from being Fore-man. He was dismiss'd; and Mr. William Torrey was put in. Mr. Attorney and Capt. Belchar went to the Grand-Jury to forward the Bill against those that made the unlawfull Assembly. Just after Mr. Cumby was dismiss'd, Capt. Belchar made a motion that he might be sworn as a Witness. I look'd upon it as an indignity, he having been hardly enough dismiss'd from the Grand-jury: and nothing led to the calling him forth but his Situation. So I oppos'd it, and it was not done. I insisted it most convenient to proceed with a few and not to seek to inflame the Reckoning by multiplying Articles. And Col. Foster complain'd that twas almost like an Inquisition; the manner of Capt. Belchars pursuing it in Council.

This Midweek morn, Mr. Pemberton stood in his Gate, and occasion'd my going in with him. He spake very warmly about the Unlawfull Assembly: I said such motions ought to be suppress'd; the thing should be thorowly and effectually dealt in. I said twas an ill office in Capt. Belchar to send away so great a quantity of Wheat (about 6000 Bushels besides Bread) in this scarce time. Mr. Pemberton said I cherish'd those evil seditious Motions by saying so. I said he unjustly charged me. He that withholds Corn, the people will curse him, though I did not affirm that Scripture Justified the Rioters. I mention'd something of God's people, that though they brought themselves into Straits by their own fault; yet God pitied and help'd them. Mr. Pemberton said, with much fierceness, They were not God's people but the Devil's people that wanted Corn. There was Corn to be had; if they had not impoverish'd themselves by Rum, they might buy Corn. I was stricken with this furious Expression. Mr. Pemberton also spake very sharply and upbraidingly, that he was invited to Dinner, and then not sent for at Dinner-time; was sick with waiting; lost his own Dinner; knew not where we din'd; 'twas indecent to ly lurking at the ordinary; wanted not a Dinner.

Novʳ 28. p. m. When the President and Mr. Pemberton[18] came to Dinner, I was in my Apartment, Mr. Mayhew and my Son with me. The President and Mr. Pemberton being come to us; Mr. Pemberton quickly begun to say, What you have been hold-

ing a Court to day! Had it over again; I was a little amus'd at
the word Court; however, I began to relate what had been done.
Mr. Pemberton with extraordinary Vehemency said, (capering
with his feet) If the Mathers order'd it, I would shoot him thorow.
I told him he was in a passion. He said he was not in a Passion.
I said, it was so much the worse. He said the Fire from the Altar
was equal impartial. Upbraiding me, very plainly, as I understood it, with Partiality. The President said, The Governour was
barbarously Treated (meaning Dr. Cotton Mather's Letter to his
Excellency). I answered; That was put to the Council. Mr. Mayhew told me afterward, that I said his Carriage was neither becoming a Scholar nor Minister. The Truth is I was surpris'd to see
my self insulted with such extraordinary Fierceness, by my Pastor,
just when I had been vindicating two worthy Embassadors of
Christ (his own usual Phrase) from most villanous Libels. And I
dônt know any syllable intimating that I had done Well. As for
the Letter, the Govr was not in humor to trust me about it; because
I just then Fil'd my Reasons for withdrawing my Vote. [In mar-
gin] Mr. Pemberton speaks hard Words, and very reflecting. We
went to Dinner, I sat next Mr. Pemberton and ask'd him to crave
a Blessing; He also Return'd Thanks, the President declining it.
Mr. Sergeant came into our Company. The President walked on
his right hand to the Council-chamber; I and Mr. Pemberton
went next. In the Way Mr. Pemberton charg'd me again, I was
griev'd and said, What in the Street! He answer'd, No body hears.
But Mr. Sergeant heard so much, that he turn'd back to still us.
Mr. Pemberton told me that Capt. Martin, the Commadore, had
abus'd him, yet I took no notice of it: I answer'd, you never laid
it before me. He said, You knew it. I said, I knew it not. (For
every Rumor is not ground sufficient for a Justice of Peace to
proceed upon; and Mr. Pemberton never spake word of it to me
before). He said Capt. Martin call'd him Rascal in the Street, and
said had it not been for his coat, he would have cân'd him. Mr.
Pemberton said I excluded him, or he was excluded from Dining
with the Superior Court by the Invitation of Capt. Martin. I said
'twas with difficulty that his Company was obtain'd at our Dinner.
The matter of Fact was this: Upon Midweek Novr 8., as I take
it, twas nois'd that General Nicholson was going out of Town to
Pascataqua, in order to his Voyage home: Hereupon the Justices

agreed to wait upon his Honor at his Lodgings; to take Leave of
him if going, to invite him to Dinner if he staid in Town so long:
(The Chief Justice was at New London), Sewall, Hathorne, Walley, Corwin went in the morning to the House of Mr. John Borland;
When the Gen¹ came, and we had Saluted him, and understood
his Honor staid in Town that day; We invited him to Dinner to
the Green Dragon; and Mr. Myles being there, I invited him;
and enquired of the Gen¹ if there were any we should ask to Dine
with him? He mention'd Capt. Martin, the Comadore. Accordingly we sent, and for Major Handy.

Mid-week, Jan.ʸ 31. [1710/11] Went and heard Mr. Bridge,
and Dr. Cotton Mather pray and preach, at the said Dr's House.
Mr. Bridge's Text was about God's lifting up a Standard, when
Enemy breaks in as a Flood. Dr. Mathers, The whole world lyes
in Wickedness. Had Cake and Butter and Cheese, with good
Drinks, before parting. As I went home, I heard Col. Vetch was
arriv'd from Annapolis.

Feb.ʳ 1. As I go to Lecture, I wait on Govʳ Vetch and con-
gratulat his Safety; He thanks me for my Respect to him and to
his Spouse.

At 3. p. m. The Council meets according to Adjournment.
Upon Conference with Col. Vetch, the Expedition is set forward
by Water. Mr. Secretary reads a paper given him by Col. Vetch,
Certifying that the Government of Annapolis Royal had not
Traded with the Indians as they were aspers'd, but with all in a
vile manner loading New-Engld with Calumnies; a spirit of Witchcraft, and now 7 fold a Spirit of Lying, haters of Monarchy,
regretting Her Majesties success in Taking Port-Royal. I took it
of the Secretary, and read it, and mov'd several of the Council
that they would speak to it. I told them it would otherwise be
taken as a tacit License to print it. When no body spake, and
Col. Vetch was going away, I pray'd him to stay a little; and said
I fear'd the reading that paper without being spoken to, would
be taken as a tacit Licensing of it. I was for the Certificat so far
as it vindicated their innocency; but was against the Reflections
on New-England, they would be dishonorable to Nova Scotia,
and New-England. I was against printing it with them. Col. Vetch
said, if it could not be printed here, he would have it printed elsewhere; Copies of it were sent to England, I said it was Raillery

unbecoming a Government. When Col. Vetch was gone, I pray'd the Govr to forbid the printing it unless those Reflections were first taken out. The Govr said, he could not hinder it; they might take their own way. And yet own'd twas Raillery. I don't know but Col. Vetch may reckon that he has a tacit License to print the Certificat just now read in Council. I am very free the Substance of the Certificat, relating to their own innocency, may be printed: But to print the bulky Reflections would be dishonorable to Annapolis, and Boston. And I can no way consent to it. I think it should be spoken to.

Febr. 28. 1710/11 Midweek: This being my Marriage-day, and having now liv'd in a married Estate Five and Thirty years, notwithstanding my many Sins and Temptations, I spent some time in Meditation and Prayer in the Castle-Chamber. I was much encouraged by reading in Course the 32^d Psalm at family prayer without any foresight of mine. And when I came to pray I was much heartened to ask Forgiveness of God for my multiplied Transgressions, seeing He had directed Peter a sinfull Mortal to forgive to 70. times 7. I hope God will forgive and do as the matter may require. While I was thus employ'd Maxwell warn'd me to Council; but I ventur'd to keep in my Closet; and I understand by the Maj^r Genl they did nothing in Council.

March, 4. Lord's Day; To my apprehension God assists my Son remarkably in prayer and preaching I hope tis an Answer of my prayer last Midweek. Preaches again in the Evening.

March, 29. Indian man charg'd with Ravishing an Indian Girl of 3 years old, was brought off, the principal Evidence being dead. . . . Too many Question about marrying ones Wives own Sister.

April, 3. [1711] I dine with the Court at Pullin's. Mr. Attorney treats us at his house with excellent Pippins, Anchovas, Olives, Nuts. I said I should be able to make no Judgment on the Pippins without a Review, which made the Company Laugh. Spake much of Negroes; I mention'd the problem, whether should be white after the Resurrection: Mr. Bolt took it up as absurd, because the body should be void of all Colour, spake as if it should be a Spirit.

April, 4. Wadlin comes in from Salt-Tertuda [Tortugas], in whom comes Mr. Josiah Willard, who has been twice taken. Used

civilly at first by the Privateer; but suffer'd hardship in Prison
at Martineco. After, was going to Barmudas, was taken, Strip'd,
and us'd Roughly.

April, 13. Dr. Mather visited me, I return'd his little Book out
of which I reprinted the Case of Conscience against a man's marrying his Brother's [?] sister.[19] He went into Chamber and Pray'd
with my wife and family, particularly for Joseph, who was there.
Joseph returns to Cambridge in the afternoon.

Friday, May, 4. Mr. Charles Chauncey dyes. Mr. Evans's Jury
Acquit Pastre of Fornication, and Maria, Mr. Wm Hutchinson's
Indian woman, of Murdering her Child, by letting it fall into the
House of Office.

Augt. 24. 1711. Sharp debates about the Province Gally. Deputies sent in a first vote Earnestly to desire the Govr to send her out
in defence of the Coast infested. Afterward sent a 2^d, wherein twas
Resolv'd that the Galley, being built at the Province charge, for
defence of the Coast, cânt be put to any other use without Consent
of the Genl Court. No forwardness in putting either of these to
vote. But Mr. Secretary suddenly drew up a vote, That it being
Her Majesties express and positive Command that the Galley
should go in the Expedition; a Sloop should be taken up and
Man'd. This was non-Concurr'd in the House of Deputies. Rejected Fire-Ships, and Hulk to Sink.

Midweek March, 26 [1712] Oyster Island is by Review Confirmed to Nathan and Zacheus Wicket, Indians, &c.

Hittee, an Indian Girl, found Guilty of Burning her Master
Little's Dwellinghouse. Adjourn'd to the Meetinghouse by reason
of the Press of people, and there the Negro Betty was Try'd for
Concealing the death of her Bastard-Child: Found Guilty.

[March 27, 1712] Betty Condemn'd. Hittee's Master pray'd she
might not be Condemn'd; was under sixteen years old. Upon this
she was remanded to Prison, and the Court adjourn'd to Six
a-clock next morning.

March, 28. Court met: order'd Oyster-Island not to be sold;
but the Attorney, Mr. Parker, to represent the state of it at the
next Term. Upon reading Hittee's Indenture (which was now
brought), Left her in Prison uncondemned; and order'd Col. Otis
her first master, and Major Basset, to take Affidavits concerning

her Birth. Adjourn'd *sine die*. Left my Statute Book with Capt. James Warren. Came homeward; Rain'd hard.

[June 13, 1712] I am put upon a Comittee about Volunteers; Col. Pynchon pleads mightily for it: 12.ˢ a week besides Subsistence: I argued, I fear'd it might become a Trade; what we did now might be drawn into Example afterward; knew not who might be our Capt. General. If persons should not be spirited by Love to their wives, Children, Parents, Religion, twas a bad Omen: fell below the heathen Romans. At last brought it to 12.ˢ 6.ᵈ Wages and Subsistence; and I prevail'd that stand, forces, Marching and in Garrison might have the same Encouragement as to Scalp Money, their danger being as great or greater. Skin for Skin. I sign'd as Chair-man. Council would have had Subsistence and £100 Scalp-money. But Deputies insisted on their own vote; till this Return of the Committee of both Houses, which they comply'd with. As soon as twas pass'd, the Govʳ propos'd to set up two Captains in each County; which startled me; I said, Will not that be too much? His Excellency Laugh'd, and said, would drop those that could not raise a company.

July, 29. Went alone to the Ferry in the Coach, Capt. Samˡ Gookin, the under-Sheriff, met me at Charlestown, and Mr. Bordman the Steward. Before Mr. Lynde's Commission was read I said, Although the Court be not so full as we could have desired, yet through the good providence of GOD there is a Court, a Court consisting entirely of such as have been brought up in the Society happily founded in this place by our Ancestors: Our Alma Mater will Grace us; it behooves us that we do not disgrace our Alma Mater. One worthy Member of this Court has been removed by death. Another has given us a further Instance of his Integrity by resigning his place because he apprehended himself incapable of sustaining it by reason of the Infirmities of his Age, (hardness of hearing). . . . In the Gentleman present I hope we shall have an Instance of the Advantage of an Inns of Court education superadded to that of Harvard College.

Febr. 12, [1712/13] Sam. comes not to Town as he intended. In the Afternoon Devotion informs my wife of his very uncomfortable Circumstances, and of the Necessity of fetching him to Boston.

Friday, Febr. 13. Joseph and I ride in Mr. Stoddard's Coach to Brooklin, got thither at Eleven a. m: find Sam abed. In a little while got him up, din'd there, came away. I was somwhat afraid, by reason his [Joseph's] Pulse was disorder'd. But the Coach being close, Harry drove us home well about 4. p. m. At Brooklin I saw the Lambs, encourag'd Tom. to be faithfull in his Masters business, which he promis'd. Told him he could not obey his Master without obedience to his Mistress; and *vice versa;* bid him take that as a Rule. Gave him a Two-shilling Bill of Credit. When my daughter alone, I ask'd her what might be the cause of my Son's Indisposition, are you so kindly affectioned one towards another as you should be? She answer'd, I do my Duty. I said no more. At parting I pray'd God to be with us going, and with them staying.

Febr. 19. Lecture-day, son S. goes to Meeting, speaks to Mr. Walter. I also speak to him to dine. He could not; but said he would call before he went home. When he came he discours'd largly with my Son; I also spake to him: His advice was, that Ilsly should be put away; some Friends talk to them both and so come together again.

Midweek, April 29 [1713] Council held at 11. a. m; ordered so many to attend the Govr Eastward as to make a Council there. Saml Penhallow's Petition read, as to importing Indians [as slaves] contrary to Law, craves relief; Govr. urged the Council vehemently: Mr. Commissary question'd the Council's power. I said if Mr. Secretary would admit him to his oath, I should not blame him. If he could not do it lawfully, the council could not make it Law. Voted not for it. Govr would have had the Council order'd the Sheriff to have Took them out of the hands of those they were sold to at Plimouth.

Tuesday, May 5, 1713. *mane.* Dr. Cotton Mather makes an Excellent Dedication-Prayer in the New Court-Chamber. Mr. Pain, one of the Overseers of the Work wellcom'd us, as the Judges went up Stairs. Dr. Cotton Mather having ended Prayer, The Clark went on and call'd the Grand-Jury: Giving their Charge, which was to enforce the Queen's Proclamation, and especially against Travailing on the Lord's Day; God having return'd to give us Rest. [In the margin. My speech to Grand jury in new Court House.] I said, You ought to be quickened to your Duty,

in that you have so Convenient, and August a Chamber prepared
for you to doe it in. And what I say to you, I would say to my
self, to the Court, and to all that are concern'd. Seeing the former
decay'd Building is consum'd, and a better built in the room, Let
us pray, May that Proverb, Golden Chalices and Wooden Priests,
never be transfer'd to the Civil order; that God would take away
our filthy Garments, and cloath us with Change of Raiment; That
our former Sins may be buried in the Ruins and Rubbish of the
former House, and not be suffered to follow us into this; That a
Lixivium may be made of the Ashes, which we may frequently
use in keeping ourselves Clean: Let never any Judge debauch
this Bench, by abiding on it when his own Cause comes under
Trial; May the Judges always discern the Right, and dispense
Justice with a most stable, permanent Impartiality; Let this large,
transparent, costly Glass serve to oblige the Attornys always to set
Things in a True Light, And let the Character of none of them
be *Impar sibi;* Let them Remember they are to advise the Court,
as well as plead for their clients. The Oaths that prescribe our Duty
run all upon Truth; God is Truth. Let Him communicat to us of
His Light and Truth; Let the Jurors and Witnesses swear in Truth,
in Judgment, and in Righteousness. If we thus improve this House,
they that built it, shall inhabit it; the days of this people shall be
as the days of a Tree, and they shall long enjoy the work of their
hands. The Terrible Illumination that was made, the third of
October was Twelve moneths, did plainly shew us that our GOD
is a Consuming Fire: but it hath repented Him of the Evil. And
since He has declar'd that He takes delight in them that hope in
his Mercy, we firmly believe that He will be a Dwelling place to
us throughout all Generations.

The Church Meeting was begun before I could get to it; Major
Fitch and Mr. Oliver Nominated. Then were chosen by lifting up
the Hand. Then Mr. Pemberton call'd on them to Nominat another; Som body said, Capt. Savage (I understood it of Ephraim);
but Capt. Habijah Savage stood up and disabled himself because
of the Dispute between his Unkle and him about the Pue. Then
some body mentioned Mr. Phillips. After awhile, I said, Some
have thought it might be convenient to have one of the Congregation. Mr. Pemberton assented. Mr. Jeffries was Nominated and
voted. Mr. Pemberton said, Mr. Phillips was Nominated; but I

had carried it over to the Congregation: whereas 'twas what he himself had introduc'd at the Meeting of the Overseers at his House. And I reckon'd Mr. Phillips not so fit because of the Controversy about the Pue. Concluded with Prayer: Pray'd that my son now call'd to more Constant Work might be blessed of GOD.

Midweek, May 20. The Rain hinder'd my Return. Visited Dr. Hale at Beverly who, oppress'd with Melancholy, was a-bed at. 5. p. m. Visited Mr. Blower. Got to Brother's at Salem about 7. and lodg'd there. By this means I was not Entangled with the Riot Committed that night in Boston by 200 people or more, breaking open Arthur Mason's Warehouse in the Common, thinking to find Corn there; Wounded the L! Govr and Mr. Newton's Son; cry'd Whalebone. Were provoked by Capt. Belchar's sending Indian Corn to Curasso. The Select-men desired him not to send it; he told them, The hardest Fend off! If they stop'd his vessel, he would hinder the coming in of three times as much.

May, 27. Col. John Appleton and I administer the Oaths &c. to the Deputies. . . . Din'd at the Green Dragon. Went late to the Election. 102 Voters at first: Mr. Addington had all but his own, 101. Col. Hutchinson and I had 97. each. But tis to be lamented that Maj^r Genl Winthrop had but 46. and was left out. He was the great Stay and Ornament of the Council, a very pious, prudent, Couragious New-England Man. Some spread it among the Deputies, that he was out of the province, and not like to Return. (Has been absent ever since April, 1712. but through Sickness.) Lieut Govr said he was a Non-Resident. Staid the Election; but voted not, said 'twas against his principles; the Councillors ought not to vote. Said of voting by papers, It was a Silly way! I took no notice of it. Thus Mr. Winthrop is sent into Shade and Retirem't while I am left in the Whirling Dust, and Scorching Sun.

> So falls that stately Cedar! whilest it stood
> It was the truest Glory of the Wood.

May, 28, 1713. The Four Churches [of Boston, including Sewall's Old South Church] Treat the Ministers, and Councillors in Town at the Exchange Tavern.

Thorsday, May, 28. All the Councillors are sworn except Major

Brown, who was not in Town. In the Afternoon I declar'd to the Council, that Prayer had been too much neglected formerly; we were now in a New House, we ought to Reform; without it I would not be there. Mr. Secretary assented, and I was desired to see it effected. I rode with Col. Hutchinson in his Coach, and earnestly solicited Dr. Increase Mather to begin, and give us the first Prayer: He disabled himself by his Indisposition; He must take Pills. I press'd him, and came away with some hope; obliged Cuffee to call for him.

May, 29. Dr. Increase Mather prays Excellently in the Council. L! Gov' at the Castle. Went to Dr. Cotton Mather, and engag'd him.

May, 30. 1713. Dr. Cotton Mather prays very Excellently. Adjourn'd to June 2. because of the Artillery.

Octob: 13. 1713. *Feria tertia.* Last night was very Tempestuous, with Lightening, Thunder, Rain. Morning Cloudy: A Council was warn'd, which made us too late to Charlestown. Mr. Stevens ordained. Mr. Stephens was in his Sermon—from Dan¹ 12. 3. The Seats were so fill'd that I went into Col. Phillips Pue, and Mr. Secretary follow'd, where had good Hearing and View. Mr. Bradstreet Pray'd; and declar'd that Dr. Increase Mather was desired to Ordain, and be Moderator in the Affair, which he perform'd. He, Dr. Cotton Mather, Mr. Bradstreet, Mr. Brattle, Mr. Barnard of Andover laid on Hands. Dr. Incr. Mather pray'd, Ordain'd, Charg'd, pray'd; Declar'd Mr. Stephens to be a Minister of Christ and a pastor of the Church in that place. Dr. Cotton Mather made an August Speech, shewing that the Congregational Churches early declar'd against Independency, that all the Reformation of the Continent of Europe ordain'd as New England did; shew'd that their Ordination had no other Foundation. Declar'd what was expected of the Ordained person, what of the church, and then gave the Right Hand of Fellowship. 3 last Staves of the 32ᵈ PS. sung. Capt. Phips set the Tune, and read it.

Octob: 16. 1713. I went to see the portentous Birth; it seems to be two fine Girls to whom an unhappy Union has been fatal. The Heads and Necks, as low as a Line drawn from the Arm-pits, are distinct. A little below the Navel, downward again distinct, with distinct Arms and Legs; Four of each. I measured across the perfect Union about the Hips and found it to hold about

eight Inches. Oh the Mercies of my Birth, and of the Birth of
Mine! *Laus Deo!* Dr. Cotton Mather introduc'd me and Mr. John
Winthrop to this rare and awfull Sight.

Octob.ʳ 19. Mr. Winslow of Marshfield comes to Town; Set
out so long before Sun-rise that he was here about 3. p. m. and
in the Council-Chamber, in his own Hair.

Octobᵖ 20. He appears with a Flaxen Wigg, I was griev'd to
see it, he had so comly a head of black Hair.

Octobᵖ 25. In the Night after 12. Susan comes, and knocks at
our chamber door, said she could not sleep, was afraid she should
dye. Which amaz'd my wife and me. We let her in, blew up the
Fire, wrapt her warm, and went to bed again. She sat there till
near day, and then return'd; and was well in the morning. *Laus
Deo.* I was the more startled because I had spilt a whole Vinyard
Can of water just before we went to Bed: and made that Reflection
that our Lives would shortly be spilt.

Novʳ 2. Sam. is somthing better, yet full of pain; He told me
with Tears that these sorrows (arising from discord between him
and his wife) would bring him to his Grave. I said he must endeavour to be able to say, O Death, where is thy sting? O Grave,
where is thy victory? He is refresh'd by discoursing with Simon
Gates of Marlborough, and Amos Gates.

Satterday, Novʳ 19. A Council is call'd; Sit round the Fire:
Genˡ Nicholson blames the observing a Fast without the order of
Authority; the Queen was Head of the Church: seem'd to be
Warm. The Lieut Governour seem'd to intimat that their Church
[King's Chapel], the members of it, were Treated as if they were
Heathen. Genˡ Nicholson mention'd it as graviminous that the
Shops were shut up. The Governour said, Twas voluntary; none
was order'd to shut up his Shop. Country-men brought wares to
Town as on other days; that he himself came to Town as suppos-
ing the Episcopal Church had observed the Fast: when he saw
they did not, he went to Mr. Colman's; I was surpris'd with this
uncomfortable Talk, and said Nothing! At length a Motion was
made, I think by Genˡ Nicholson, that there might be a Genˡ
Fast. I was of Opinion there was great need of it, and readily
voted for it. The Govʳ pitch'd upon the 14ᵗʰ January.

[December] 24. Dr. C. Mather preach'd of God's Punishing Sin
with Sickness.

Dec.ʳ 25. Being moderat weather, A great abundance of provisions, Hay, wood, brought to Town; and Shops open as at other times. In the Afternoon I went to the Funeral of Mr. Francis Clark's daughter Hannah, between 9 and 10 years old, a desirable Child. Were 3. Funerals in the South-burying place together.

Jan.ʸ 30. 1713/14. Serene Cold Weather. Last night Ephraim Becon, going over the Neck with his Sled, Wandered to the Left hand, towards Dorchester, and was frozen to Death. One of the Horses is found dead.

I presented my Son and daughter with six silver spoons, cost about 21ˢ a piece, bought of Capt. Winslow this day: and 6. Alchimy [alloy] spoons, of Mr. Clark, cost 3. 6.ᵈ

Feb.ʳ 6. I went to the Town-house on the occasion of the Queen's Birthday; Mr. Bromfield and I sat a-while in one of the windows, Table being full; afterward sat in. A little before Sunset I went away. . . . My neighbour Colson knocks at our door about 9. or past to tell of the Disorders at the Tavern at the South-end in Mr. Addington's house, kept by John Wallis. He desired me that I would accompany Mr. Bromfield and Constable Howell thither. It was 35. Minutes past Nine at Night before Mr. Bromfield came; then we went. I took Æneas Salter with me. Found much Company. They refus'd to go away. Said were there to drink the Queen's Health, and they had many other Healths to drink. Call'd for more Drink: drank to me, I took notice of the Affront to them. Said must and would stay upon that Solemn occasion. Mr. John Netmaker drank the Queen's Health to me. I told him I drank none; upon that he ceas'd. Mr. Brinley put on his Hat to affront me. I made him take it off. I threaten'd to send some of them to prison; that did not move them. They said they could but pay their Fine, and doing that they might stay. I told them if they had not a care, they would be guilty of a Riot. Mr. Bromfield spake of raising a number of Men to Quell them, and was in some heat, ready to run into Street. But I did not like that. Not having Pen and Ink, I went to take their Names with my Pensil, and not knowing how to Spell their Names, they themselves of their own accord writ them. Mr. Netmaker, reproaching the Province, said they had not made one good Law.

At last I address'd my self to Mr. Banister. I told him he had been longest an Inhabitant and Freeholder, I expected he should

set a good Example in departing thence. Upon this he invited
them to his own House, and away they went; and we, after them,
went away. The Clock in the room struck a pretty while before
they departed. I went directly home, and found it 25. Minutes
past Ten at Night when I entred my own House.

About 5. in the Morning there was a cry of Fire; Bells rung.
Son J. Sewall came to our Chamber door and acquainted us. But
quickly after our rising, the Bells left off ringing, and I saw no
Light. Mr. Webb's Malt-house, near Mr. Bronsdon's, was burnt
down. Twas a great Mercy that the Fire was not spread all over
the North-End. Part of the House of Mr. Bronsdon, the Landlord,
began to burn.

Monday, Feb: 8. Mr. Bromfield comes to me, and we give the
Names of the Offenders at John Wallis's Tavern last Satterday
night, to Henry Howell, Constable, with Direction to take the
Fines of as many as would pay; and warn them that refus'd to
pay, to appear before us at 3. p. m. that day. Many of them pay'd.
The rest appear'd; and Andrew Simpson, Ensign, Alexander Gor-
don, Chirurgeon, Francis Brinley, Gent. and John Netmaker,
Gent., were sentenc'd to pay a Fine of 5ˢ each of them, for their
Breach of the Law Entituled, An Act for the better Observation,
and Keeping the Lord's Day. They all Appeal'd, and Mr. Thomas
Banister was bound with each of them in a Bond of 20ˢ upon
Condition that they should prosecute their Appeal to effect.

Capt. John Bromsal, and Mr. Thomas Clark were dismiss'd
without being Fined. The first was Master of a Ship just ready to
sail, Mr. Clark a stranger of New York, who had carried it very
civilly, Mr. Jekyl's Brother-in-Law.

John Netmaker was fin'd 5ˢ for profane cursing; saying to ——
Colson, the Constable's Assistant, God damn ye; because the said
Colson refus'd to drink the Queen's Health. This he paid presently. Then Mr. Bromfield and I demanded of the said Netmaker
to become bound in a Bond of Twenty pounds, with two Sureties
in Ten pounds a-piece, to Answer at the next Genˡ Session of
the Peace for Suffolk, his Contempt of Her Majesties Government
of this Province and vilifying the same at the house of John Wallis,
Innholder in Boston, last Satterday night. Mr. Banister declin'd
being bound; and none else offer'd (To imbarrass the Affair as I
conceiv'd). Upon this Mr. Netmaker was dismiss'd, giving his

Word to appear on Tuesday. at 10. m. that he might have Time
to provide Sureties.

Tuesday, March, 9th. Mr. Bromfield and I waited till past
11. and dismiss'd the Constables Howell and Feno, supposing No
body would come. Constable met Mr. Netmaker at the door, and
came back again with him: He came all alone. Mr. Bromfield and
I spent much time with him to bring him to some Acknowledgment of his Error, but all in vain. Offer'd not so much as his own
Bond: which constrain'd us to Write a Mittimus, and send him
to Prison. Angry words had pass'd between him and Const. Howell; he Threatn'd Const. Howell what he would do to him; or his
Servants for him. For this reason I dismiss'd Constable Howell;
sent for Mr. John Winchcomb, and gave him the Mittimus, out
of respect to Mr. Netmaker; and he took it kindly. This about ¼
past 12. at Noon by my Clock. Went into Town; Mr. Wᵐ Pain
spake with me near the Townhouse; express'd himself concern'd
that Mr. Netmaker was in prison; he would pay his Fine that he
might be releas'd. I told him there was no Fine. Went on, visited
Hannah Parkman, saw the place, where the Malt-house was burnt
down. . . . It was late and Duskish, and Col. Elisha Hutchinson
went away before any thing was Voted. Sat round a little Fire;
I happen'd to sit next Genˡ Nicholson. He apply'd himself to me
and Mr. Bromfield, ask'd whether did not know that he was here
with the Broad Seal of England? I answer'd, Yes! Ask'd whether
did not know that Mr. Netmaker was his Secretary? I answer'd,
Tis generally so receiv'd. Then with a Roaring Noise the Genˡ said,
I demand JUSTICE against Mr. Sewall and Bromfield for sending my Secretary to prison without acquainting me with it! And
hastily rose up, and went down and walk'd the Exchange, where
he was so furiously Loud, that the Noise was plainly heard in
the Council-Chamber, the door being shut. The Governour vehemently urg'd the Discharge of Netmaker; argued that Genˡ Nicholson was as an Embassador; his Servant ought to have been delivered to him. I said, Mr. Netmaker was upon his Parole from
Monday to Tuesday; in which time he might have acquainted Genˡ
Nicholson with his Circumstances. The Govʳ said, Mr. Bromfield
and I ought to have acquainted him our selves. Would have had
the Vote so Worded. Would have had us that committed Mr.
Netmaker to have released him. I objected to that; saying, we

had committed him: but I did not know that we had power to release him. Then the Keeper was sent for with the Mittimus, which Mr. Secretary read by Candle-Light, in these words;

(Seal.)   MASSACHUSETTS,
                        SUFFOLK ss.
(Seal.)   To the Keeper of Her Majesties Goal in Boston,
                                    Greeting,
            We herewith send you the body of John Netmaker, Gent: who being Order'd by our selves, two of Her Majesties Justices for Suffolk, to give Bond with Sureties, to appear at the next General Sessions of the Peace to be held for the County of Suffolk, to make Answer for his Contempt of Her Maj' Government of this Province, and Vilifying the same at the house of John Wallis, Innholder, in Boston in the Night Between the Sixth and Seventh of this Instant February: Refus'd so to doe;

You are therefore in Her Majesties Name required to receive the said Netmaker, and him safely keep till he be discharged by due course of Law. . . .

                                                SAMUEL SEWALL.
                                                EDW. BROMFIELD.

The Diary

VOLUME III
(1714–1729)

Aug.[t] 5th [1714] Fast for Rain at the Lecture. I keep at home by reason of my swell'd face, though tis something fallen from what twas yesterday. Note. about 2. p. m. Hannah was coming hastily down the new Stairs, fell, and broke the Pan of her Right Knee in two;[1] one part went upward, the other downward. I got her down and set her in my chair, sent for Dr. Cutler: who told us how it was; we led her up into her Chamber: Neighbour Hamilton and others came in and got her to bed, then Dr. Cutler bath'd it, with spirits of Wine, put on a large Plaister, then with two bolsters and large Swathing bound it up tite to bring the broken pieces together, and Unite them. Madam Davenport sent for him before he had done. Before Four a-clock Scipio comes and tells me that my daughter Hirst is brought to Bed of a son. I gave him a good shilling. Hannah is glad to hear of this.

This day Augt 5. the Ship arrives that brings news of the death of the Princess Sophia of an Apoplexy May, 28. Æt. 84. Bill against Dissenters keeping Schools pass'd both Houses. Mr. Dudley Bradstreet quickly after he had received Orders, dy'd of the small Pocks.

Lord's-day, Augt 29. Beard arrives, who brings the Act of Parliament against Dissenters keeping School; which ordains that no Catechism shall be taught in Schools, but that in the Common prayer Book.

I could not observe that Mr. Pemberton so much as used the Common form of praying for him that was to speak in the Afternoon: only pray'd God to be with us in our coming together.

I suppose Mr. Watts brings the News that Mr. Henry dyed the day the Royal Assent was given to the Bill against the growth of Schisme. Dy'd by a fall from his Horse riding to preach at Nantwich, being on a visit at West-Chester.[2]

Aug.[t] 31. I read the Act against Schism at Selby's Coffee-house. About 4. p. m. visited Mr. Peter Thatcher,[3] Milton. He was very glad to see me, said twas a Cordial: got home well a little after 9. *Laus Deo*. Carried him two China Oranges.

[September] 6. Visited Mrs. Lord under her Indisposition at the widow Dyer's. Went to the Meeting of the owners of the Saltworks[4] at the Sun-Tavern. Col. Byfield was there. Agreed to pay £10. apiece towards a Boylery; the said Byfield to buy Iron pans in England; two of them.

Dec.ʳ 25. Shops open, &c as on other days, very pleasant weather. . . .

Mrs. Bradstreet of Newbury, her killing her Negro woman is much talked of.

Lord's Day, Decembʳ 26. Mr. Bromfield and I go and keep the Sabbath with Mr. John Webb, and sit down with that Church at the Lord's Table. I did it to hold Communion with that Church; and, so far as in me lay, to put Respect upon that affronted, despised Lord's Day. For the Church of England had the Lord's Supper yesterday, the last day of the Week: but will not have it to-day, the day that the Lord has made. And Gen! Nicholson, who kept Satterday, was this Lord's Day Rummaging and Chittering with Wheelbarrows &c., to get aboard at the long Wharf, and Firing Guns at Setting Sail. I thank God, I heard not, saw not any thing of it: but was quiet at the New North. I did it also to Countenance a young small Church, and to shew that I was pleas'd with them for having the Lord's Supper once in four Weeks, and upon one of the Sabbaths that was vacant. Had a very comfortable Day.

Dec.ʳ 27. My Son tells me that Thomas Sewall went to the Church of England last Satterday: He expostulated with him about it.

Dec.ʳ 31. Very pleasant day after the Snow; visit Mr. Wadsworth. Thank him for his Lecture Exercises. Visit Mr. Addington,[5] who takes Physick, though he took some this week before; complains for want of Breath. Of his own accord Talk'd to me, About the Circumstances of the Government; what should do, if no orders should come by the first of February: Said, ought to think before hand; I consented with him and had some discourse. I desired to see the Letter about the president of the Council; and pray'd him to let me see the Act at large which continues commissions for half a year after the Queen's death.[6]

New-years-day, 1714/15. In the morning read in Course that awfull portion of Scripture, Isa. 24. Mr. Addington being at his office, shew'd me the Record of the Queen's order dated May, 3. 1707, which is thus concluded:

"The Eldest Councillor who shall be, at the time of your death or absence, residing within our said Province of the Massachusets Bay,

shall take upon him the Administration of the Government, and
execute our said Commission and Instructions, and the several Powers
and Authorities therein contained, in the same manner, and to all
intents and purposes, as other our Govr or Commander in Chief
should or ought to do, in case of your Absence, till your return; or in
all cases untill our further pleasure be known therein. So we bid you
farewell.

"By Her Maj^s Command,   SUNDERLAND."

Midweek, Jany 12. Genl Council. It being mov'd: Council were
of opinion the Genl Court was dissolv'd; because Prorogued before met, which was not agreeable to Charter. Now declared it to
be dissolv'd. Govr mentioned the renewing Commissions. I mov'd
to adjourn to the 2^d Febr. But the Govr adjourned to the 26th
Jany. I mov'd that Lt Col. Sommersby might be sent to transmit
a copy of his Inquest about Mrs. Bradstreet's Negro. Govr oppos'd
and check'd me, said twas to accomplish a diligent search. Col.
Noyes inform's what was done, which gave me occasion to speak.
Mr. Pemberton and Mr. Colman in their Lectures pray God to
continue the Govr, if it may be.

Jany 26. Genl Council; Govr offers a Proclamation to be voted
to continue all Officers till the K. pleasure known. Mr. B. Lynde,
Major Genl W., Col. Hutchinson opos'd it. Consideration was desired till morning. Then it was Negativ'd; but 2 or 3 for it. I
spake for it on Wednesday, saying it enter'd not into the Question
act [on account of?] the 6. Moneths end. But now I voted with
my Brethren, for I saw twas so worded as to tie up the hands of
the Council from making any Alteration though the Government
should be devolved on them next week.

Jany 30. Cold day. Mr. Pemberton prays that God would Govern the Succession of the Government.

[February 1, 1714/15] . . . When were together in the Closet,
I mollified [critics] a little by saying we were not a Council, but
some Gentlemen of the Council met together upon an extraordinary occasion. . . . After a pretty deal of Talk, I motion'd that
we might send to the Governour to enquire whether he had received any Orders; which was readily agreed to. . . . Got thither a
little after Five, only the Governour's Lady was there; Mr. W^m
Dudley received us, and call'd the Govr After a-while I rose up,

and began to do the Message, Gov' would have me sit down. The Message was this; May it please your Excellency, whereas the Six Months given by the Parliament of Great Britain, for continuing persons in their Civil and Military Offices; do expire this day: These are humbly to enquire whether your Excellency has received Orders from our Soveraign Lord King George, enabling you to sustain the place of Governour of this Province longer? If you have receiv'd no such Orders, we are of opinion that Authority is devolv'd upon His Maj' Council, by the direction of our charter; and that we are oblig'd in obedience thereunto, and for the welfare of His Majesties Subjects here, to exert our selves accordingly.

We humbly thank your Excellency for your good Services done this people which are many; and for your Favour to our selves in particular, and take leave to subscribe our selves your Excellency's most humble and faithfull Servants. . . .

The Governour's Answer was, I have received no Orders: and express'd an Aversion to enter into discourse. I said, If [it] was out of the Province, this [matters?] much more. Gov' said that was a Jest; might be out of the Province at a great distance, at Virginia, and yet give Orders in writing. Twas more to be at Cascobay, than at New Hampshire. Drank to me, saying, Judge Sewall. 'Twas Candlelight, went to the door and crav'd Excuse for not going to the Gate. And sent no body with us.

Gov' said there were Thirty Canada Indians at Piscataqua, he was listening after it.

When return'd, found our Company Waiting for us. When we had related the Governour's Answer, and they perceived by his declining to argue the matter, he design'd to hold his place, it put the Gentlemen to it. Col. Hutchinson said, There must be a Council Call'd, all seem'd to be of that mind; Mr. Winthrop would have had the Secretary write Letters; but he said, 'Twas no Council, he could not doe it. I said Let us write and all subscribe. Mr. Winthrop was so knockt that he said it could not be done, if the Secretary declin'd. The L' Gov' and Secretary left us. At last resolv'd to Write, and writ Five Letters; To Situate, Marble-head, Salem, Ipswich, Newbury.

Febr. 14. I wait on Dr. Incr. Mather to have a Commissioners Meeting appointed to morrow, at 3 aclock. But when I came to Dr.

C. Mather, he said should be employ'd in the Afternoon; so appointed it in the Morning: Gave Flagg the List to warn, because Maxwell was Cast out of the Church yesterday, and is superannuated.

In the Afternoon, Col. Townsend, Mr. Bromfield, Mr. Addington, Davenport and I visited the Governour, who Treated us with good Drink and Apples. No body went with us to the Gate. Gov.ʳ Hunter's Proclamation comes to Town dated Jan.ʸ 29. ordering those of pernicious principles to be apprehended and punished, who assert that Commissions are void at the end of the Six Moneths.

Midweek, Febr. 16. Council . . . vote to give New Commissions to Civil Officers.

[February] 18. Dr. Cotton Mather, Mr. Pemberton, Colman, come into Council and intimat what was discours'd last night at Mr. Winthrop's. Council order me and Mr. B. Lynde to give their Answer, viz, That 'tis agreeable to them, and they wish it may be gone forward with. We went immediately but can't find them, went to Mr. Pemberton's, Colman's. At last as were going to Mr. Mather's, Mr. Lynde call'd at his Brother's and found the Dr. there. We went in, drank Tea, after we had done our Message. A commission was drawn and sign'd for Mr. Wᵐ Dudley as Sheriff; he was sent for, to offer it to him, He said he had one already from the Govʳ and Council and saw no reason to take another, with a Little seeming Banter he said his had a Seal, This had none.

Monday, Febr. 21. Son Sewall intended to go home on the Horse Tom. brought, sent some of his Linen by him: but when I came to read his wive's Letter to me, his Mother was vehemently against his going: and I was for considering. I took the Horse and rode to Timᵒ Harris of Brooklin. Staid there so long that twas almost dark before I got to Roxbury Meeting house, yet call'd and saw Mrs. Mary Mighell. Visited Mr. Walter, staid long with him, read my daughters Letters to her Husband and me: yet he still advis'd to his going home. Went home in the dark between 7 and 8. My Wife can't yet agree to my Son's going home.

March, 20. Lt.ᵗ Govʳ comes to my house, shews me the printed Copy from the London Gazett in Govʳ Hunter's hand at New-York. It seems Mr. Paul Dudley bestirr'd himself to have his

Father pray'd for as Govr, and that the Order for the Fast might not be Read. Mr. Pemberton Spake to me as [he] went by the foreseat in the morning. I Spake against it as I could so on a sudden surprise, mention'd the Exception, or provision be made. Mr. Sewall pray'd as formerly. Mr. Pemberton ask'd if I had read it, I said yes: Said he should have seen it! At Noon I carried it to him borrowed of Mr. Newton. . . . Said he was amaz'd I should speak as I did; twas as far from it as East from West: New-England, he fear'd, would pay dear for being Fond of Government. I say'd unless he knew those that were Fond of Government he did ill so to Censure. Said I came only to give him a sight of the Proclamation, he might use his Freedom. He thank'd me and I went away.

P. m. Mr. Pemberton acquainted the Congregation that he had received an Order for a Fast from Civil Authority, he had it not with him, Spake of reading it next Lord's Day. He never said a word that I know of, though the President and Three others of the Council were of his Church, and before him: he saw not fit to advise with them. Pray'd for those that were or might be called to the Government. A little before night Mr. Paul Dudley, and Mr. Wm Dummer come to my house; call to Speak with me. Mr. Dudley acquaints me that the Govr intended to be here in Town about Eleven a-clock to publish the proclamation, that I might be there; said would goe to every one of the Council. I said, but is this sufficient, meaning the Copy. His eyes Sparkled, Said he had no orders to dispute, there had been great Friendship between him and me. I said I had done nothing to forfeit it. As was going out said his Father would come to Town with two Troops of Horse.

In the evening most, or all the Councillors in Town met at the Chief Justices. . . . All seem'd to express themselves satisfied, that their Fatigue was almost over. Capt. Belchar said he would hinder the coming of the Troops.

Monday, March, 21. Govr comes to Town with Four Troops in stead of two. Twelve of the Council were there at the proclamation. I was not there, I used to be with Mr. Addington; and was griev'd at the forbidding to read the Fast; *i. e.* Mr. P. Dudley writ to the Ministers to pray for his father, and not to read the Order for the Fast. I knew nothing of the Fast, till Mr. Pemberton declin'd reading it. . . . Dr. C. Mather said it was sign'd by the hon'ble Wait Winthrop esqr. the president of the Council and 17. more of the council, and Countersign'd &c.

Satterday, July, 2. When I got home was grievously surpris'd to find Hannah fallen down the Stairs again, the Rotula of her Left Knee broken, as the other was; and a great Gash Cut a cross her Right Legg just below the Knee, which were fain to stitch. Much blood issued out. The Lord Sanctify this Smarting Rod to me, and mine. This cloud returning after the Rain! Broke her Right Knee-pan the fifth of August 1714.

July, 3. Put up a Note for Hannah to be pray'd for, in the morning.

[July 6, 1715] This day it is Fifty four years Since I first was brought ashoar to Boston near where Scarlet's wharf now is, July, 6, 1661, Lord's Day. The Lord help me to Redeem the Time which passes so swiftly. I was then a poor little School-boy of Nine years and ¼ old. This day I have written a Letter to my Cousin Joseph Moodey, student in Harvard College, mending a Copy of his verses shewed me by his Father.

Feria Secunda, Augt 1. 1715. Dr. Increase Mather visits us, Discourses in a very Friendly obliging manner. At my desire prays with Hannah, and speaks Comfortably to her: Prays for me, my Wife, eldest Son present, the family. *Laus Deo.*

p. m. Mr. Pemberton pray'd, Dr. Cotton Mather preach'd from Isa. 5. 6. latter clause, I will command the clouds &c. Excellently; censur'd him that had reproach'd the Ministry, calling the Proposals Modalities of little consequence, and made in the Keys; call'd it a Satanick insult, twice over, and it found a kind Reception. Dr. Increase Mather concluded, Sung the 3^d part of the 68th PS. Gibson set the Low Dutch Tune, Dr. Incr. Mather gave the Blessing. All excellently; only I could wish the extremity of the censure had been forborn—Lest we be devoured one of another. Neither the Govr (though in Town) nor Mr. Paul Dudley present.

Monday, Augt 8. Set out at 11. at night on Horseback with Tho. Wallis to inspect the order of the Town.

[October] 11th Went with Mr. Daniel Oliver to Natick; from the Falls in Company with the President and Tho. Oliver esqr. and Mr. John Cotton. At Natick the Indians of the Committee executed the Parchment Deed for the Land at Magunkaquog: and paid the Proprietors Three pounds apiece.

[October] 12. Solomon Thomas acquaints me that Isaac Nehemiah [a Natick Indian], one of the Committee, had hang'd himself. Ask'd what they should doe. I sent him to the Crowner. A while after I went to Cous. Gookin's in order to go home. When there, Solomon came to me again, and earnestly desired me to go and help them. Mr. Whitney join'd to solicit for him, by reason of the distance from Cambridge. So I went, Mr. Baker accompanied me. The Jury found Isaac Nehemiah to be *Felo de se*. Hang'd himself with his Girdle, 3 foot and 4 inches long buckle and all. 'Twas night before had done, so went to Sherbourn again, and lodg'd at Cousin Gookin's.

Third-day, [October] 18. The Govr prorogues the Genl Court to the 23^d Novr. I and Mr. Clark voted against it. Govr pretended Deference to Govr Burgess in doing it, in expectance of his Arrival; but in the Proclamation, never read to the Council, he said nothing of it, which was gravaminous to some. . . . Now about Dr. Mather shews me a Copy of Govr Dudley's Signing a Petition for a Bishop as the only means to promote Religion here.

Novr 6. The day for reading the Order for the Thanksgiving according to the usual custom; Mr. Pemberton told the Congregation, There was an order to keep the 17th as a Thanksgiving; should read it the next Lords-day.

[November] 9th. Govr Saltonstall sued for his Father's estate as eldest Son and therefore sole Heir. I said 'twas contrary to our Law, the Law of Nature and the Law of GOD. It went against the Govr in all the three Causes.

Jany 5. [1715/16] Mr. Pemberton not having been at Lecture, I visit him: He is very warm about the Agent [Dummer], say'd the Lt Govr is an Usurper; not fit for the Chair. I said to whom does the Chair belong; To Govr Dudley, reply'd Madam Pemberton. . . . The people made light of the errand of God's people hither; indifferent.

Jany 6. Lt Governour delivers the Chief Justice, Mr. Davenport and me our Commissions as Judges of the Superiour Court: Gave the Oaths: The Lord help us, me especially, to keep them better than ever.

Lord's Day, Jany 15. An Extraordinary Cold Storm of Wind and Snow. Blows much worse as coming home at Noon, and so holds on. Bread was frozen at the Lord's Table: Mr. Pemberton administered. Came not out to the Afternoon Exercise. Though twas so Cold, yet John Tuckerman was baptised. At six a-clock my ink freezes so that I can hardly write by a good fire in my Wive's Chamber. Yet was very Comfortable at Meeting. *Laus Deo.*

March, 31. Great Storm of Snow on the Ground, and falling: and Jury not agreed; yet about Noon got away, the Weather clearing.

Note. The Jury bringing in for Mr. Hugh Adams against Haws, in the Action of Defamation. I said to Adams: Seeing you have Justice done you, hope it will incline you to Govern your Tongue, and govern your Pen. And if I were capable to advise you, I would counsel you to pay a great Deference to the Council of Churches held at Chatham.

To Mr. Joseph Otis brought in, Not guilty! I said, The providence of God in clearing you, will I hope melt your heart: for what you did, was notoriously Criminal.

April, 6. Capt. Arthur Savage arrives this day; come from the Downs March, 8. He was upon the Scaffold, and saw the Lords Derwenwater and Kenmure beheaded.[7] He and his wife came into the Meeting.

April, 17. I see plenty of them. Hannah visits her Bro^r and Sister Sewall. This is the furthest Walk she has taken since her Lameness.

I warn my eldest Son against going to Taverns.

April, 19. The Lt Govr comes to my House in the morn, and shows me the Accusation of Sir Alexander Brand against Mr. Agent Dummer, as if he had made the Knight drunk, and pick'd his pocket of 26. Guineas and brought in two Lewd Women into the Cross-Keys [Inn]. I presently thought on the Soldiers set to guard our Saviour's Tomb, their Tale; and said, If Sir Alexander were drunk, how could he tell who pick'd his Pocket? And as to the Women, I said, My Kinsman might be seen going in, and vile Women might press in so close after him, as to make a semblance of his introducing them. Seem'd to ask my advice Whether he ought not to acquaint the Govr of Cont [Connecticut?] that they

might discard him from being their Agent. In the Letter Shewed,
Mr. Agent Dummer is call'd this Fellow, Rascal. I went to Mr.
Pemberton to enquire into the matter, he refer'd me to Mr. White;
I went thither, who shew'd me Mr. William Willard's Letter of
March, 5th much exploding the Story.

Lord's Day, Ap. 22. My Wife and daughter Hannah goe to the
Solemn Assembly after long Restraint. I put up a Note for them.
Hannah fell down, but had no great hurt, blessed be God.

May, 1. Super. Court held at Boston by all the Five Justices.

Note. at this Court, the Chief Justice being indispos'd I was
obliged to Condemn the Negro.

May, 13. In the evening I had an inkling that two Merchants
came from Ipswich. I said, How shall I do to avoid Fining them?
I examined Richard Gerrish. As I understood him, they lodg'd
at Major Epes's on Satterday night, and went to the publick Worship there; and when the Afternoon Exercise was over, came to
Newbury. They Travailed not in Service Time: and had a Ship
at Portsmouth ready to sail which wanted their Dispatch. Alleg'd
that Mr. Peter La Blond was gone sick to Bed. I took his word to
speak with me in the morning. I consulted with Col. Thomas,
who inclin'd to admonish them as young, and strangers, and let
them go.

Newbury, May, 14. 1716. By long and by late I spake with
Mr. Richard Gerrish jun[r], and Mr. Peter La Blond, by whom I
understand they were at Mr. Wigglesworth in the morning, and
at Ipswich Meeting in the Afternoon. Being in a strait, I had
pray'd to God to direct. I consider'd Col. Thomas was not a Justice there; that this Profanation of the Sabbath was very great;
and the Transgressors fleeting from Town to Town and County
to County could rarely be Censured. On the other hand they were
young, Mr. La Blond's Mother my Neighbour, Mr. Gerrish had
a smell of Relation: both of them of another Province; and I
fear'd lest my Cousin's Custom might be lessn'd by it, because I
had the Information from her Husband, whose wife, my Cousin,
was a Gerrish, and Cousin to this Rich[d] Gerrish, only Child of
Capt. Rich[d] Gerrish of the Bank.[8] Mr. La Blond appear'd brisk
as if he ail'd Nothing. I came to this Resolution, that if they would
make such a submission as this I would let them pass; viz: We do

acknowledge our Transgressions of the Law in Travailing upon the Lord's Day, May, 13. 1716. And do promise not to offend in the like kind hereafter, as witness our Hands

RICHARD GERRISH,
PETER LA BLOND.

This Offer they rejected with some Disdain, and Mr. La Blond paid me a 30ˢ and 10ˢ Bill of Credit for both their Fines. I immediately paid it to Samuel Moodey, Selectman of Newbury (They have no Town-Treasurer). Cousin Moses Gerrish rode before and brought him to his Mother's. And then conducted us to his house on the North side of the River.

Superʳ Court at Ipswich, May 19. Here Mr. Hern informs me that Gerrish and La Blond went from Platt's at Salem on the Lord's Day morn; He spake to them against it; They said they could but pay 5ˢ Ferryman told me, Two were carried over about the time of going to Meeting. Crompton informs me that they were at his house, and went not to Meeting at Ipswich: Went away late in the Afternoon: So that they Travail'd 22. Miles or more that day. I hope God heard my Prayer, and directed me to do Right, and Accepted me.

June, 20. I went over to Charlestown in the morn, and drave a Pin in Charlestown Meetinghouse, in the Corner-post next Mr. Bradstreet's. . . . I sat in the nearest Shop, and saw them raise the 3ᵈ post towards the Ferry from the Corner-post. Gave me a Cool Tankard. Gave Mr. Graves one of my Son's Books. Got to the Council Chamber before Ten.

I essay'd June, 22, to prevent Indians and Negros being Rated with Horses and Hogs; but could not prevail. Col. Thaxter brought it back, and gave as a reason of the Non-agreement, They were just going to make a New Valuation.

I had drawn up a Dissent in these Words, "Whereas Two and Twenty Thousand pounds of the Bills of publick Credit of this Province were emitted by the General Court in the year 1711; And the Impost and Excise, and a Tax of £22,000. on Polls and Estates, to be Raised this May Sessions, 1716. were Granted as a Fund for drawing them into the Treasury again; We are humbly of Opinion that the now Resolving to Raise Eleven Thousand pounds only, is an unwarrantable diminution of the General Court's Grant; and tends greatly to weaken the publick Credit;

if the Province should stand in need of the like Anticipation for the future: For which reason they cannot come into it."

I show'd this to Col. Hutchinson; but did not find that I could get him or any, to join with me. I was hereby confirm'd in my Resolution to Sign no more Bills. And when the £5000 Emission came up, to be paid 1719, I said to the Council,

Gentlemen, I thank you for the Employment given me thus long, which has been very pleasant and profitable to me. But I am sensible that it wears my Eyes much; and there are many can do it better than I. And therefore I entreat you to think of some other person: Forasmuch as I am uncapable of engaging any further in that Service.

Some desired me to serve longer. I offered to carry up the privat Bill with some minute amendment, respecting Col. Phips, his Changing his Name from Bennet to Phips; and to carry back the Emission of £5000. to have the Plates mentioned on which they were to be made. And by this means took the advantage of saying the same to the Deputies I had said to the Council.

June, 23. An order comes up for the Plates; and Adam Winthrop esqʳ is put in my place.

July, 7. Dr. Increase Mather prays Excellently for daughter Hirst in the Counting-Room. Son Joseph and I present.

July, 8. I put up a Note for her in the South Congregation. Mr. Pemberton prays for her Excellently.

July, 10. Son Sewall prays in the Counting Room. Afterwards Mr. Colman prays there. Then I go to Mr. Pemberton to ask his Prayers. My wife goes home in the Coach after Nine; was willing that I should stay all night. When I went into my daughter's Chamber, she lay upon her Left side next the Pallat Bed, I went to her there. She complain'd of Cold, and call'd for a Gown to be laid on her, and warm Linen Cloaths to her Hands. I went to the other side again. Not long after she desired to be turn'd on her right Side. I ask'd her whether her pain took her Right Arm that Caus'd her to turn: She said No, all was quiet; but she was weary with lying on that Side. The Watcher, Mrs. Welsteed, and the Nurse had much adoe to turn her; at last my daughter was satisfied: but begun to be uneasy; yet call'd for something to drink; which she had much adoe to take though given her in a Spoon. I said, when my flesh and my heart faileth me, God is the strength

of my heart and my portion for ever. Said, I am just a-going, Call
Mr. Hirst. She Moan'd lower and lower till she dyed, about Midnight.

I lay in Mr. Hirst's Bed, that I might not disturb my family at
home. Thus have I parted with a very desirable Child not full
Thirty five years old. She liv'd desir'd and died Lamented. The
Lord fit me to follow, and help me to prepare my wife and Children for a dying hour.

Augt, 10. Goe to the Saltworks with Mr. Stoddard. Saw the
Pans boyling.

Oct.ʳ 16. p. m. Went a foot to Roxbury. Govʳ Dudley was gon
to his Mill. Staid till he came home. I acquainted him what my
Business was; He and Madam Dudley both, reckon'd up the
Offenses of my Son; and He the Vertues of his Daughter. And
alone, mention'd to me the hainous faults of my wife, who the
very first word ask'd my daughter why she married my Son except
she lov'd him? I saw no possibility of my Son's return; and therefore asked, that he would make some Proposals, and so left it.
Madam Dudley had given me Beer as I chose; G. Dudley would
have me drink a Glass of very good Wine; and made a faint of
having the Horses put in, to draw me; but with all said how many
hundred times he had walked over the Neck. I told him I should
have a pleasant journey; and so it prov'd; for coming over with
Mrs. Pierpoint, whose maiden name was Gore, had diverting discourse all the way. Met Mr. Walter in his Calash with his wife
returning home, were very glad to see one another, he stopping
his Calash. 'Twas quite night before we got to our house.

[October] 20. Celebrats the Coronation-day. I was at the Council-Chamber, but drank no Health.

[October] 21. Unusually, and awfully dark. There was not one
Man in the Fore-Seat of the Old Meetinghouse.

Tuesday, Dec.ʳ 25. Shops are open, and sleds come to Town
as at other times. I went to Cambridge to wish Mr. Brattle Joy;
and found the Ferry-boat crowded much with passengers coming
to Town: and so going back at my Return.

Dec.ʳ 28. Capt. Barrel's upper chamber next Newbury Street
falls on fire; with much adoe Capt Tim. Clark and others quench
it. Wait on the Govʳ and he appoints Janʸ 2. for a Meeting of the
Commissioners of the Indian Affairs.

Jan.ʳ 6. [1716/17] Great Rain last night; but fair, moderat Weather. Hannah Sewall taken into the South Church. Lord grant it may be in order to her being taken into Heaven!

[January] 8. Cool N. East wind, but holds up, and is Moderat. Great Assembly at the New South, which is the first. Dr. Increase Mather began with an excellent Prayer. . . . 'Tis sad it should be so, but a virulent Libel was starch'd on upon the Three Doors of the Meeting House, containing the following Words;

TO ALL TRUE-HEARTED CHRISTIANS.
Good people, within this House, this very day,
A Canting Crew will meet to fast, and pray.
Just as the miser fasts with greedy mind, to spare;
So the glutton fasts, to eat a greater share.
But the sower-headed Presbyterians fast to seem more holy,
And their Canting Ministers to punish sinfull foley.

[March 12, 1717] Order for a Fast drawn up by Col. Winthrop, is voted, to be Apr. 4th. I put in Losses by Sea of Lives and Estates; New Jerusalem. Govʳ propounded it might be Religious and Civil Liberties. I said Religious was contain'd under Civil; arguing that Civil should go first. Capt. Hutchinson spoke that Religious might go first.

March 31. Now about 'tis propounded to the Church whether Capt Nathan¹ Oliver's Confession should be before the Church, or before the Congregation: I opposed the former as not agreeing with the universal Practice: 'Twas brought on by our late Pastor with the design that it should be before the Congregation. Not fit that the penitent should prescribe before what Auditory his Confession should be. Some said there was little difference: I said twas the more gravaminous that Capt. Oliver should insist on it. I think it was the Congregation's due, all being Offended: when a person is admitted, the Congregation are acquainted with it. 'Twas carried for Capt. Oliver, and he was restor'd, but I did not vote in it. When he spake to me, I said, you did run well, who hindered you? He mention'd the advice of some Friends. I suppose Col. Paige. When Mr. Williams spake to me, I said let him as a Capt. take Courage and make it before the Congregation.

Apr. 24th. Mrs. Hedge and her Ethiopian woman were dismissed their Attendance. Note. Zeb. Thorp was accused by this

Negro of Ravishing her. All were bound over. Throop [Thorp?] had said, if he were guilty he wish he might never get alive to Plimouth. He was a very debauch'd man; being presented to Barnstaple Court Ap. 16. He went Drunk into Court; so that he was ordered to Goal till where he lay till next day, and then was proceeded with. He was said to be in Drink when he fell, riding Swiftly: had 19. £ odd, Mr. Little found in's pocket: some say, he brought £50. from Yarmouth.

Apr. 29. 30. We have the good News of the Pirat's being broken to pieces on the Cape on Friday-night. 24. Guns. On Friday Apr. 26. Zeb. Throp [Thorp] was brought dead to Plimouth and buried there.

Thorsday May, 2.ᵈ Mr. Sewall in his Thanksgiving on Account of the dissipation of the Pirats, mentions Job 34. 25. Knewest the works overturned them in the Night. Text, Mal. 4. Sun of Righteousness.

[May] 10. Try'd in the Old Meetinghouse. Mr. Auckmooty was Counsel for the Prisoner and had family with him in the Foreseat of the Women, though he be bound over for notorious words against the Government. About 14. of the Jury were challenged peremptorily. Was brought in Guilty a little before night. Tryal held about five hours.

May, 11. I pass'd Sentence upon Phenix, the Chief Justice being absent.⁹ This was done in the Court-Chamber.

[May(?)] Hearing of Nantucket Indians complaining of Wrong done them by the English.

7.ᵗʰ day, [October] 19. Call'd Dr. C. Mather to pray, which he did excellently in the Dining Room, having Suggested good Thoughts to my wife before he went down. After, Mr. Wadsworth pray'd in the Chamber when 'twas suppos'd my wife took little notice. About a quarter of an hour past four, my dear Wife expired in the Afternoon, whereby the Chamber was fill'd with a Flood of Tears. God is teaching me a new Lesson; to live a Widower's Life. Lord help me to Learn; and be a Sun and Shield to me, now so much of my Comfort and Defense are taken away.

Nov.ʳ 22. Son prays in the Council. The Governour makes a very sharp Speech, Chiding with the Deputies because they gave him no more Money. . . . Went to Major Walley's to shew Mr. Brown of Narragansett the Deed for the School and the Certificat of its being Recorded in their Town. He Thank'd me for it, and Acknowledged their error in not gratefully accepting it at first.

Monday, [December] 9th Do a great Mornings work in the office of Probate. Am much refreshed with Mr. Sol. Stoddard's Letter of Condolence, which is excellent. I soked it in Tears at reading. Sent to enquire of Col. Hutchinson, who grows worse. . . . I take Mr. Stoddard's Letter to be an Answer to my Prayer for God's gracious looking upon me.

Jan. 29, [1717/18] m. Mr. Bradstreet read to me Chrysostom's going out of Constantinople into Banishment; and I read his Return; both in Latin, very entertaining. 'Twas occasion'd by my mentioning the two folios I had given him. I offered to give Dr. Mather's Church History for them and put them into the Library. It seems Mr. Bradstreet has all the Eton Edition.

Febr 6. This morning wandering in my mind whether to live a Single or a Married life; I had a sweet and very affectionat Meditation Concerning the Lord Jesus; Nothing was to be objected against his Person, Parentage, Relations, Estate, House, Home! Why did I not resolutely, presently close with Him! And I cry'd mightily to God that He would help me so to doe!

Lord's Day, Feb. 23. Mr. Foxcroft preaches. I set York Tune, and the Congregation went out of it into St. David's in the very 2d going over. They did the same 3 weeks before. This is the 2d Sign. I think they began in the last Line of the first going over. This seems to me an intimation and call for me to resign the Praecentor's Place to a better Voice. I have through the divine Long-suffering and Favour done it for 24. years, and now God by his Providence seems to call me off; my voice being enfeebled. I spake to Mr. White earnestly to set it in the Afternoon; but he declin'd it. After the Exercises, I went to Mr. Sewall's, Thank'd Mr. Prince for his very good Discourse: and laid this matter before them, told them how long I had set the Tune; Mr. Prince said, Do it Six years longer. I persisted and said that Mr. White or Franklin might do it very well. The Return of the Gallery where Mr. Franklin sat was a place very Convenient for it.[10]

Tuesday, Feb. 25. Went to Roxbury to speak to Mr. Walter about my eldest Son. He advises to his going home to his wife. Went first to Jno Ruggles, lyeing Sick.

Feb. 27. I told Mr. White Next Sabbath was in a Spring Moneth, he must then set the Tune. I set now Litchfield Tune to a good Key.

Feb. 28. I told Mr. Nathan[1] Williams My voice was much Enfeebled; He said twas apparently so. I bid him tell Mr. White of it. p. m. My Son Sam[1] Sewall and his Wife Sign and Seal the Writings in order to my Son's going home. Gov.r Dudley and I Witnesses, Mr. Sam. Lynde took the Acknowledgment. I drank to my Daughter in a Glass of Canary. Gov.r Dudley took me into the Old Hall and gave me £100. in Three-pound Bills of Credit, new ones, for my Son; told me on Monday, he would perform all that he had promised to Mr. Walter. Sam agreed to go home next Monday, his wife sending the Horse for him. Joseph pray'd with his Bro.r and me. Note. This was my Wedding Day. The Lord succeed and turn to good what we have been doing.

March 14. Deacon Marion comes to me, sits with me a great while in the evening; after a great deal of Discourse about his Courtship—He told [me] the Olivers said they wish'd I would Court their Aunt.[11] I said little, but said twas not five Moneths since I buried my dear Wife. Had said before 'twas hard to know whether best to marry again or no; whom to marry. Gave him a book of the Berlin Jewish Converts.

[July] 25. [1718] I go in the Hackny Coach to Roxbury. Call at Mr. Walter's who is not at home; nor Gov.r Dudley, nor his Lady. Visit Mrs. Denison: she invites me to eat. I give her two Cases with a knife and fork in each; one Turtle shell tackling; the other long, with Ivory handles, Squar'd, cost 4s 6d; Pound of Raisins with proportionable Almonds. Visited her Brother and Sister Weld. Came home by Day-light in the Coach, which staid for me at the Gray-Hound.[12]

[July] 26. Go to Council about the Pirat Sloop, which has Chased some.

Aug.t 6. Visited Mrs. Denison, Carried her, her Sister Weld, the Widow, and Mrs. Weld to her Bro.r Mr. Samuel Weld, where we were Courteously entertained. Brought Mr. Edmund Weld's wife home with me in the Coach; she is in much darkness. Gave Mrs. Denison a Psalm-Book neatly bound in England with Turkey-Leather.

27. 4. I ride and visit Mrs. Denison, leave my Horse at the

Gray-Hound. She mentions her discouragements by reason of Discourses she heard: I pray'd God to direct her and me.

Sept. 14. 1718. Lord's day, Mr. Dwight pray'd and preach'd very well. . . . When the Authority over us require that which is unlawfull of us, we must be Noncompliers and Dissenters. Mention'd the Cross in Baptisme. They are to be Commended who stood out in 1662.[13] Is it not somthing to have our Names put into a Book of Martyrs in addition to the 11th Hebr.

Midweek, Octob. 1. The Gov. sets out for Piscataqua. Ordination of Mr. Thomas Prince. Mr. Wadsworth began with Prayer, very well, about ½ past Ten. Mr. Prince preached from Heb. 13 —17. Mr. Sewall pray'd. Dr. Incr. Mather ask'd if any had to object: ask'd the Church Vote who were in the Gallery fronting the Pulpit. Ask'd Mr. Prince's Acceptance of the Call. Dr. Increase Mather, Dr. Cotton Mather, Mr. Wadsworth, Colman, Sewall lay their Hands on his head. Dr. Incr. Mather Prays; Gives the Charge, Prays agen. Dr. Cotton Mather Gives the Right Hand of Fellowship. . . . Entertainment was at Mr. Sewall's, which was very plentifull and splendid. Went to the Funeral of Mrs. Abigail Perry.

Wednesday, Oct. 15. Visit Mrs. Denison on Horseback; present her with a pair of Shoe-buckles, cost 5s 3d. Went and gave my Condolence to Madam Watler on account of the death of her Son Increase at Jamaica, which she took well. Hold the privat Meeting at my house.

Oct. 18. Grant a Hearing next Court in order to Two Prohibitions; one on account of a Charterparty made at Lisbon: the other in behalf of a poor Sailer imprison'd for reproachfull words spoke to a Capt of a Ship in Boston Harbour near the Long Wharf.

[November] 1. My Son from Brooklin being here I took his Horse, and visited Mrs. Denison. Sat in the Chamber next Maj. Bowls. I told her 'twas time now to finish our Business: Ask'd her what I should allow her; she not speaking; I told her I was willing to give her Two [Hundred] and Fifty pounds per annum during her life, if it should please God to take me out of the world before her. She answer'd she had better keep as she was, than give a Certainty for an uncertainty; She should pay dear for dwelling at Boston. I desired her to make proposals, but she made none. I

had Thoughts of Publishment next Thorsday the 6th. But I now
seem to be far from it. May God, who has the pity of a Father,
Direct and help me!

Nov. 12. Overseers Meeting, to petition the Court to make the
College 100. foot long. One calling for the Memorial to the end
of the Table, I stood up, and said what the hon^ble^ Commissioners
had in hand was of great moment, but I apprehended there was an
affair of greater moment. I had heard Exposition of the Scriptures
in the Hall had not been carryed on, I enquired of the President
[John Leverett] whether 'twere so or no. Was silence a little while;
then the President seem'd to be surprised at my Treating of him
in that manner; I did not use to do so; neither did he use to Treat
me so: This Complaint was Twice at least. Many spake earnestly
that what I did was out of Season. Mr. Attorny stood up and
Seconded me very strenuously. When I was fallen so hard upon,
I said I apprehended The not Expounding the Scriptures was a
faulty Omission, and I was glad I had that Opportunity of shewing
my dislike of it. President said, he had begun to take it up agen;
I said I was glad of it. At another time said, If he were to Expound
in the Hall, he must be Supported. It went over. The Memorial
was voted: Then Mr. Belcher stood up, and mov'd earnestly that
Exposition might be attended. At last Mr. Wadsworth stood up
and spake in favour of it, and drew up a vote that the president
should *as* frequently *as he could* entertain the students with Expositions of the holy Scriptures; and read it. I mov'd that *as he
could* might be left out; and it was so voted. Mr. President seem'd
to say softly, it was not till now the Business of the President to
Expound in the Hall. I said I was glad the Overseers had now the
Honour of declaring it to be the President's Duty.

Nov. 19. Mr. President spake to me again pretty earnestly; and
intimated that twas not the President's Duty to Expound before
this Order: I said Twas a Shame that a Law should be needed;
meaning *ex malis moribus bonae Leges.*

Friday, [November] 28. 1718. Having consulted with Mr. Wal-
ter after Lecture, he advised me to goe and speak with Mrs.
Denison. I went this day in the Coach; had a fire made in the
Chamber where I spake with her before, [November] the first:
I enquired how she had done these 3 or 4 weeks; Afterwards I
told her our Conversation had been such when I was with her

last, that it seem'd to be a direction in Providence, not to proceed any further; She said, It must be what I pleas'd, or to that purpose. Afterward she seem'd to blame that I had not told her so [November] 1. [November 28, 1718] Because the man had been there several times to take the Living, and she [Mrs. Denison] knew not what Answer to give. I said I knew not but that intended to Let the Living although she lived single. I repeated her words of [November] 1. She seem'd at first to start at the words of her paying dear, as if she had not spoken them. But she said she thought twas Hard to part with *All,* and have nothing to bestow on her Kindred. I said, I did not intend any thing of the Movables, I intended all the personal Estate to be to her. She said I seem'd to be in a hurry on Satterday, 9.ʳ 1., which was the reason she gave me no proposals. Whereas I had ask'd her long before to give me proposals in Writing; and she upbraided me, That I who had never written her a Letter, should ask her to write. She asked me if I would drink, I told her Yes. She gave me Cider, Apples and a Glass of Wine: gathered together the little things I had given her, and offer'd them to me; but I would take none of them. Told her I wish'd her well, should be glad to hear of her welfare. She seem'd to say she should not again take in hand a thing of this nature. Thank'd me for what I had given her and Desired my Prayers. . . .

My bowels yern towards Mrs. Denison; but I think God directs me in his Providence to desist. The first time that I mention'd making an Agreement, She said if we could not agree we must break off. . . . Note. Mrs. Denison told me she came afoot to Lecture; but I saw her not, nor knew anything of it till she told me.

Nov.ʳ 30. Lord's-day. In the evening I sung the 120. Psalm in the family. About 7 a-clock Mrs. Dorothy Denison comes in, her Cousin Weld coming first, saying she desired to speak with me in privat. I had a fire in the new Hall, and was at prayer; was very much startled that she should come so far a-foot in that exceeding Cold Season; She enter'd into discourse of what pass'd between us at Roxbury last Friday; I seem'd to be alter'd in my affection; ask'd pardon if she had affronted me. Seem'd to incline the Match should not break off, since I had kept her Company so long. Said Mr. Denison spake to her after his Signing the Will, that he would not make her put all out of her Hand and power, but reserve somwhat to bestow on his Friends that might want. I told her She might keep all. She excus'd, and said 'twas not such an all. I Commended the estate. I could not observe that she made me any offer of any part all this while. She mention'd two Glass Bottles she had. I told her they were hers, and the other small things I had given her, only now they had not the same signification as before. I was much concern'd for her being in the Cold, would fetch her in a plate of somthing warm: (for I had not sup'd), she refus'd. However I Fetched a Tankard of Cider and drank to her. She desired that no body might know of her being here. I told her they should not. Sam. Hirst went to the door, who knew not her Cousin Weld; and not so much as he might stay in the room while we talked together. She went away in the bitter Cold, no Moon being up, to my great pain. I Saluted her at parting.

Dec.ʳ 1. Had much probat Business. . . . Dr. Clark says the Small pocks is in Town. Capt Sargent of Newbury, his daughter, has it in Charter-Street. The Lord be Mercifull to Boston![14]

Jan.ʸ 23 [1718/19] A notorious Counterfeiter of the New Twenty-shilling Bill, is apprehended; had his plate made in London, and came over in Clark. . . . He went to England on purpose to get it done.

Jan.ʸ 29ᵗʰ Many went over to Boston. Mr. Cooke, Mr. Attorny Genˡ, Mr. Auchmuty, Robinson, Capt. Fullam being invited went to Capt. Douse's (Mr. Cooke lodg'd there). They drank severall Bowls of Punch: At last Mr. Cook looked Mr. Auchmuty in the face and ask'd him if he were the man that caus'd him to be put out of the Council? A. answered No! I could not do it; but I endeavour'd it, I endeavoured it! Cooke, The Govʳ is not so great a Blockhead to hearken to you.

Feb. 5ᵗʰ At the Council after Lecture, Mr. Cooke was call'd and Mr. Attorny Vallentine, and Mr. Auchmuty. He had offer'd to put it off as if he said, he himself was not such a Block-head: But now he own'd the Truth of the written Affidavits, and so they were not sworn. Capt. Fullam being sent to, writ a Letter to the same effect, which was produc'd, and read by Mr. Secretary. His Excellency left the Council. They voted, that Mr. Cook's words were rude, injurious, and Reflecting on the Gov.ʳ, which the Govʳ directed to be entred the next Council-day.

March, 12. Dr. Cotton Mather prays again. . . . For my part, the Dr. spake so much of his visions of Convulsion and Mutiny, mentioning our being a dependent Government, and the danger of Parliamentary Resentments: that I was afraid the printing of it might be an Invitation to the Parliament, to take away our Charter. Gov.ʳ would have it put to the vote; but when he saw how hardly it went, caused the Secretary to break off in the midst. Court votes the Governour's sending out Sixty Men as a Marching Company to cover and encourage the New Settlement at the Eastward. Gov.ʳ and Council appoint a Fast to be kept Apr. 2ᵈ. Order Mr. Dudley and me to draw up the Order. Court is prorogu'd to April 22. Staying by Candle-light with Mr. Dudley to draw up the Fast [Proclamation], it snow'd hard before I got home.

March, 13. Between 1 and 2 or 3. last night There was great Lightening with sharp Thunder. Sam and Grindal came down into my daughter's Chamber. I humbly and Thankfully bless God that we saw the quick and powerfull Fire; heard the Terrible Voice, and yet we live!

April, 1. In the morning I dehorted Sam. Hirst and Grindal Rawson from playing Idle Tricks because 'twas first of April; They were the greatest fools that did so. N. E. Men came hither to avoid anniversary days, the keeping of them, such as the 25th of Dec.ʳ How displeasing must it be to God, the giver of our Time, to keep anniversary days to play the fool with ourselves and others. p.m. John Arcus brings me a superscribed paper, wherein were a pair of very good white Kid's Leather Gloves, and a Gold Ring with four peny weight wanting 3 Grains, with this Motto, *Lex et Libertas*. A. T. I have received 4. Presents lately; 4 Oranges, 2 Pieces of Salmon, Madam Foxcroft's Wedding Cake; and this which is a very fair Present indeed. I have hardly any to compare with it. The good Lord help me to serve faithfully the Supream Donor!

[September] 16. After the Meeting I visited Mrs. Tilly.

[September] 18. ditto.

[September] 21. I gave Mrs. Tilly a little booke entitled *Ornaments for the daughters of Sion.*[15] I gave it to my dear Wife Aug.ᵗ 28. 1702.

23ᵈ 24ᵗʰ eat Almonds and Reasons with Mrs. Tilly and Mrs. Armitage; Discoursed with Mrs. Armitage, who spake very agreeably, and said Mrs. Tilly had been a great Blessing to them, and

hop'd God would make her so to me and my family. At my coming
home am told that Col. Wm Dudley had Call'd and said that Judith
was sick of the Fever and Ague at the L^t. Gov^rs

[September] 25. Visited Madam Pemberton to enquire after
Judith: She applauded my Courting Mrs. Tilley: I thank'd her
for her Favour in maintaining what I did. Met with the Lt Govr
there beyond expectation: Thank'd him for his Kindness to my
daughter: He received me very courteously. Discours'd with my
Son the Minister about this, and Hannah's Motion to have Ministers pray with her. Discours'd with Mr. Cutler, president [of
Yale College]. Son and Daughter visit us from Brooklin and dine
with us. Visited Mrs. Sewall and enquired of her Sick Son. Visited
Mrs. Tilley. When came home they told me Mr. Stoddard had
invited me to eat Salt-Fish with him.

[September] 26. Col. Wm Dudley calls, and after other discourse,
ask'd me [leave?] to wait on my daughter Judith home, when 'twas
fit for her to come; I answered, It was reported he had applyed to
her and he said nothing to me, when rode with me to Dedham. As
came back, I call'd at his house as I had said, and he was not at
home. His waiting on her might give some Umbrage: I would
Speak with her first.

Octob.^r 29. Thanks-giving-day: between 6 and 7. Brother
Moodey and I went to Mrs. Tilley's; and about 7, or 8, were married by Mr. J. Sewall, in the best room below stairs. Mr. Prince
pray'd the 2^d time. . . . Cous. S. Sewall set Low-dutch Tune in a
very good Key, which made the Singing with a good number of
Voices very agreeable. Distributed Cake. Mrs. Armitage introduced me into my Bride's Chamber after she was a-bed. I thank'd
her that she had left her room in that Chamber to make way for
me, and pray'd God to provide for her a better Lodging: So none
saw us after I went to bed. Quickly after our being a-bed my Bride
grew so very bad she was fain to sit up in her bed; I rose to get
her Petit Coats about her. I was exceedingly amaz'd, fearing lest
she should have dy'd. Through the favour of God she recover'd in
some considerable time of her Fit of the Tissick, spitting, partly
blood. She her self was under great Consternation.

Friday, [October] 30. Govr Shute, Govr Dudley and his Lady,
Councillors and Ministers in Town with their Wives dined with us,
except Dr. Incr. Mather and Mr. Belcher. Had a very good Dinner,

at Four Tables, Two in the best Room. Many Coaches there. In the evening Mr. Oliver invited me and my Bride to Mr. Prince's Wedding. We went half way up the Hill, and my Bride could go no further; but was fain to return back by reason of her great Cold and Shortness of breath.

May, 26. [1720] Went to Bed after Ten: about 11 or before, my dear Wife was oppressed with a rising of Flegm that obstructed her Breathing. I arose and lighted a Candle, made Scipio give me a Bason of Water (he was asleep by the fire) Call'd Philadelphia, Mr. Cooper, Mayhew. About midnight my dear wife expired to our great astonishment, especially mine. May the Sovereign Lord pardon my Sin, and Sanctify to me this very Extraordinary, awfull Dispensation.

May, 29. God having in his holy Sovereignty put my Wife out of the Fore-Seat, I apprehended I had Cause to be asham'd of my Sin, and to loath my self for it; and retired into my Pue. . . . I put up a Note to this purpose; Samuel Sewall, depriv'd of his dear Wife by a very sudden and awful Stroke, desires Prayers that God would sanctify the same to himself, and Children, and family. Writ and sent three; to the South, Old, and Mr. Colman's. Mr. Prince preaches p. m.

[October] 1. Satterday, I dine at Mr. Stoddard's: from thence I went to Madam Winthrop's just at 3. Spake to her, saying, my loving wife died so soon and suddenly, 'twas hardly convenient for me to think of Marrying again; however I came to this Resolution, that I would not make my Court to any person without first Consulting with her. Had a pleasant discourse about 7 [seven] Single persons sitting in the Fore-seat. . . . She propounded one and another for me; but none would do, said Mrs. Loyd was about her Age.

Octob⸍ 3. Waited on Madam Winthrop again; 'twas a little while before she came in. Her daughter Noyes being there alone with me, I said, I hoped my Waiting on her Mother would not be disagreeable to her. She answer'd she should not be against that that might be for her Comfort. I Saluted her, and told her I perceiv'd I must shortly wish her a good Time; (her mother had told me, she was with Child, and within a Moneth or two of her Time). By and by in came Mr. Airs, Chaplain of the Castle, and hang'd up his Hat, which I was a little startled at, it seeming as if he was to lodge there. At last Madam Winthrop came too. After a considerable time, I went up to her and said, if it might not be inconvenient I desired to speak with her. She assented, and spake of going into another Room; but Mr. Airs and Mrs. Noyes presently rose up, and went out, leaving us there alone. Then I usher'd in Discourse from the names in the Fore-seat; at last I pray'd that Katharine [Mrs. Winthrop] might be the person assign'd for me. She instantly took it up in the way of Denyal, as if she had catch'd at an Opportunity to do it, saying she could not do it before she was asked. Said that was her mind unless she should Change it, which she believed she should not; could not leave her Children. I express'd my Sorrow that she should do it so Speedily, pray'd her Consideration, and ask'd her when I should wait on her agen. She setting no time, I mention'd that day Sennight. Gave her Mr. Willard's Fountain open'd with the little print and verses; saying, I hop'd if we did well read that book, we should meet together hereafter, if we did not now. She took the Book, and put it in her Pocket. Took Leave.

[October] 5. Although I had appointed to wait upon her, M^m Winthrop, next Monday, yet I went from my Cousin Sewall's thither about 3. p. m. The Nurse told me Madam dined abroad at her daughter Noyes's, they were to go out together. I ask'd for the Maid, who was not within. Gave Katee a penny and a Kiss, and came away. Accompanyed my Son and dâter Cooper in their Remove to their New House. Went to tell Joseph, and Mr. Belcher saw me by the South Meetinghouse though 'twas duskish, and said I had been at House-warming, (he had been at our house).

[October 10, 1720] In the Evening I visited Madam Winthrop, who treated me with a great deal of Curtesy; Wine, Marmalade. I gave her a News-Letter about the Thanksgiving.

[October] 11th I writ a few Lines to Madam Winthrop to this purpose: "Madam, These wait on you with Mr. Mayhew's Sermon, and Account of the state of the Indians on Martha's Vinyard. I thank you for your Unmerited Favours of yesterday; and hope to have the Happiness of Waiting on you to-morrow before Eight a-clock after Noon. I pray GOD to keep you, and give you a joyfull entrance upon the Two Hundred and twenty ninth year of Christopher Columbus his Discovery; and take Leave, who am, Madam, your humble Servt.   S. S.

[October 12, 1720] Mrs. Anne Cotton came to door (twas before 8.) said Madam Winthrop was within, directed me into the little Room, where she was full of work behind a Stand; Mrs. Cotton came in and stood. Madam Winthrop pointed to her to set me a Chair. Madam Winthrop's Countenance was much changed from what 'twas on Monday, look'd dark and lowering. At last, the work, (black stuff or Silk) was taken away, I got my Chair in place, had some Converse, but very Cold and indifferent to what 'twas before. Ask'd her to acquit me of Rudeness if I drew off her Glove. Enquiring the reason, I told her twas great odds between handling a dead Goat, and a living Lady. Got it off. I told her I had one Petition to ask of her, that was, that she would take off the Negative she laid on me the third of October; She readily answer'd she could not, and enlarg'd upon it; She told me of it so soon as she could; could not leave her house, children, neighbours, business. I told her she might do som Good to help and support me. Mentioning Mrs. Gookin, Nath, the widow Weld was spoken of; said I had visited Mrs. Denison. I told her Yes! Afterward I said, If after a first and second Vagary she would Accept of me returning, Her Victorious Kindness and Good Will would be very Obliging. She thank'd me for my Book, (Mr. Mayhew's Sermon), But said not a word of the Letter. When she insisted on the Negative, I pray'd there might be no more Thunder and Lightening, I should not sleep all night. I gave her Dr. Preston, The Church's Marriage and the Church's Carriage, which cost me 6^s at the Sale. The door standing open, Mr. Airs came in, hung up his Hat, and sat down. After awhile, Madam Winthrop moving, he went out. Jno Eyre look'd in, I said How do ye, or, your servant Mr. Eyre: but heard no word from him. Sarah fill'd a Glass of Wine, she drank to me, I to her, She sent Juno home with me with a good Lantern, I gave her 6^d and bid her thank her Mistress. In some of our Discourse, I told her I had rather go to the Stone-House adjoining to her, than to come to her against her mind. Told her the reason why I came every other night was lest I should drink too deep draughts of Pleasure. She had talk'd of Canary, her Kisses were to me better than the best Canary.

[October] 17. In the Evening I visited Madam Winthrop, who Treated me Courteously, but not in Clean Linen as sometimes. She said, she did not know whether I would come again, or no.

I ask'd her how she could so impute inconstancy to me. (I had
not visited her since Wednesday night being unable to get over
the Indisposition received by the Treatment received that night,
and *I must* in it seem'd to sound like a made piece of Formality.)
Gave her this day's Gazett.

[October] 18. Visited Madam Mico, who came to me in a
splendid Dress. I said, It may be you have heard of my Visiting
Madam Winthrop, her Sister. She answered, Her Sister had told
her of it. I ask'd her good Will in the Affair. She answer'd, If her
Sister were for it, she should not hinder it. I gave her Mr. Homes's
Sermon. She gave me a Glass of Canary, entertain'd me with good
Discourse, and a Respectfull Remembrance of my first Wife. I took
Leave.

[October] 19. Midweek, Visited Madam Winthrop; Sarah told
me she was at Mr. Walley's, would not come home till late. I gave
her Hannah 3 Oranges with her Duty, not knowing whether I
should find her or no. Was ready to go home: but said if I knew
she was there, I would go thither. Sarah seem'd to speak with pretty
good Courage, She would be there. I went and found her there,
with Mr. Walley and his wife in the little Room below. At 7
a-clock I mentioned going home; at 8. I put on my Coat, and
quickly waited on her home. She found occasion to speak loud
to the servant, as if she had a mind to be known. Was Courteous
to me; but took occasion to speak pretty earnestly about my keeping a Coach: I said 'twould cost £100. per annum: she said
twould cost but £40. Spake much against John Winthrop, his
false-heartedness. Mr. Eyre came in and sat awhile; I offer'd him
Dr. Incr. Mather's Sermons, whereof Mr. Appleton's Ordination
Sermon was one; said he had them already. I said I would give him
another. Exit. Came away somewhat late.

[October] 20. At Council, Col. Townsend spake to me of my
Hood: Should get a Wigg. I said twas my chief ornament: I wore
it for sake of the Day. . . . Madam Winthrop not being at Lecture,
I went thither first; found her very Serene with her dâter Noyes,
. . . sitting at a little Table, she in her arm'd Chair. She drank to
me, and I to Mrs. Noyes. After awhile pray'd the favour to speak
with her. She took one of the Candles, and went into the best
Room, clos'd the shutters, sat down upon the Couch. . . . She
spake somthing of my needing a Wigg. Ask'd me what her Sister

said to me. I told her, She said, If her Sister were for it, She would not hinder it. But I told her, she did not say she would be glad to have me for her Brother. Said, I shall keep you in the Cold, and asked her if she would be within to morrow night, for we had had but a running Feat. She said she could not tell whether she should, or no. I took Leave. As were drinking at the Governour's, he said: In England the Ladies minded little more than that they might have Money, and Coaches to ride in. I said, And New-England brooks its Name. At which Mr. Dudley smiled. Govʳ said they were not quite so bad here.

[October] 21. Friday, My Son, the Minister, came to me p. m by appointment and we pray one for another in the Old Chamber; more especially respecting my Courtship. About 6. a-clock I go to Madam Winthrop's; Sarah told me her Mistress was gon out, but did not tell me whither she went. She presently order'd me a Fire; so I went in, having Dr. Sibb's Bowels with me to read. I read the two first Sermons, still no body came in: at last about 9. a-clock Mr. Jnᵒ Eyre came in; I took the opportunity to say to him as I had done to Mrs. Noyes before, that I hoped my Visiting his Mother would not be disagreeable to him; He answered me with much Respect. When twas after 9. a-clock He of himself said he would go and call her, she was but at one of his Brothers: A while after I heard Madam Winthrop's voice, enquiring somthing about John. After a good while and Clapping the Garden door twice or thrice, she came in. I mention'd somthing of the lateness; she banter'd me, and said I was later. She receive'd me Courteously. I ask'd when our proceedings should be made publick: She said They were like to be no more publick than they were already. Offer'd me no Wine that I remember. I rose up at 11 a-clock to come away, saying I would put on my Coat, She offer'd not to help me. I pray'd her that Juno might light me home, she open'd the Shutter, and said twas pretty light abroad; Juno was weary and gon to bed. So I came hôm by Star-light as well as I could. At my first coming in, I gave Sarah five Shillings.

Octobᵣ 24. I went in the Hackny Coach through the Common, stop'd at Madam Winthrop's (had told her I would take my departure from thence). Sarah came to the door with Katee in her Arms: but I did not think to take notice of the Child. Call'd her Mistress. I told her, being encourag'd by David Jeffries loving eyes, and sweet Words, I was come to enquire whether she could find in her heart to leave that House and Neighbourhood, and go and dwell with me at the South-end; I think she said softly, Not yet. I told her It did not ly in my Lands to keep a Coach. If I should, I should be in danger to be brought to keep company with her Neighbour Brooker, (he was a little before sent to prison for Debt). Told her I had an Antipathy against those who would pretend to give themselves; but nothing of their Estate. I would a proportion of my Estate with my self. And I suppos'd she would do so. As to a Perriwig, My best and greatest Friend, I could not possibly have a greater, began to find me with Hair before I was born, and had continued to do so ever since; and I could not find in my heart to go to another. She commended the book I gave her, Dr. Preston, the Church Marriage; quoted him saying 'twas inconvenient keeping out of a Fashion commonly used. I said the Time and Tide did circumscribe my Visit. She gave me a Dram of Black-Cherry Brandy, and gave me a lump of the Sugar that was in it. She wish'd me a good Journy. I pray'd God to keep her, and came away.

Nov.ʳ 2. Midweek, went again, and found Mrs. Alden there, who quickly went out. Gave her [Madam Winthrop] about ½ pound of Sugar Almonds, cost 3ˢ per £. Carried them on Monday. She seem'd pleas'd with them, ask'd what they cost. Spake of giving her a Hundred pounds per annum if I dy'd before her. Ask'd her what sum she would give me, if she should dy first? Said I would give her time to Consider of it. She said she heard as if I had given all to my Children by Deeds of Gift. I told her 'twas a mistake, Point-Judith was mine &c. That in England, I own'd, my Father's desire was that it should go to my eldest Son; 'twas 20 £ per annum; she thought 'twas forty. I think when I seem'd to excuse pressing this, she seem'd to think twas best to speak of it; a long winter was coming on. Gave me a Glass or two of Canary.

Nov.ʳ 4ᵗʰ Friday, Went again about 7. a-clock; found there Mr. John Walley and his wife: sat discoursing pleasantly. I shew'd them Isaac Moses's [an Indian] Writing. Madam W.[inthrop] serv'd Comfeits to us. After a-while a Table was spread, and Supper was set. I urg'd Mr. Walley to Crave a Blessing; but he put it upon me. About 9. they went away. I ask'd Madam what fash-

ioned Neck-lace I should present her with, She said, None at all.
I ask'd her Whereabout we left off last time; mention'd what I had
offer'd to give her; Ask'd her what she would give me; She said
she could not Change her Condition: She had said so from the
beginning; could not be so far from her Children, the Lecture.
Quoted the Apostle Paul affirming that a single Life was better
than a Married. I answer'd That was for the present Distress. Said
she had not pleasure in things of that nature as formerly: I said,
you are the fitter to make me a Wife. If she held in that mind, I
must go home and bewail my Rashness in making more haste than
good Speed. However, considering the Supper, I desired her to be
within next Monday night, if we liv'd so long. Assented. She
charg'd me with saying, that she must put away Juno, if she came
to me: I utterly deny'd it, it never came in my heart; yet she
insisted upon it; saying it came in upon discourse about the Indian
woman that obtained her Freedom this Court. About 10. I said I
would not disturb the good orders of her House, and came away.
She not seeming pleas'd with my Coming away.

Monday, Nov: 7.ᵗʰ My Son pray'd in the Old Chamber. Our
time had been taken up by Son and Daughter Cooper's Visit; so
that I only read the 130.ᵗʰ and 143. Psalm. Twas on the Account
of my Courtship. I went to Mad. Winthrop; found her rocking her
little Katee in the Cradle. I excus'd my Coming so late (near
Eight). She set me an arm'd Chair and Cusheon; and so the Cradle
was between her arm'd Chair and mine. Gave her the remnant
of my Almonds; She did not eat of them as before; but laid them
away; I said I came to enquire whether she had alter'd her mind
since Friday, or remained of the same mind still. She said, There-
abouts. I told her I loved her, and was so fond as to think that
she loved me: She said had a great respect for me. I told her, I
had made her an offer, without asking any advice; she had so many
to advise with, that twas a hindrance. The Fire was come to one
short Brand besides the Block, which Brand was set up in end;
at last it fell to pieces, and no Recruit was made: She gave me a
Glass of Wine. I think I repeated again that I would go home and
bewail my Rashness in making more haste than good Speed. I
would endeavour to contain myself, and not go on to sollicit her
to do that which she could not Consent to. Took leave of her. As

came down the steps she bid me have a Care. Treated me Courteously. Told her she had enter'd the 4th year of her Widowhood.
I had given her the News-Letter before: I did not bid her draw
off her Glove as sometime I had done. Her Dress was not so clean
as somtime it had been. Jehovah jireh!

Nov.ʳ 15. Sewall, Davenport, Fitch, Dudley were sent into the
Deputies with Amendments on the Bill for making the Counterfeiting Bills of Credit a Capital Crime. I spake against taking in
the Bills of the other Governments; we knew not that they themselves would make them so; theirs were not upon so good a foundation, as New-Hampshire; Mr. Eliakim Hutchinson, who was a
good Standard in things of that nature, was of that Opinion. By
keeping to our Province we should pursue the method we ourselves
had taken in making the 2ᵈ Conviction Capital, 13ᵗʰ of Qu. Anne,
p. 246. Twould be good to go leisurely in a thing of so great Consequence in a sanguinary Law. I think after the rest had spoken,
I said we had not heard that twas made capital to Counterfeit the
Exchequer Bills in England.

Afterward in Council, I said our friends and Foes spake of our
losing our Charter; This Law would be an edg'd Tool, and we
knew not into whose hands it should be put.

Jan.ʸ 10. [1721/22] Overseers of the College, their Meeting at
the Council Chamber, to consider of Mr. Hollis's Proposals as to
his Professour of Divinity. Debate was had in the Fore-noon about
that Article, "He shall be a Master of Art, and in Communion
with a Church of Congregrational, Presbyterian, or Baptists." I
objected against it, as chusing rather to lose the Donation than to
Accept it. In the Afternoon I finally said, One great end for which
the first Planters came over into New England, was to fly from
the Cross in Baptisme.

For my part, I had rather have Baptisme administered with the
incumbrance of the Cross, than not to have it Administered at all.

This Qualification of the Divinity Professour, is to me, a Bribe
to give my Sentence in Disparagement of Infant Baptisme: and I
will endeavour to shake my hands from holding it.

When it came to the Vote, but very few appear'd in the Negative. I desired to have my Dissent enter'd. The Governour deny'd
it with an Air of Displeasure, saying, You *shânt* have it, . . .

Copy of a Letter to Mrs. Mary Gibbs, Widow, at Newtown, Jan.ʸ 12.ᵗʰ 1721/22.

Madam, your Removal out of Town, and the Severity of the Winter, are the reason of my making you this Epistolary Visit. In times past (as I remember) you were minded that I should marry you, by giving you to your desirable Bridegroom. Some sense of this intended Respect abides with me still; and puts me upon enquiring whether you be willing that I should Marry you now, by becoming your Husband; Aged, and feeble, and exhausted as I am, your favourable Answer to this Enquiry, in a few Lines, the Candor of it will much oblige, Madam, your humble Servᵗ

MADAM GIBBS.   S. S.

Friday, Jan.ʸ 19. I rode in Blake's Coach, and visited Mrs. Mary Gibbs at Mr. Cotton's at Newton, told her that in my Judgment she writ incomparably well; ask'd her acceptance of a Quire of Paper to write upon. It was accompanied with a good Leather Inkhorn, a stick of Sealing Wax, and 200. Wafers in a little Box. Gave her little Granddaughter, Mary Cotton, a 12ᵈ Bill; some of Meers's Cakes. Gave 3ˢ among the Servants. Carried 2. 6ᵈ Loavs. Din'd with Mr. Cotton, Mrs. Gibbs, Mrs. Cotton, Mrs. Anne Noyes; Mrs. Cotton, Mr. Cotton's Sister. Came away about 4. p. m. Had a very Comfortable Journy out, and home. Set out about ½ hour past Ten.

Midweek, Jan.ʸ 24. Overseers Meeting. Mr. Edward Wigglesworth is presented by the President and Fellows of Harvard College, elected by them the Professor of Divinity, who was approv'd by them by Papers Written Yes, No. 'Twas voted it should be done in that manner. Were 11. Yeas, 3 Nos. Directed that he be called the Hollis Professor.

Friday, Jan.ʸ 26. I rode to Newtown in the Coach, and visited Mrs. Gibbs. Spake of the proposals I had intimated per Mr. H. Gibbs; for her Sons to be bound to save me harmless as to her Administration; and to pay me £100. provided their Mother died before me: I to pay her £50. per annum during her Life, if I left her a Widow. She said 'twas hard, she knew not how to have her children bound to pay that Sum; she might dye in a little time. Mr. Cotton, whom she call'd, spake to the same purpose, spake of a Joynture. I said I was peremptory as to the indemnifying

Bond; Offer'd to take up with that alone, and allow her £40. per annum; Scolly's Tenement yielded but £33., and then I made no question but that there must be a Deduction for Repairs. She said she would consider of it: I said, I would also Consider. Afterward she excus'd her speaking to me. I suppose she meant the word Hard. Carried her a pound of Glaz'd Almonds, and a Duz. Meers Cakes; Two bottles of Canary. Visited Mrs. Cotton, wish'd her Joy of her young daughter Elizabeth. Gave little Mary 2.ˢ Had a very good Legg of Pork, and a Turkey for Dinner. Mrs. Gibbs help'd me on with my Coat at Coming away; and stood in the Front door till the Coach mov'd, then I pull'd off my Hat, and she Curtesied. I had moved to be published next Thorsday; to carry in our names to Col. Checkley.

Janʸ 25. When I ask'd H. Gibbs what was the effect of his proposals, He answer'd, What his Mother would have done the Children would agree to it.

Janʸ 31. Ask'd Mr. H. Gibbs whether Mrs. Gibbs were come to Town; He said he had sent to her to know when she would come. Just as I was ready to go to Dorchester, he came in, and deliver'd me his Mother's Letter of the 30ᵗʰ Current; and took mine lying in the Window ready Sealed up, to send to his Mother. May God provide! and Forgive, and Doe as the Matter may Require.

[February 2, 1721/22] I took the Opportunity to speak plainly to him about Mrs. Gibbs; that her Children were not so Releas'd, but must be Bound to indemnify me as to former Debts, her Administration. Told, I hoped she was not so Attach'd to her Children, but that she would carry it Tenderly to me; or else there would soon be an end of an old Man. I said, supposed they would Clothe her, Answered, no question; And would be Tender of me. Shew'd him both her Letters.

To Mrs. Mary Gibbs at Newtown.

Febr 10ᵗʰ 1721/22. Madam, These are kindly to salute you, and to say, that the Omission of Answering one or two of my Letters, and of coming to Town, makes it needful for me to enquire, what the plain meaning of your Letter of Janʸ 30.ᵗʰ may be "I do chuse to comply with your last proposal, of Releasing my children, and Accepting of the sum you proposed."

The last Proposal was, For your children, or some in their behalf, to give Bond to indemnify me from all debts contracted by you before the Marriage; and from all matters respecting the Administration. This I told you, I peremptorily insisted on. I was to secure you Forty pounds per annum during the term of your natural Life, in case of your Survival.

This proposal must be taken entirely, every part of it together. And if the words *Releasing my Children,* intend a Releasing them from this Bond, my last Proposal is not accepted by you; and my Letter of Febr. the sixth, rests upon a mistaken foundation. I would prevent Misunderstanding, and therefore I thus write; praying an Answer as soon as conveniently can be. My Service to Madam Cotton. I am, Madam, your humble servant,   S. S.

    To Mrs. Mary Gibbs at Newton, Feb. 16. 1721/22.

Madam, Possibly you have heard of our Publishment last Thorsday, before now. It remains, for us to join together in fervent Prayers, without ceasing, that God would graciously Crown our Espousals with his Blessing. A good Wife, and a good Husband too, are from the Lord. I am bound as far as Deacon Brewer's to-day. The Council sits in the Afternoon next Monday. And I am to wait on the Committee of the Overseers of the College next Tuesday the 20th Inst. Please to accept of Mr. Mitchel's Sermons of Glory, which is inclosed. With my Service to Madam Cotton, I take leave, who am, Madam, your humble Servt.   S. S.

March 29th. Samuel Sewall, and Mrs. Mary Gibbs were joined together in Marriage by the Revd Mr. William Cooper, Mr. Sewall pray'd once.

Friday, Decr 21. p. m. The Govr took me to the window again looking Eastward, next Mrs. Phillips's, and spake to me again about adjourning the Court to next Wednesday. I spake against it; and propounded that the Govr would take a Vote for it; that he would hold the Balance even between the Church and us. His Excellency went to the Board again, and said much for this adjourning; All kept Christmas but we; I suggested K. James the first to Mr. Dudley, how he boasted what a pure church he had; and they did not keep Yule nor Pasch.

Mr. Dudley ask'd if the Scots kept Christmas. His Excellency protested, he believ'd they did not. Govr said they adjourn'd for the Commencement and Artillery. But then 'tis by Agreement. Col. Taylor spake so loud and boisterously for Adjourning, that 'twas hard for any to put in a word; Col. Townsend seconded me, and Col. Partridge; because this would prolong the Sessions. Mr.

Davenport stood up and gave it as his opinion, that twould not be Convenient for the Govr to be present in Court that day; and therefore was for Adjourning. But the Govr is often absent; and yet the Council and Representatives go on. Now the Govr has told us, that he would go away for a week; and then return'd and if he liked what we had done, He would Consent to it. Govr mention'd how it would appear to have Votes pass'd on Decr 25. But his Excellency need not have been present nor sign'd any Bill that day. I said the Dissenters came a great way for their Liberties and now the Church had theirs, yet they could not be contented, except they might Tread all others down. Govr said he was of the Church of England. I told Mr. Belcher of his Letter to me. He answer'd, He thought he had been a Dissenter then. Govr hinted that he must be free on Monday because of the Communion the next day.

Midweek, Jany 2. 1722/3, His Honour the Lt Govr [Dummer] takes the Oaths in Council, as to the Acts relating to Trade and of his Office. After Mr. Checkley had pray'd, the Lt Govr sent for the Deputies-in and made his Speech. When the Representatives were return'd to their own Chamber, I stood up and said, "If your Honour and this honourable Board please to give me leave, I would speak a Word or two upon this solemn Occasion.—Altho the unerring Providence of God has brought you to the Chair of Government in a cloudy and Tempestuous Time; yet you have this for your Encouragement, that the People you Have to do with, are a part of the Israel of God, and you may expect to have of the Prudence and Patience of Moses communicated to you for your Conduct. It is evident that our Almighty Saviour Counselled the First Planters to remove hither, and Settle here; and they dutifully followed his Advice; and therefore He will never leave nor forsake them, nor Theirs: so that your Honour must needs be happy in sincerely seeking their Interest and welfare; which your birth and Education will incline you to do. *Difficilia quae pulchra!* I promise my self that they that sit at this Board, will yield their Faithfull Advice to your Honour, according to the Duty of their Place."

The Lt Govr and Council would stand up all the while, and they express'd a handsom Acceptance of what I had said.

Lord's Day, Novr 24. [1723] Govr Saltonstall is here. Mr. Prince Prays that God would convert the Jews, and Mahometans.

Saturday, February the First, [1723/24] John Valentine esqr. went out in the morning to speak with Mr. Auchmuty, but found him not at home. He staid so long before he returned home that his Family grew uneasy, and sent to many places in the Town to enquire after him. At last they search'd his own house from chamber to chamber, and closet to Closet. At last Mr. Bowdoin look'd into the cockloft in the North end of the House, that had no Light but from the Stairs; and there, by his Candlelight, saw him hanging. This was about 7. a-clock, when the Town was much alarum'd to hear that Mr. Valentine was become a Deserter, and had Conveyed himself away by means of a Halter patched up with his Leathern Girdle, and the Neck of his Neck-cloth. He pass'd his Girdle within the Neck of his Neck-Cloth, then buckled it, and Cast the other Bend over a Pin of the Post that bore up the Roof, and stole away. He was upon his knees. When some help was Called in, they took him down, laid him on a Bedstead; call'd Capt. Pollard, the Coroner, who gave a Constable a Warrant to Summon a Jury. 18. were empanell'd and sworn, Mr. Samuel Waldo, Merch^t, Foreman. Some Justices and many Attorneys were present. The Jury returned that he was *Non Compos*. Notwithstanding all this Bustle, I heard not the least inkling of it before the Lord's day morning, when Scipio came from Watching, and told of it. At Capt. Tim^o Clark's motion, I Writ a Permit for Mrs. Valentine's Negro to ride to Free-Town to tell her Son that his Father died last night. In the evening following the Lord's Day, when all was perfected, the Coroner shewed me the Indent of the Jury. I told him he should have taken the Affidavits of the Witnesses in Writing, which I think he afterwards did. His Honour, the Lieut-Govr was at the Castle: No application was made to his Honor (as he assured me) nor to any body else that I know of, respecting the Funeral.

Satterday, Augt 15. [1724] Hambleton and my Sister Watch, I get up before 2 in the Morning of the L.[ord's] Day, and hearing an earnest Expostulation of my daughter, I went, down and finding her restless, call'd up my wife. Sent for her Bro^r the Min^r who pray'd with her. I read to her the 23^d Psalm, and pray'd with her, (Mr. Prince I think, pray'd in the evening). Mr. Cooper pray'd. I read the 34th Psalm, and the first and last of the 27th, I do not remember the exact order of these things. I put up this Note at the

Old [First Church] and South, "Prayers are desired for Hannah Sewall as drawing Near her end." Her Bro^r pray'd with her just before the morning Exercise. Finding that I could do her little or no Service, I went to Meeting, and join'd with Mr. Prince praying excellently for her. The Lord's Supper was Celebrated. When I came home I found my Daughter laid out. She expired half an hour past Ten. Her pleasant Countenance was very Refreshing to me. I hope God has delivered her from all her Fears! She had desired not to be embowelled. In the Afternoon I put up this Note at the Old South, "Samuel Sewall desires Prayers, that the Death of his Eldest Daughter may be Sanctified to him, and to the Relatives."

Ap. 27. [1725] Court is open'd . . . At this Court, Josiah Challenge, an Indian was found guilty of murdering his fellow Sailer Isaac Monokuit. Trial was Ap. 29. Condemnation, Ap. 30. Murder was Committed June, 10, 1724. more than 10. Moneth's agoe, and yet the Prisoner, Witnesses, Capt. Thomas Newton and John Harris; Justice, Doct^r Little and all concern'd, were present which made the Cause clear as the Noon-Day. This was an Answer of frequent and fervent Prayer!

Notes

1. Adrian Heerboord's *Metaphysics* (Amsterdam, 1665).
2. Daniel Gookin was a fellow of Harvard College who joined with Sewall in dealing with the question of ranking (or seating) students.
3. This reference to sexual perversion suggests the discussion of the same habits a few decades before in William Bradford's *Of Plymouth Plantation*.
4. The Reverend Urian Oakes was a pastor of Cambridge Church and later a president of Harvard. Oakes, who was then a college fellow at odds with President Hoar, feared that if Sewall carried out his threat to resign his fellowship, this would be blamed upon him.
5. This reference to the Reverend Thomas Thacher of South Church, who "commonplaced" his presentation, meant that he reduced, or arranged, various topics in theology, philosophy, etc. under certain "commonplaces," or heads, an exercise expected of resident Bachelors.
6. One can only guess as to Sewall's reference to the "external" causes for the "lownes" of Harvard College at the time. There was no doubt of Harvard's current decline in students, the deterioration and closing of several buildings, and general dissatisfaction.
7. This is probably a reference to the Reverend John Woodbridge of Andover.
8. "Southton" refers to Southampton.
9. The Reverend Thomas Parker, pastor of Newbury Church, now blind, had taught Latin, Greek and Hebrew to Sewall and others. (See Introduction.)
10. King Philip's War of 1675–77, which devastated much of New England, was provoked by the English seizure of Indian lands and their disruption of tribal hunting. United for a time with the powerful Narragansetts, King Philip's Wampanoags and their allies used firearms effectively against the Puritan settlements until the New England Confederacy, assisted by "praying" (converted) Indians, crushed the rebellion.
11. Sewall's decision as to whether to enter the ministry or business was a difficult one. (See entry for February 23, 1676/7.)
12. Thanksgiving was of course an *ad hoc* holiday rather than the permanent, relatively fixed festivity it has since become.
13. This is one of numerous references to the Quakers of this era and their (then) militant tactics of conversion. Canonicus may have been the descendant of the famous sachem of that name who had ceded Rhode Island to Roger Williams.
14. This reference to Boston's greatest fire should read "second greatest," since the catastrophe of 1653 easily ranks first. This 1676 fire destroyed the large North Meetinghouse and consumed entire streets. Forty-six homes were burned including that of Increase Mather, although his noted library escaped.
15. The Reverend Samuel Willard (1640–1707) was Samuel Sewall's pas-

tor of the Old South Church in Boston, a vice-president and head of Harvard during the absence of Increase Mather, and a leading exponent of the moderate Puritan Covenant theology.

16. *Antapologia* was written by the Reverend Edwards, a minister of Christ Church, London, in reply to a pamphlet of 1643, prepared by the Independents, entitled "Apologetical Narration."

17. Solomon Stoddard (1643–1729), the famous Congregational clergyman, was born in Boston, graduated from Harvard, and became the first librarian of Harvard (1667–74) before assuming the pastorate of Northampton (1672–1729). Recognizing the need for compromise in an era when the old orthodox Puritanism was yielding to a more secular atmosphere, he had accepted the Halfway Covenant in 1662 by which persons not fully qualified for church membership could secure baptism for their children. His "Stoddardeanism" permitted professing Christians to take Communion and to enjoy the privileges of full church membership. As the indubitable pope of the Connecticut Valley, he fought the orthodoxy of the Mathers and gave hell-fire sermons, thus preparing the way for his grandson, Jonathan Edwards, the adoption of the induced conversion, and the Great Awakening. He expressed the frontier idea that church membership must not be limited to formal conversions. He was a lifelong friend of Judge Sewall, who arranged for him, when in Boston, to give the Thursday lecture or the election sermon. Like Sewall, he opposed the vogue for wigs and sponsored sumptuary laws.

18. Major John Pynchon (1626–1703) was a merchant, large landowner, and military hero during King Philip's War, when he saved the inhabitants of Hadley.

19. Refers to Graham, the pirate. When the volunteers for the brigantine failed to materialize, the General Court offered free plunder to enlistees.

20. Colonel Percy Kirke (1646–1691) was notorious for his cruelty to the Puritan rebels at Sedgemoor, where the Duke of Monmouth was defeated by the followers of James II.

21. William Stoughton (1630–1701), then an Assistant on the Massachusetts Council, later became Lieutenant Governor, and the presiding judge in the Salem witchcraft trial. He was a conservative power in the colony.

22. There are numerous references to the recurrent outbreaks of smallpox. England's Royal Society was instrumental in overcoming these plagues. Jonathan Edwards was to die of the inoculation itself, for which scientific advance Cotton Mather did battle against Boston doctors during the epidemic of 1721.

23. Michael Wigglesworth (1631–1705) was an English-born clergyman and poet who came to America as a boy. While pastor at Malden, Massachusetts, he wrote the long didactic poem *The Day of Doom* (1662), which dealt with God's wrath toward sinning mankind and justified infant damnation. The poem was a colonial best-seller and

(Day of Doom)

was praised by Cotton Mather as the Book of the Ages. A former Harvard tutor, he was no rigid Predestinarian, for he suggested light punishment and the hope of salvation for those willing to do something to be saved.

24. The Duke of Monmouth (1649–1685), illegitimate son of the late Charles II, rebelled against James II and was crushed. Archibald Argyle (1629–85) led an unsuccessful invasion of Scotland and had also been beheaded.

25. Governor Joseph Dudley (1647–1720), a power in colonial politics, became Sewall's kin when his daughter Rebecca married Samuel Sewall Jr. Dudley was a member of the General Court during 1673–76, took an active part in King Philip's War, and won election every year to the upper house of the legislature until the old Massachusetts charter was revoked. He had tried vainly to avert the loss of the charter when he left for England in 1682, but aroused severe criticism because of his strong imperial loyalties. In 1686, he became Governor of Massachusetts despite widespread local suspicion of his motives, especially because of his close association with Sir Edmund Andros. A rich landowner as well as perennial officeholder, he extended various benefits of office to Sewall and usually secured the support of the influential Mathers.

26. The Mathers were far more conservative regarding mixed dancing than their kinsman John Cotton had been. The latter had written in 1625, "Dancing (yea, though mixt) I would not simply condemn—only lascivious dancing to wanton ditties and in amorous gestures and wanton dalliances, especially after great feasts, I would bear witness against." Puritans usually agreed in condemning "unchast touches and Gesticulations" seen in mixed dancing among the sexes.

27. As already noted, the date of Thanksgiving, like those of the various days of fasting and humiliation, was determined from time to time by specific community events. Not until the mid-nineteenth century did the date of Thanksgiving become fixed—at least relatively.

28. Nurse Goose, wife of Isaac Goose, has sometimes been considered to be the original Mother Goose of nursery fame, but this is unproved. Hey !!

29. Sewall, as a strict Puritan, rarely forgot to point out annually that Christmas was virtually ignored by Bostonians. Christmas was suspect as a pagan day unconnected with the birth of Christ.

30. A reference to the second edition of a pamphlet issued by Boston ministers and printed by Samuel Green (who did such jobs for Sewall). The full title was "An Arrow Against Profane and Promiscuous Dancing. Drawn Out of the Quiver of the Scriptures." By Increase Mather.

31. James Morgan, being condemned for murder, was required by Puritan custom to be brought to the meetinghouse as an object lesson for a sermon on the Sunday preceding the execution, or at the Thursday lecture.

32. Sewall, ever a Puritan literalist, repeatedly attacked the English custom of taking an oath by holding or kissing the Bible.

33. Sewall referred frequently to the custom of distributing gloves or scarves at funerals.

34. William Johnson of Woburn, Massachusetts, was the son of the noted Captain Edward Johnson, author of *The Wonder-Working Providence of Sion's Savior in New England* (1654).

35. Sewall's Puritan party and the local Anglican officials quarreled over the efforts of the latter to administer this sacrament at the Town House.

36. Sewall and the Mathers were especially incensed by such Anglican symbols as the use of the Cross in a way as to savor of idolatry and popery. Anglicans looked at this attitude as outright colonial defiance of English authority.

37. There are repeated references to this quarrel between Sewall's local Puritans and the Boston Anglican officials over the latter's use of the Meetinghouse, even a small part of it, for Church of England services.

38. Madam Rebecca Taylor, wealthy heiress of the Stoughton family, was the influential widow of a leading Boston merchant.

39. Apparently a popular old English Catholic sport associated with Shrove Tuesday.

40. This concern over the pagan symbol of the maypole suggests, of course, the old Bradford quarrel over Merrymount.

41. Increase Mather was charged by Edmund Randolph with writing a libelous letter, but Mather denied its authorship. The latter evaded arrest in order to leave for England as a colonial agent.

42. Lima, Peru, was devastated by an earthquake on October, 1687.

43. Sir William Phips (1651–95), the first royal governor of Massachusetts, was born on the Maine frontier, worked as a ship's carpenter, and rose socially when he married the widow of John Hull, Sewall's mother-in-law. He was now a wealthy contractor and a protégé of Charles II, and had been knighted after his successful discovery of a treasure off the coast of Hispaniola. While in England he had helped Increase Mather in a vain effort to recover the old Massachusetts charter; and Mather had nominated him for the governorship. In this post, he terminated the witchcraft frenzy and shifted his influence increasingly to Congregationalism.

44. Thomas Papillon, an eminent merchant and parliamentarian of Huguenot descent, whom Sewall visited in London in an effort to recover the charter.

45. Increase Mather spent a year in England to urge the ministers of James II and then of William III to restore the Massachusetts charter which contained many local rights.

46. Emmanuel College, Cambridge University, is famous as the model for Harvard and as the college of so many first generation American Puritans, such as John Cotton and Thomas Hooker.

47. A reference to news of the Glorious Revolution in Boston and also to the fall of Governor Edmund Andros.

48. Alexander Kick's letter to Queen Mary on "The State of New England" had been published by Increase Mather.

49. Thomas Pound was the pirate leader of the frigate *Rose;* William Coward headed another such group of pirates.

50. There are surprisingly few references to the notorious Salem witch-craft trials. Samuel Sewall shared the general Puritan shock at the "evidence" of witchcraft in New England, and served with Deputy Governor Stoughton and four other magistrates to examine the accused. Nearly a hundred victims were then in jail awaiting trial. When Governor Phips returned from a military expedition he appointed a Special Commission under Stoughton, as chief, assisted by six associates, including Sewall; none were lawyers and the rules of evidence seemed to be improvised at times. This Special Court of Oyer and Terminer was appointed June 13, 1692, with jurisdiction over Suffolk, Essex and Middlesex. The Court opened hearings in Salem during the first week of June, 1692. Nineteen suspected witches and similar malefactors were executed, all asserting their innocence. In January, 1693, a grand jury brought bills against fifty, but all were acquitted save three, and these had their sentences reprieved.

51. Giles Corey, then eighty-one, had a wife who was executed as a witch, three days after his death, and in whose guilt he believed. While in jail he had made a will conveying property; but he preserved silence during an indictment against himself, believing that his entire estate would be confiscated if he pleaded guilty. Thereupon he suffered the old English penalty of being pressed to death.

52. Dorcas Hoar was among some fifty five defendants who confessed and won immunity from execution.

53. Increase Mather's work entitled *Cases of Conscience Concerning Evil Spirits,* as this indicates, apparently circulated a year before the publication date of 1693. Mather was in England when the Salem trials began, and when he returned he attacked "the spectral evidence" used to convict. Although he did not doubt that witches existed, he persuaded Governor Phips to halt the executions. However, his thirty-year-old son, Cotton Mather, had been busily publicizing his first-hand observations regarding witches, though he too opposed the so-called spectral evidence and urged the judges to show greater caution. Enemies of the Mathers nevertheless put the blame for the Salem affair on them, thus weakening their influence thereafter. Increase, then Rector of Harvard College, was currently unpopular for his alleged charter concessions to the Crown, especially for agreeing to make the governor an appointee of the King. Actually he had preserved the power of the Massachusetts popular assembly even if he was associated with the conservative ruling theocracy.

54. "A Dialogue Between Whig and Tory, alias Williamite and Jacobite," published in 1693.

55. A reference to evidence given in a Salem witchcraft case of "preternatural strength."

56. The Massachusetts General Court decided to appoint January 14, 1697, a day of fasting and prayer regarding "the late tragedy raised among

us by Satan and [his] instruments, through the awful judgment of God."
This was obviously no confession of error regarding the slaughter of
the innocents, but the community was swayed by Sewall's open confession and soon reacted sharply against the trials.

57. The Reverend John Cotton was the son of the famous Puritan leader
of that name. He was dismissed and went to Charleston, South Carolina, in November, 1698, dying there of yellow fever.

58. Samuel Sewall was a lifelong friend and a Harvard classmate of Edward Taylor (1633–1729), a minister and physician of Westfield. Only
in 1937 did the historian Thomas H. Johnson discover Taylor's remarkable manuscripts, which contained his religious poems, revealing
talent of a high literary order among the Puritans. Taylor kept his
poems a secret, except on such occasions as this, when he sent a poem
to Sewall, and the latter persuaded Cotton Mather to incorporate it
in a printed sermon on the death of Sewall's son.

VOLUME II

1. Here is the most striking of Sewall's numerous references to the pirates
of his day—the case of Captain William Kidd of Scotland (1645–
1701), who had recently turned pirate and was now pleading with his
one-time sponsor, Governor Bellomount of New England, to secure
him a pardon. In 1697 Bellomount had commissioned Kidd to war
upon the pirates who infested East India shipping, but a mutinous
crew (it was said) forced Kidd to give up privateering, which was
respectable, for piracy, which was not. Two of the pirates mentioned
here, Joseph Bradish and Tee Wetherly, had escaped from Boston but
were recaptured. Kidd was tried in London and hanged at Newgate,
but he refused to reveal the names of his aristocratic backers. He left
behind a tale of vast treasures in the Caribbean, greater than those
seized with him near Boston, and had offered to help Bellomount find
them if he were freed. This legend of Captain Kidd's treasure has in-
trigued treasure-hunters ever since.

2. If Sewall kept these New England Sabbaths, he meant the descendants
of the Pilgrims.

3. Originally published in June 24, 1700, *The Selling of Joseph* was re-
printed in the *Proceedings of the Massachusetts Historical Society* for
October, 1863. For all his religious and economic conservatism,
Sewall was indeed a progressive on slavery by the standards of his day.
As his *Diary* reveals, slaveholding was not uncommon among his fel-
low-Puritans.

4. From this entry and the ensuing letter, one may infer some of Sewall's
informal activity in the way of matchmaking.

5. Sewall's favorite diatribe against wigs seem to have been indorsed by
such eminent ministers as Michael Wigglesworth, author of *The Day
of Doom,* and Solomon Stoddard, grandfather of Jonathan Edwards.

6. From this point on, for the ensuing year, there are references to the

resentment of Increase and Cotton Mather against Sewall and his party for blocking the former's path to the presidency of Harvard. The reference to Negroes relates to Sewall's recent antislavery pamphlet, *The Selling of Joseph.*

7. Rebekah Dudley was the daughter of the controversial and powerful Governor Joseph Dudley, who aided Sewall on occasion with his patronage.

8. Cotton Mather's history, the *Magnalia,* whose appearance was the occasion for a day of Thanksgiving.

9. Here begin some of the episodes of Queen Anne's War (1702–13), which was especially savage on the northern frontier, with French and Indian border raids such as the Deerfield Massacre. Massachusetts used effective frontier scouts equipped with snowshoes and succeeded in capturing Port Royal, Nova Scotia.

10. Longfellow's poem "The Jewish Cemetery at Newport" speculates upon the disappearance of the 200 Israelite families during the Revolution. This cultured elite, with a classical synagogue that was a showplace for colonial visitors, thrived on the manufacture of furniture, soap, and the fortunes of privateering.

11. This was an exciting chase for pirates which ended in the trial and execution of John Quelch, commander of the brigantine *Charles,* and his crew for piracy and murder. A second group of pirates were likewise executed. Sewall's brother, Major Stephen Sewall, swiftly pursued one group of these cutthroats and seized them and their treasure, for which he was rewarded by the Governor.

12. The Reverend Samuel Myles was rector of King's Chapel.

13. The miscegenation bill that Sewall feared was passed with strict provisions against fornication as well as marriage between the races. However, he succeeded in securing this mitigating proviso: "And no master shall unreasonably deny marriage to his negro with one of the same nation, any law, usage, or custom to the contrary notwithstanding."

14. The Reverend John Williams published "The Redeemed Captive Returning to Zion," which was often reprinted.

15. Sewall refers to the early invasion failures before Massachusetts succeeded in capturing Port Royal permanently.

16. The election of John Leverett (1662–1724) to the presidency of Harvard meant the defeat of the clerical conservatism of the Mathers and the victory of the first lay president of Harvard (1707–24), who had been a college tutor, a practicing lawyer, and judge of the Superior Court. In 1714 he was elected a member of the Royal Society, reflecting his sympathy for the new science of Isaac Newton. Sewall, however, was suspicious of President Leverett's friendliness to certain high-church tendencies and of his liberalism.

17. Even the humane Sewall shared the contemporary English prejudices against social contact with Indians, including educated Christians.

18. The Reverend Ebenezer Pemberton of Sewall's own South Church

was the successor of Samuel Willard and colleague of Samuel's son
Joseph, who succeeded him as pastor. Pemberton was temperamentally
given to outbursts of anger and was hardly qualified to act in a pas-
toral capacity for Sewall; the latter's comments on Pemberton were
anything but objective after Sewall's son became a rather active com-
petitor for Pemberton in the Old South ministry.

19. This apparently refers to the pamphlet of 1695, "Case of Conscience,
Whether it is Lawfull for a Man to Marry his Wives Own Sister." It is
signed by the Mathers, Samuel Willard, and other noted Bostonians.

VOLUME III

1. Sewall suffered from severe cases of smallpox and measles. Hannah
Sewall was indeed accident-prone and died within a few years from
complications arising from this injury to her knees.

2. Sewall here spoke disparagingly of the Reverend Pemberton for failing to make any reference to young Sewall, his colleague. The Reverend Matthew Henry was an expositor, or commentator.

3. The Reverend Peter Thatcher was a Harvard classmate of Sewall's,
very popular in the Boston community judging by the unusual crowd
at his funeral. The dreaded Schism Act never took effect. It required
all schoolmasters and teachers to declare conformity to the Church
of England, receive its sacrament of Communion, secure the license
of a bishop, and affirm the oaths of allegiance and supremacy.

4. About this time Sewall joined a group of merchants who held the
exclusive and apparently profitable privilege of making salt ("in the
French manner") for a limited period in the province.

5. The Reverend Benjamin Wadsworth, president of Harvard, and a lifelong friend of Sewall. Isaac Addington, a popular leader against the
imperial party, was a member of the Governor's Council associated
with Sewall at least from the time of the Salem witchcraft trials and
now was a judge of Suffolk Probate Court.

6. The *Diary* for many pages refers to the constitutional issues that arose
following the death of England's sovereign, Queen Anne, especially
in regard to the future status of colonial commissions, such as that of
the Governor, and the question of interim authority for the Council
and the status of the Massachusetts charter. Sewall was of course concerned with the power of the General Council of which he was a
member.

7. The lords were beheaded on Tower Hill, London, for high treason as
participants in the Jacobite rebellion.

8. Sewall, as in this case, was not above the practice of stretching the
law a bit to help a relative. The law was quite specific in forbidding
travelers, peddlers, and their servants to travel on the Sabbath.

9. Jeremiah Phenix, a Boston tradesman, killed a ropemaker with an
iron hatchet.

10. The Reverend Thomas Prince (1687–1758), Increase Mather's bright

student at Harvard and future historian of New England, now became a pastor of Sewall's Old South Church. The reference to a "second Sign" apparently means Sewall's growing conviction that his musical gifts were inadequate for his congregation. As a precentor he apparently took an active part in encouraging the quality of congregational singing.

11. Their aunt was the widow Katharine Winthrop, already urged upon Sewall as an eligible wife.

12. Sewall's courtship of the widow of William Denison seemed favored by considerable affection on both sides, but it ran afoul of practical financial considerations affecting Mrs. Denison's sense of obligation to her kindred.

13. Sewall refers to the dissenting ministers removed under the Act of Uniformity.

14. The smallpox epidemic in Boston caused the death of 1,100 by 1721.

15. The book was written by Cotton Mather in 1691.